Trail of Blood

Trail of Blood
A Father, a Son and
a Tell-tale Crime Scene Investigation

Wanda Webb Evans
in collaboration with James Dunn

New Horizon Press
Far Hills, New Jersey

Evans, Wanda and James Dunn
    Trail of Blood:
    A Father, a Son and a Tell-tale Crime Scene Investigation

Cover Design: Wendy Bass
Interior Design: Susan M. Sanderson

Library of Congress Control Number: 2004108086

ISBN: 0-88282-261-6
New Horizon Press

Manufactured in the U.S.A.

2009   2008   2007   2006   2005   /   5   4   3   2   1

For Scott—
The son he was and the man he would have become.

Authors' Note

This book is based on the experiences of James Dunn and reflects his perceptions of the past, present and future. The personalities, events, actions and conversations portrayed within the story have been taken from his memories, court documents, interviews, testimony, research, letters, personal papers, press accounts and the memories of some participants.

In an effort to safeguard the privacy of certain people, names and a few identifying characteristics have, in some cases, been changed. Events involving the characters happened as described. Only minor details have been altered.

Table of Contents

Acknowledgements

The journey I began the day I learned that my son Scott was missing would have been unbearable and fruitless if I'd had to travel alone. I am grateful for those who walked with me; sometimes leading the way, sometimes following; sometimes by my side; always supporting me, comforting me, and urging me to keep going.

My thanks go to all the men and women who participated, first in the search for Scott, then in the investigation that resulted in the arrest and conviction of his murderers, and finally, in the ongoing search for his body. Of that group of dedicated experts, I pay special tribute to several, beginning with Detective Tal English of the Lubbock Police Department. Tal threw himself unstintingly into the investigation. For six years, he refused to give up, and his dedication and determination kept my hopes alive and strengthened my own determination. Former LPD Detective George White partnered with Tal, bringing to the investigation unlimited energy, vast experience and expertise.

My everlasting thanks also go to Richard Walter, the forensic psychologist who is one of the founders of the Vidocq Society. Richard provided impetus and direction at critical times when the search investigation appeared to have stalled; he became my good friend as well as my ally.

My thanks, also, to Bill Fleisher, my first contact at Vidocq, who brought Richard and me together.

Thanks to Rusty Ladd of the Lubbock County Criminal District Attorney's Office (now Judge Ladd), whose diligent efforts resulted in exacting justice for Scott.

Pam Alexander, the Director of the Lubbock Victim Assistance Services, Inc., was a lifesaver for me and for my wife, Barbara. Without her presence, her optimism, her knowledge of the Criminal Justice System, we would have been lost in that complex organization.

My longtime friend W. R. Collier provided unswerving support throughout the long ordeal. He and our mutual friend Derry Harding, who paved the way for me to assist in the investigation, have my enduring gratitude.

Without Wanda Evans, who wanted to tell our story, and did so with skill, compassion, and reverence for our family relationships, this book would not have been possible.

James Dunn

Some events in life are too excruciating to be reduced to the printed page, and for a long time, I thought this was one of those. It haunted me, though, until I knew I had to try, at least, to write the story of Jim Dunn's long, agonizing ordeal. I was both pleased and challenged when Jim agreed with me, and we set our feet on the path that would lead to this book. I can only say, thank you, Jim, for sharing the story of your pain-and your courage-with me.

I echo Jim's appreciation for all those who had any part in bringing his search for justice to its bittersweet conclusion. We haven't yet found Scott, but we continue to believe it will happen.

In addition, thanks to Connie Teer and my sister, Nan Honeycutt, for proofreading the manuscript at every stage of preparation, and their expert advice whenever I took a wrong turn.

Wanda Webb Evans

Prologue

Sunday night. Jim Dunn pushed away from the desk, stretching, smoothing out the small knot that had formed between his shoulder blades. Barbara, his wife, had gone to bed an hour or so earlier, while he stayed downstairs in the office, puttering, filing, planning for work the following week. He knew the days ahead would be hectic, but he would love every minute. The idea of having their own business still seemed almost unbelievable to Jim and Barbara. Their database marketing company, Comprehensive Marketing, was almost three years old. Barbara was treasurer and Jim was president; already, they had added salespeople, even though they didn't have a place for their offices. That would come soon. They were searching for suitable office space, affordable office space, where they could continue to expand. Every day was fulfilling to them.

From another part of the house, chimes signaled the hour. Midnight. Jim couldn't help smiling as the last note faded into night. Throughout his childhood, he had been lulled to sleep at night and awakened in the morning by the sound of those notes from the grandfather clock that had stood in the living room of the little Texas farm house where he lived with his grandparents. Granddad and Ma were gone now and so the clock stood in the foyer of Jim's Pennsylvania home, reminding him, on the hour and the half hour, of the years he had spent in their care and all the things he had learned from them, values that had made him the man he was today. Before going upstairs, he lingered, savoring his surroundings, savoring his life.

On the wall over his desk, a certificate framed in bronze proclaimed that James H. Dunn III had been named Distinguished Alumnus by the School of Agricultural Science at Texas Tech University. A small, warm thrill went through him every time he looked at it. His former college buddy and still his best friend, W. R. Collier, had nominated him for the honor and no one had been more surprised than Jim when he was selected. Rarely had he felt so proud and so delighted at the same time. A few years later, Jim had nominated W. R., who also won the award. W. R. still lived in Lubbock, Texas, where he was president of the city's largest locally owned bank. Even now, so many years after their graduation from Tech, their friendship was still strong.

Jim's eye fell on two photographs angled toward each other on one corner of the desk. There was Barb, her blonde hair burnished by the photographer's artful lighting. Their marriage of ten years—his second marriage, actually—had made him happier than he ever could have dreamed possible. Facing it was an enlarged snapshot of Jim standing next to his younger son, Scott. Scott was a little taller than Jim and his below-collar length hair was blond, where Jim's had been black until it turned white prematurely.

Jim Dunn sighed, truly contented. Their family had been through some rocky times in the past, but life was good today. Getting better every day, in fact. The business was going great, the marriage even better. He could not remember ever being happier. What more could a man ask for?

The telephone on the desk rang once and Jim grabbed it, hoping to avoid waking Barbara.

"Hello," he said softly, wondering who would be calling so late on Sunday night. Probably Scott, he thought with amusement. It was an hour earlier in Texas and Scott had little concept of time.

"I'm trying to locate Scott Dunn's mother or father." The voice was a woman's; the words spoken in a wooden, flat tone sent sharp icicles of anxiety through Jim's chest. Through the years, he had answered other middle-of-the night calls from and about his charming, happy-go-lucky younger son, but none had filled him with the sense of dread this distant, unfamiliar voice created with those few words. Before he could calm down enough to respond, the woman continued.

"I don't know who I'm calling, but I found this number on the telephone bill. I assume since the number wasn't one I called that it belongs to Scott's mother or father." Her sharp words indicated one who was accustomed to getting people's attention. She definitely had Jim's.

"I'm his father. Who are you?" Jim asked, bewildered.

"My name is Leisha Hamilton and Scott has disappeared. I wondered if you'd heard anything from him."

Jim felt stunned. When he found his voice, it sounded ragged. "Disappeared? What makes you think he's disappeared?"

There was no change in the disembodied voice. "I've been living with Scott for a while now. He left the apartment sometime on Thursday, while I was at work, and I haven't heard from him since then. I thought he might have told you where he was going."

Jim shook his head in denial, as if she could see him, but his mind was racing. Was this some sort of a practical joke? Who was this woman? Scott had never mentioned her. In fact, his son hadn't said that he was living with anyone. Only a week earlier, Scott had called and excitedly told Jim he had just gotten engaged to a girl named Jessica. He had met her the previous summer, when she had been a high school senior, a few years younger than he, but they had broken up when she went off to college at Mississippi State. Scott said, "She came back to Texas on spring break and we've gotten back together. I'm having a ring made for her." She was planning on moving to the Dallas area as soon as the semester ended and they were going to get married. Scott wanted to bring her to Pennsylvania to meet his dad and Barb. In an upbeat voice he told his dad about all the other plans he had. At the end of the call he'd revealed how much his dad's support had meant to him and said they'd talk soon.

That happy conversation was only a week ago and now some strange woman was saying she had been living with Scott and he had suddenly disappeared! This made no sense. Trying to get his thoughts in order, Jim took a deep breath and exhaled slowly. "Leisha, I have to be honest with you. I've never heard of you."

"I've been living with Scott since March," she answered. "Mr. Dunn, I just don't know where he went. He had the flu for two days.

In fact, he got so sick at Max's Monday night that he stayed over there." Jim knew that Max Gianoli was Scott's boss.

"He didn't go to work Tuesday, and Tuesday night I had to go get him," Leisha continued. "He was so weak; I had to help him walk. He stayed in bed Wednesday and was still sick Thursday morning, so before I went to work, I gave him some medicine and a glass of water. When I came home, he was gone." She might have been reading a shopping list, for all the feeling in her voice. She paused for a few moments, but Jim didn't say anything. Finally, she went on.

"Like I said, when I came back, he was gone. But he left the jeans he had been wearing. His car keys and the keys to the apartment were in the pocket."

Jim felt frozen. Now this woman was making even less sense. Four days had passed. Jim shook his head, pondering, Scott would never go anywhere without his car. He was especially attached to the car, which he had named "Yellow Thunder." The name was an apt description of how it must have seemed to Scott, speeding down the highway, the Camaro's high-performance engine roaring, his high-performance stereo blasting.

"Isn't this the weekend," Jim asked, perplexed, "Scott was going to change the motor from the yellow Camaro to the white one?"

"Yes. It's down at the place where he works. It's half torn apart already. I know it doesn't make sense, but I have the keys right here in my hand." She sounded impatient—the first emotion Jim had detected in her voice.

Jim was unnerved. Doubts echoed. Scott would not go *anywhere* without his car. And he would not pick *this* weekend to go away. He was involved in a major project, transferring the motor from Yellow Thunder into a white Camaro he had just bought. The body of the white car was in better condition than the yellow one, but the motor in Yellow Thunder was better. From the two, Scott would create a car superior to either one.

More uncertainties reverberated: discussing his plans the last time Jim and his son had talked, Scott had also told his dad that he was entering another Crank It Up competition for the electronics store where he worked as a car stereo installer. The goal of the competition was to install a stereo in a vehicle in a way that would get the best performance at the highest decibel level without distortion of the sound. Scott was a genius at this sort of thing and had won dozens of first place trophies as evidence of his creativity. In fact, he had told Jim, with a grin in his voice, he had been given the nickname "Ice Man," because he had figured out that by putting blocks of ice on the tops of the speakers, he could increase the quality of sound at exceptionally high decibel levels. Jim couldn't understand what was going on. Scott would not miss one of those competitions. Nor would he just take off without letting Jim know he was going to do it. He *always* kept in touch. And this strange woman was telling him four days had passed since Scott had left.

"Why did you wait so long to call me?" Jim demanded.

"I was mad at Scott for leaving like that," she said bluntly. "I figured he'd be back home in a couple of days. But now I'm starting to worry. He hasn't been to work. He hasn't called his boss. No one's seen him anywhere."

"Do you know if he was seeing other women?" Jim asked, thinking of Jessica, the girl Scott had spoken of.

"No," she snapped. "I don't know. It's possible, I guess."

Jim took a deep breath and let it out slowly before he answered. He didn't want to jump to conclusions. Perhaps all this was just a misunderstanding. Perhaps Scott would surface momentarily and his father would feel foolish when he heard some perfectly reasonable explanation. He didn't want to cause Scott problems at work now that everything appeared to be going so well for his son. "Let's give it a couple more days," he said hesitantly. Leisha agreed and gave him her phone number at the restaurant where she worked.

chapter one

Dark Doubts

After hanging up, Jim sat, motionless, thoughts racing round and round in his head. Scott had pulled his share of pranks through the years, but not this kind. Scott was so enthusiastic, so funny, so clever, that everyone liked to be around him. His twinkling blue eyes, daredevil smile and amiable manner drew people to him. It was almost impossible not to like him. Girls, especially, were drawn to his blond good looks.

Throughout his school years, Scott had trouble studying because he was dyslexic and that made him a poor reader. After high school, Scott served a short stint in the Army. Despite his academic problems, Jim knew Scott had what it takes to be a success—the brains, the personality, the motivation. He was a genius with anything electronic; it was almost as if he had a sixth sense. He knew every circuit, every wire and how they all connected. He could take any gadget apart and put it back together again.

For a while he floundered and couldn't seem to find himself. When Jim's grandfather died, Jim asked Scott if he would like to live in his great-grandfather's house in Shallowater, Texas, a Lubbock suburb, and go to college. Scott agreed, moved into the house and entered South Plains College in Levelland, Texas.

However, it became apparent that Scott still could not hack academic life. He continued to have difficulty keeping up and his grades were not good. He was a doer, not a student. He wanted to be out there creating things, not studying them. Moving to Abilene, Texas, Scott worked for the original ProSound Electronics store. Impressed with Scott's ingenuity, Max Gianoli, the owner of the store, created an entire new department for Scott, installing car stereo systems. This soon became his primary business. The shop was so successful that Gianoli opened a branch store in Lubbock and told Scott he would be the manager when the store was established. To Jim's delight, Scott settled once more in the very place where he wanted his son to live—his home town.

In fact, with Scott's announcement that he was planning to marry Jessica, Jim felt everything seemed to be working out for Scott. Business at ProSound was booming; he had made a television infomercial for the store and his competition stereos were winning a lot of awards.

Moreover, he saw signs that his and Scott's relationship was reaching a new level of communication. During their last telephone conversation, Scott had told Jim about his insight. "Dad," he said, "I was listening to this country song on the radio. It was by George Strait and it reminded me of you. It said, *'Daddies don't love their children every now and then. It's love without end, Amen.'*

"I'm beginning to understand just what that song means," he told his father. "I know you have always loved me and you always support me in whatever I do. Listen," Scott said, obviously excited by his idea of bringing his dad closer, "why don't you move to Lubbock? I know you have such a flame in your heart for this town. I wish you would move back. You don't belong in Pennsylvania. It's just not Texas. We could open a father/son car stereo store here and I guarantee it will make a lot of money."

His words had touched Jim's heart. Jim felt that, at the age of twenty-four, Scott was maturing into a caring, introspective adult.

What had happened to his son in the interval since they spoke?

Although he had told Leisha Hamilton they should wait before making any formal inquiry, Jim sat worrying, his thoughts flying back and forth. It was possible that Scott had simply gone to Dallas to be with Jessica. She might be home from school by now. Or maybe he had flown to Mississippi to help her drive back to Texas. That would explain his leaving his car behind. Four days was just a long weekend, Jim told himself.

A few minutes later, he wasn't so sure. Something could have happened to Scott. He might be badly hurt. He might be sick. *Should I call the police?* Jim wondered, but he knew the police probably wouldn't take Scott's disappearance seriously after only these few days.

Jim pushed himself out of his chair, his thoughts clouded by fear. He picked up the picture of Scott and himself and felt strangely cold. The snapshot had been taken the last time Jim and Barb had gone to Texas, to attend a family wedding. Now, Jim remembered standing on his cousin Diann's front lawn, watching Scott's car roar off down the street. As he watched, Jim had been seized by a sudden chilling thought: this was the last time he would ever see Scott.

He hadn't seen his son since that day and now he wondered, heavy hearted, if his momentary foreboding had come true. Jim shook off the misgivings, replaced the photo on the desk and went to bed, but he could not sleep. He lay awake in the dark, only vaguely aware of Barbara breathing softly beside him. His mind was in turmoil. He longed to talk to Barbara about the troubling telephone call, but he knew she would want to immediately go to Texas and see about Scott. It wasn't as if Yardley, Pennsylvania were only a short drive from Lubbock, Texas. They couldn't just pop in and ask Scott's friends if they had seen Scott. Okay, so Barbara would. She had been Scott's friend and staunch ally since the day she married Jim, when Scott was fourteen years old. Distance would be no barrier to her, if Scott needed help.

But once again Jim hesitated, weighing what he should do. He just couldn't bring himself to report Scott's disappearance yet.

Hopefully, Scott was spending some time with friends. Maybe Scott had decided to move out of the apartment he was sharing with Leisha, because of his engagement to Jessica. Jim decided he would not tell Barbara for a few days, hoping Scott would turn up.

The decision didn't resolve Jim's anxieties. He still could not sleep. Through his mind passed snapshots of the past. Jim remembered the day Scott was born, the first time he held his son. He had looked into that wrinkled little face and vowed he would always be there for his son. Jim had hardly known his own father; his grandparents had raised him. They had become his parents after he had been abandoned by his birth parents. Even after all these years, there was an aching emptiness inside Jim, because he had never known his father. He made a commitment that he would be a real father to his son. Scott would never have to wonder where his father was; Jim's children would never have to question whether he supported them wholeheartedly in their every endeavor. Their world would be different from his: their father would be an integral part of their everyday lives. However, because of the divorce this hadn't been possible.

Nevertheless he had tried to show his children the love he felt in his heart. And now, when Scott was about to become the warm, caring, successful man his potential indicated he could be, was all that potential, that promise, cut down so prematurely?

Jim turned to face the wall and punched his pillow. Had something happened to Scott that would rob him of the opportunity to be the man he yearned to be? Jim was filled with fear that it had.

Monday morning, Jim got up and tried to go about his work as if nothing unusual had happened. He didn't mention the late night telephone call to Barbara; he didn't want to worry her. But he couldn't stop thinking about it. He slogged through the day, trying to focus on work, but his anxiety about Scott lurked just below the surface and he kept waiting, torn between hope and dread, listening for the telephone to ring. It didn't.

The hours dragged by. Then another sleepless night. On Tuesday, when he hadn't heard from Scott and nothing more from Leisha, Jim called her at work. He had two reasons for calling the woman: to see if she had heard from Scott and to see if she had been telling him the truth about who she was and where she worked.

Leisha didn't sound at all happy to hear Jim's voice. "No, I have not heard from Scott," she snapped. "And furthermore, I don't have time to talk to you."

Her rudeness took Jim by surprise. She hadn't been overly friendly when she called on Sunday night, but she certainly had been a little more cordial than she was today. Was her rudeness because she really was too busy to talk or was it because she wasn't concerned about Scott's whereabouts any longer?

Jim didn't know. He had no sense of what was going on in her mind, but he determined that if she wouldn't talk to him, it was time to find someone who would. He called Scott's employer, Max Gianoli, at ProSound Electronics. If Leisha was telling the truth and Scott really had disappeared, Gianoli might have some inkling about where the young man might have gone. If Scott's leaving had come as a surprise to Gianoli, he might be worried too.

Gianoli wasn't worried. He was furious. "Scott let me down big time," he snarled. "He knew we had a big show last weekend and I needed his help on it. I'm pissed as hell that he ran off like that."

Jim tried to interrupt and ask Gianoli if he had any idea what had happened to Scott, but the man wasn't listening. "Scott's got to learn that he can't come and go as he pleases. I've got a business to run."

"Does this mean Scott's fired?" Jim asked.

"It sure as hell does. He's out of here," Gianoli growled and hung up.

For a few more days, Jim's thoughts bounced back and forth as he tried to make a decision. Normally logical and decisive, Jim felt frustrated that he couldn't settle on what to do about Scott. Or if he should do anything. Call the police. Don't call the police.

Finally, Jim decided that if Scott hadn't returned home by the weekend, he would report him missing.

On Friday night, Leisha Hamilton called. Jim felt a surge of hope when he recognized her voice. In spite of his apprehension at hearing her, he was praying that she had good news about Scott. She quickly disillusioned him of that idea.

"I just wanted to tell you that I picked Scott's car up from ProSound Electronics. Max called me up and threatened to tow the car if I didn't come and get it."

Remembering Max Gianoli's frame of mind when he talked to him on Tuesday, Jim wasn't too surprised that the man was angry about Scott's car being left at ProSound. On second thought, however, it seemed too soon for him to get excessively upset about the car. Max had no way of knowing Scott wouldn't be back any minute to pick up the car. He certainly wouldn't go away forever and leave it behind.

"When did you get the car?" Jim asked Leisha.

"Yesterday. Like I said, Max wanted it off the lot. And I have the keys, you know."

Jim's fear was quickly giving way to anger at the idea of this stranger driving his son's car around, as if she owned it and not Scott.

"Are you driving the car?" he asked.

"Not much. I have my own car, but I like having Scott's car here. It reminds me of him."

She sounded sincere and Jim tried to control his misgivings. "Leisha, what do you think happened to Scott?"

"I really don't know," she said. "At first, I thought he might have run off with that Jessica. But I already called her and she hasn't heard from him, either."

For a couple of heartbeats, Jim was speechless. The last time they had talked, Leisha had indicated she didn't know about Jessica. She had said there was no other woman in Scott's life. Now, she was telling Jim she had called Jessica. He could only imagine how Jessica must have felt getting a telephone call from her. He wondered if

Jessica had known about Leisha prior to Scott's disappearance. All week, he had been trying to think of a way to find Jessica, to see if she knew what had happened to Scott. He didn't know her last name, though, and had no way to reach her. "If you'll give me her name and phone number, I'll call her," he told Leisha.

"I already told you. She doesn't know anything."

"Maybe she just didn't want to talk to you. She might talk to me, though. Especially if Scott is with her." In his heart, though, Jim had begun to fear that his son wasn't anywhere safe. Scott absolutely would not have left his possessions behind. Unless he intended to come back soon…

"Let me give her a call," Jim said.

"Her name's Jessica Tate. I threw away the number, but she's enrolled at Mississippi State. Maybe you can find her," Leisha said grudgingly.

"Is there anyone you know who had a grudge against Scott? Anyone who might be angry at him?"

"There may have been." She sounded disinterested. "I don't really know."

Jim persisted. "Did he owe money to anyone?"

"No, I don't think so. Not a lot of money, anyway."

Clearly, they weren't getting anywhere. Frustrated, Jim tried another approach. "Do you know of anyone who was jealous of him?"

Silence was her only response. Jim's heart pounded. He was on to something. "Were you dating anyone else? Since Scott was seeing Jessica, there's no reason why you shouldn't have been seeing other people." He tried to sound casual, reasonable.

"That's true. I went out on a couple of dates with Tim Smith, who lives in our apartment complex. But I just did it to make Scott jealous when I found out about Jessica."

Jim's chest heaved. It was almost audible. Instinctively, he knew she wasn't telling the whole truth. "How well do you know this Tim?"

"Pretty well, I guess. I got locked out of our apartment one night and Tim let me stay at his place. I was so upset the day Scott went missing, I asked Tim to stay over that night and keep me company."

She didn't have to say anything else; images of what was going on, of what scene might have ensued between Leisha, Scott and this Tim, flooded his mind. Dumbfounded, he gripped the receiver, unable to speak.

"Hello? Hello?" He could hear her disembodied voice, but he was choking on his own anger; his throat was so tight he couldn't force any words out.

Finally, he asked, uttering his words carefully, "Tim spent the night in your apartment the same day Scott disappeared?"

"Yes. He slept on the floor and I slept on the couch." Jim wondered if she thought him a fool. Ignoring his silence, she continued, saying there had been a break-in on the day following Scott's disappearance. She recited a list of Scott's things that were missing.

Jim tried to follow her words, but dark thoughts spun through his mind. First, she says Scott disappears. Then she takes up with another man immediately, as though she knows Scott isn't coming home that night. Surely, Scott had gone places before without telling her. How did she know he wasn't just off with one of his friends and wouldn't return at any minute?

When Jim finally told Leisha he couldn't talk anymore and hung up the phone, he realized he couldn't keep the truth from Barbara any longer. He hadn't told Barb of Scott's disappearance for a week and the secrecy was eating him up. It had been almost impossible to carry on as usual, as though nothing was wrong. To smile in all the right places, to tussle with day-to-day business decisions, which suddenly seemed so trivial. Jim hadn't wanted to tell his wife, because he kept hoping Scott would show up and he wouldn't have to upset her.

Telling Barbara proved to be as hard as Jim had anticipated it would be. "Why didn't you tell me right away?" she asked. As he had guessed, she wanted to catch the next plane to Lubbock.

He shook his head. "No. He's twenty-four years old. He can come and go as he pleases. We can't be sure yet that anything has happened to him. Besides, even if we went to Lubbock, what could we do there? We don't know most of Scott's new friends. We could embarrass him if he's just gone away for a short period and wants to be alone."

The question haunted them for another week. Was there some way they could locate Scott if they went to Lubbock? Could they find Scott if they searched long enough and hard enough? Jim was in a state of agitation when Leisha called again the following Sunday night.

She had no word about Scott, but she was full of other kinds of news. "Tim is following me around. He's making me nervous," she said. She thought he was weird and she was beginning to be afraid of him.

"I thought he stayed with you the night Scott disappeared." Jim said.

There was a long pause before she responded. "No—I didn't tell you he spent the night at the apartment that night, I told you he stayed with me the next night. I don't remember anything that happened the night of the sixteenth. That was the night after I found out Scott was gone."

This contradicted her earlier story, but Jim let her words pass unchallenged. "How well do you know Tim Smith?"

Again silence filled the line. Then she said, "Oh, I see him around all the time. I don't know him all that well. He makes me nervous."

Funny, she didn't sound nervous, he thought. "Then why would you let him spend the night?"

That got her attention. The irritation he'd heard in her voice the day he'd called her at work returned. "I don't know. I just needed some company, that's all. But now I can't get rid of him."

Jim decided to prod her. "Was there any trouble between Tim and Scott?"

Again, a long pause before she answered. "Well, they didn't much like each other."

Didn't much like each other. That wasn't a likely description, if Tim was interested in Leisha and thought Scott was in his way.

"Was there any real trouble between them?" Jim persisted.

"They didn't fight, if that's what you're asking," she said.

"Did Tim ever go to your apartment?"

"Once or twice. One time, I loaned him the keys to the apartment, so he could wait for a FedEx package. I guess he could've had the key copied."

At her words, another suspicion insinuated itself into Jim's mind, and he wondered if she had planted it deliberately. Was she hinting that her friend, Tim, might have done something to Scott? Why would she do that, unless she knew something had happened to Scott? What was she hoping to accomplish by telling Jim all these things?

After ending the call, Jim sat at his desk, pondering his son's fate. For days, he had been haunting the telephone, hoping against hope that it would ring and he would hear Scott's voice: "Hey, Dad! You'll never guess where I am!"

It hadn't happened and he was beginning to think it never would. It was time to call the police and report Scott missing. He picked up the phone again and called the Lubbock Police Department to file a missing persons report.

It was Sunday night and it was also the Memorial Day weekend. He knew there would be few detectives on duty, but Jim couldn't wait any longer. He had to find out the truth.

The officer who answered introduced himself as Corporal Jimmy Brazell. "Are you a relative of Scott Dunn's?" Brazell asked.

"Yes. I'm his father."

"Do you think your son has come to some harm?"

The question stirred the fear in Jim's soul. Why would the policeman immediately focus on such a thing? Did he know about an accident of some kind? Or worse? For the first time, Jim had to voice his deepest fears. "Yes. My son has been missing for several days. He's never disappeared like this before. I think it's highly possible that he's been hurt, kidnapped or in accident. I'm afraid his life might be in danger."

Brazell explained what the police routine would be. "When we get a report like this, Mr. Dunn, whoever takes the information gives it to someone in the records department, who puts it in the computer. From there, it is sent to the Crimes Against Persons Section, where it will be assigned to an investigator."

Corporal Brazell paused for a few seconds, then cleared his throat. "With this being a holiday weekend and not an emergency, chances are, it won't get assigned until Tuesday morning."

"A missing person isn't an emergency?" Jim exploded.

"I have to be honest, Mr. Dunn. At most police departments, including the LPD, when the subject of a missing persons report is an adult, it doesn't become a high priority for investigators unless there's strong suspicion that harm has come to the missing individual. Don't worry though. In most missing persons cases involving an adult, there's nothing for the family or the police to be concerned about. Most of the time, the missing person turns up within a few hours or a few days, safe and maybe a little red-faced. Chances are, this will be true in your son's case. I would be willing to bet that by Tuesday morning, your son will have turned up, alive and well, after an unscheduled vacation."

"That doesn't sound like my son," Jim insisted. Deep down, though, he hoped and prayed Brazell was right and the growing dread in his heart was only a parent's irrational fear.

chapter two

Dark Brown Stains

Detective Tal English, a tall, amiable native of Lubbock whose slow, deliberate speech, mild blue eyes and deferential attitude contrasted sharply with a quick mind and intuitive reasoning, was twenty-seven years old and had been a detective assigned to the Crimes Against Persons Department for about a year. That department is divided into two divisions, robbery and sex crimes, but the investigators in each division work on other crimes against persons as well. English was assigned to the robbery detail, partnered with a veteran LPD detective, Corporal George White.

English didn't even know that Scott Dunn had been reported missing when he reported to work on the Tuesday after Memorial Day. He parked his car in the City of Lubbock lot across the street from the square beige and brown building that housed the Lubbock police department, as well as the city's Municipal Court and Lubbock Power, Light and Water and covered the entire block between Texas Avenue and Avenue J. English walked just down the hall from his minuscule office, grabbed a cup of coffee from the department coffee pot and had just sat down at his desk, when his telephone rang.

He picked up the phone to hear Jim Dunn, wanting to know what the police had done about finding his son, Scott, over the weekend. English admitted that he didn't know what Jim was talking about. "The missing persons report has not yet made it to my desk." Jim gave the detective the same information he had given Brazell on Friday night—how unlikely it would be for his son to go off for this length of time and not tell anyone where he was. According to Dunn, Scott's boss had fired him. Dunn also told English what Scott's roommate Leisha Hamilton had said about someone breaking into Scott's apartment the day after he turned up missing.

English tried to reassure the anxious father that, most likely, Scott was all right and would eventually show up on his own. "We get tons of missing persons reports all the time and very seldom does anything pan out on them, especially on young kids like that," he told Jim. "They usually show up—in 99 percent of these missing persons incidents, victims waltz back from an unannounced vacation or an extended weekend with a new attraction—or some other explainable circumstance."

Jim informed English, "Scott has been gone too long for the extended weekend scenario and the timing is entirely wrong for the vacation theory." Jim also emphasized to English that Scott would *never, ever* have gone off for such a long period of time without his yellow Camaro.

The detective reassured Jim that he would look into the case as soon as he got the report from the records division. In the meantime, although he didn't tell the distraught father, English had another missing persons case that he considered more urgent. The other case also involved a young man, a ministerial student who had been reported missing by his family. He was a model student and a respected member of his church and school community. The prior week, he had gone to his bank and pushed a note under the teller's window, asking for all of his money, both checking and savings accounts, amounting to several thousand dollars in cash. No one had seen him since that day. None of the man's family members or acquaintances knew of any reason why he would need so much money. English had to face the possibility that the young man had been kidnapped and forced to withdraw his money. If that were the case, the concern became, how long would the man stay alive after he gave up his money? The search for the ministerial student, who appeared to be in more imminent danger than Scott Dunn did, took priority in Tal English's mind.

English got to work diligently, with his superiors at LPD and the student's family breathing down his neck, trying to find the missing boy. English had no qualms about working so hard on this case instead of the Scott Dunn matter, because Scott's case looked like the normal missing persons case where the young man would turn up in a couple of days. By the end of the day, English had not found the other missing person, however, and he went home feeling discouraged and worried.

The next morning, he walked into his office to start the search for the missing student again. Once again, as it had on the previous day, the phone rang. Jim Dunn once again was on the telephone, wanting a progress report on the investigation into Scott's disappearance. Since he had done nothing so far, to find Scott Dunn, English had nothing to report, but something about Jim Dunn's persistence got his attention. When the conversation ended, he immediatcly called the number Jim had given him for Leisha Hamilton.

Leisha answered the telephone and English identified himself. He told her he was investigating the disappearance of Scott Dunn. Sounding more angry than worried, Leisha told the detective she thought Scott had gone off with another woman. She said other girls were always calling Scott, but the calls had stopped since he left. Then Leisha informed English that she thought someone was breaking into her apartment when she went out.

"Why do you think that?" English asked her.

"The day after Scott left, I came home from work and somebody had kicked in the back door. I made a police report. Haven't you seen the report?" she asked.

Not having seen the report, English did not know anything about this.

Since that time, Leisha told the detective, she had noticed several things inside her apartment had been moved—placemats, chairs and other small things. So she felt that somebody could have been in the house.

"Is anything missing? Do you think it could have been a burglar?" English asked.

"Yes," she told him, "several items are missing." On the first day, when she discovered Scott was gone, a waterbed mattress liner, some towels, sheets, a thermal blanket, a comforter and three pillows were also missing. All the bedding had been laid out as kind of a pallet where Scott slept in the bedroom. A laundry basket full of Scott's clothes also was gone. She told English she assumed Scott had taken these things with him.

Then, on the second day, when the door had been kicked in, tools and spare parts needed to work on the Scott's remote control boat were gone. Also missing were a gas can for the boat and an empty clothes basket. In addition, Leisha Hamilton said, Scott's wallet was gone, but the jeans he had worn last were left behind, along with his car keys.

"We lived with Max Gianoli, over on Fortieth Street, when we first came to Lubbock," Leisha also told English. "Max and Scott moved here in January and I came in February. Then, when Max's wife moved to Lubbock, Scott and I moved into this apartment." Their move had been recent, "so we haven't much bedroom furniture." Max had given her the keys to the old apartment, Leisha said, and she was supposed to have turned them in to the manager, but she hadn't done so. Now, the keys were missing. "I guess Scott might have taken the keys and gone over there," she mused.

Something about Leisha's comments didn't sound quite right, English felt. He decided to check the situation out a little further. He drove to the apartment on Fortieth Street and pounded on the door, but no one responded. A check with the manager elicited the information that the locks already had been changed. The manager hadn't seen any sign of Scott Dunn since he and Leisha Hamilton had moved. It was time, English realized, that he paid a visit to Max Gianoli, Scott Dunn's employer.

Before the detective got a chance to go to ProSound Electronics, however, the Las Vegas, Nevada, Police Department called and said the missing student English had been looking for had turned up there, safe, but without the money he had brought with him. Ironically, the missing person case that on the surface appeared to be the more suspicious turned out to be okay. Meanwhile the case of Scott Dunn, which had looked innocuous, was proving to be more dangerous.

With the problem of the missing ministerial student solved, English turned his full attention to the disappearance of Scott Dunn. A visit to Max Gianoli still topped English's to-do list. During the short drive, English found himself hoping Gianoli would tell him Dunn had taken a few days off and would be back soon. At ProSound, English introduced himself to a fit, dark-haired man in his forties, half expecting an angry outburst from Gianoli, based on what the man had said to Jim Dunn about firing Scott. English was surprised that Gianoli now seemed genuinely puzzled at Scott's disappearance. He appeared to have had second thoughts on the matter.

Gianoli said it was not at all like Scott to leave so abruptly, especially not with a big Crank It Up competition coming up. He pointed out a row of statuettes that lined a shelf behind the counter. "Scott won those. He's the best. Scott can look at a wire and know where it goes. Everybody else practically has to draw a diagram showing where each wire goes. Not Scott. He can just look at the speaker and do it."

Gianoli also told English that Scott was great for his business. In fact, Scott, good-looking and articulate about his knowledge of electronics, had done a television infomercial to promote the opening of the store. Gianoli confirmed what Jim Dunn had told English, that it was totally unlike Scott to go off without his tools, his car and his prized remote-control boat. "When it comes to his stuff—*he likes his stuff* and he's not going to leave that for anybody."

English questioned two other employees at the store and got the same assessment. Scott was a great installer, a good friend, a grand guy to party with, Pat Taylor told him. Taylor insisted that Scott would not stay away for any length of time without calling and letting them know where he was.

The other installer, Mike Roberts, said the same thing. Roberts insisted that Scott would not go away and leave his tools, which were still there in the shop area of the store. In fact, Roberts currently was using them, because, he said, Scott owed him some money. Since Scott was not around to pay him back, Roberts had appropriated the tools. Roberts said he and Scott had gotten to be pretty close friends. They liked to hang around together in their free time and they were interested in many of the same things. Scott's remote-controlled boat was a favorite of both of them. The Lubbock area doesn't boast many lakes and most of them are of the small, playa variety, but they were big enough to put Scott's boat in. Mike had gone with Scott several times to put the boat in the water.

Roberts told English he had gone by to see Scott at about midnight on Wednesday and stayed for an hour, talking about work, how to get ready for the Crank It Up contest. Scott had not been at work since Monday and Roberts had been installing the stereos in the company van for the competition. Scott promised to come to work the next day. Since Scott's yellow Camaro was parked at ProSound Electronics, Roberts said he would come by the next morning and drive Scott to work. At about 8:45 Thursday morning, Roberts said, he had knocked on Scott's door, but had received no answer. He had tried for fifteen minutes to get a response, but had gotten none. At nine o'clock he left. The only unusual thing he had noticed was that the north window of Scott's bedroom was closed. Normally it was opened wide enough to allow an electric cord to go through it. Scott used the cord to jumpstart his car. Also, Roberts said, he had noticed that Tim Smith's car was parked in the lot next to Scott's apartment. He thought that was unusual, since Smith lived several buildings away.

Gianoli, Roberts and Taylor also insisted that Scott would not have gone away for this long and left his cars behind. Not the Scott they knew.

Driving away from ProSound Electronics, English didn't know what to think. In spite of what Scott Dunn's father and his friends thought, English still felt that maybe, for some reason as yet unknown, Scott had just taken off, but English could not be as sure as he had been earlier.

The following morning, English found a message on his voice mail at the office. Leisha Hamilton had called and said she was planning to go out of town for a couple of days the following week. He wondered why she would take the trouble to call. He had not suggested to her that she stay in the city or that she keep him informed of her whereabouts. Puzzled, he tucked the note into the new folder labeled *Dunn, Scott* that he had started.

His partner, Corporal George White, came into the small office they shared. White, attractive and older than English by at least a dozen years, was not quite as tall as his young partner's six-feet-plus and had graying dark hair. English told White about the Dunn case. For a while, they kicked a few ideas around. Then, since there were other pressing cases to work, they moved on. Nevertheless, a nagging suspicion about the Dunn case, heightened by Jim Dunn's repeated calls every day, began to develop.

About four o'clock on Friday afternoon the telephone rang. It was Jim Dunn again. Taking a deep breath, hating what he had to say,

English admitted to the worried father that he knew no more about his son's disappearance than he had when they had talked twenty-four hours earlier. He gave Jim a detailed account of everything he had done that week to locate Scott.

"I'm sorry I don't have any good news," he told Jim.

Jim had news for the detective and it was not good, either. He told English that Max Gianoli had called both him and Scott's mother. The information Gianoli had given him made Jim even more certain that something bad had happened to his son.

Max Gianoli had told Jim that Leisha had come into the shop on the Monday after Scott left and that she was really acting weird. She was hysterical and crying—shaking, Gianoli said. She had taken Scott's car. Gianoli had not threatened to have it towed, as she had reported to Jim, and Gianoli had wondered why she had not just left it on the parking lot if she was so sure Scott was going to come back at any moment. She had told Gianoli that she wanted Scott to have to face *her* when he came back. The only way to make sure he did that was to keep possession of the things he loved the most—his car and his boat.

Then, Leisha had calmed down enough to tell him that she was afraid of some guy named Tim. She had been dating Tim and she said she thought Tim had done something to Scott. Gianoli said that all the time she was talking, she was looking over her shoulder, as if expecting Tim to come into the store.

According to Gianoli, Leisha said Tim had been following her and was leaving threatening notes on her door. She could not get him to leave her alone. She said she was afraid to go home. Finally, she left the store; Gianoli said he was relieved to see her go.

Promising Jim Dunn that he would follow up on this information immediately, English concluded the call and turned to George White. "I think we need to pay a call on Leisha Hamilton."

White, who had not heard the full phone conversation, nodded. "Maybe we should call and see if she's at home."

English turned back to the phone and dialed Leisha Hamilton's number. The woman answered immediately. English told her he was following up some leads regarding Scott Dunn. She agreed to talk to him, launching into the story about Tim Smith that English had just heard from Jim Dunn. Tim had been coming into the restaurant where she worked, just sitting and watching her work her entire eight-hour shift. And he had been leaving notes on her car and on her apartment door. No matter what she said to him, he would not leave her alone.

"Oh, there's something else," she added. It seemed that her father, who lived three hours away, had visited on May 28 and she had cleaned up the house. When she vacuumed the living room floor, she moved the couch and discovered that a large piece of carpeting had been cut out, leaving the bare carpet padding.

English's chest felt tight. He tried to free it by taking a deep breath. Why would someone remove a piece of carpet? He couldn't think of one reason for such an act that didn't mean trouble for Scott Dunn. Something was wrong here. "Leisha, my partner and I would like to come and take a look at the apartment. All right?"

"Sure. Whatever you want."

"We're on our way," he said, nodding to White. The two grabbed their jackets from the rack and left the office, shrugging into them as they walked. They drove to the Regency Apartments, an older unit that covered about half a block. Its front was a mosaic of narrow windows, aqua-colored doors flush with the building and faded light blue siding. A small, fenced pool was next to Leisha's unit. Number 4 was the northernmost apartment on the west-facing building. The small apartment was of the mass-produced variety popular in the sixties, with a low roof and two small windows flanking the blue wooden door.

English parked in a small area adjacent to Apartment B4, walked quickly up the short sidewalk and knocked on the door. The good-looking woman who opened the door was tall, slim and dark-haired.

They stepped into a small, sparsely furnished living room. The couch sat immediately to their right, on the west wall of the tiny room. English walked across the room and, looking back at the couch, saw a tan oblong of padding underneath it, where a large chunk of the gray and green pile carpet had been removed. The thought crossed his mind that she would not have had to move the couch to see the cut-out in the carpeting. Across from the couch was a portable television on a stand and a portable stereo. A chair that matched the couch was the only other furniture in the living room. To the left was a small kitchenette, separated from the living room by a breakfast bar. The two men moved the couch and measured the area, roughly three feet by five feet, which had been cut out. A pretty big hunk of carpet, English thought.

Then his eyes opened wider. Directly in front of the stereo, the carpet was stained pink in a large, irregular pattern.

"What's this?" White asked.

Leisha shrugged. "That was here when we moved in. I have no idea what it is. Kool-Aid, maybe?"

"Why do you think you never noticed before that the carpet had been cut?" English asked.

She shook her head. "I've been sleeping on the couch ever since Scott left. I've had sheets hanging over it, so I never noticed it."

George White nodded amiably. "Mind if I look around the rest of the apartment?"

Leisha shrugged again and White went into the north bedroom. English glanced cursorily around the small kitchen.

"Tal! Come look at this!" White called from the bedroom.

Hearing the urgency in his partner's voice, English hurried into the other room. He stopped just inside the doorway and stared. The room was empty. Not a stick of furniture. A few boxes, half-filled with clothes and miscellaneous items, were scattered about the floor. George White was holding the edge of a brown afghan that was spread neatly in one corner and staring at the carpet below it. English's eyes followed White's. A half-moon shaped piece of clean carpet, about three feet long and two feet wide, had been patched into the existing carpet in the room. Along the ragged edges of the patch, where the original carpet had been cut, were large brown splotches.

Leisha had said this was the room where she and Dunn slept on the floor. White gave the patched area a closer look, then reached down and pulled at the edge of the clean carpet. The smaller piece of carpet came loose. White peeled back a small portion of it. It was stuck to the padding with duct tape that was crusted with a large amount of a dried ruby substance. Blood?

English, his heart pounding, exchanged a meaningful look with White. Then English turned around and looked through the bedroom door to where Leisha sat on the couch, watching television as if oblivious to their presence.

"Leisha," English called.

She appeared in the doorway.

"What is this?" English asked.

She shook her head. "I don't know. Maybe some mud or something Scott tracked in."

"How long has it been here?"

"I don't know. I haven't used this room since Scott left."

"You didn't put the afghan on the floor? You never moved the afghan or looked under it?" English persisted.

"No. I told you. I've been sleeping on the couch."

"Let's call the ID boys over here," White said and headed for the telephone.

While English and White were waiting for an officer from LPD's Identification Section, they examined the room in minute detail. A closer look at the bedroom wall revealed a collage of whitish smears, lighter than the surrounding wall, as if someone had tried to wash the wall and had done a poor job of it. The smears were markedly evident along the baseboard in that area, but English's eyes followed the smears higher up the wall, where he could see red-brown specks. "Blood?" he suggested to White.

"Leisha, do you know what this is?" White asked.

Leisha walked up to the wall and looked at a brown fleck just above her eye level. "It looks like blood," she said. "And look, there's a hair in it."

She volunteered that she had not noticed the spot before. She pointed to the afghan. "This is where Scott was sleeping the last time I saw him." Her voice was as cool and as calm as if she had been telling them what she had eaten for lunch.

English stared at the woman, scrutinizing her.

English continued to track the brown specks up the wall. He could see droplets on the ceiling, too. Blood spatter? With a chill in his chest, English began to feel that something bad had happened in this room.

ID Officer Gaylon Lewis arrived and began taking photographs. White showed him the bare place in the living room where the piece of carpet had been removed and Lewis photographed that area. In the bedroom, White had replaced the corner of carpet he had pulled away from the wall so that Lewis could photograph the patch in place. Then, White pulled up the half-circle of carpet again, revealing padding underneath that bore dark stains. Duct tape had been taped to the underside of the existing carpet and to the half-circle. This was a fairly neat job and undoubtedly took some time to do. Pictures were taken of the underside of the patch of carpet and of the padding underneath. Lewis collected the duct tape for processing for latent fingerprints. Then the carpet padding and sections of stained carpet were cut out for testing. The detectives noted that the area that was cut from under the couch would have been large enough to cover this semicircular area. There was a large smear of what looked like dried blood between the carpet nailing strip and the wall. A section of the nailing strip was taken up and several scrapings from the wall collected. One area near the upper center of the semicircle had another brown spot that looked a lot like dried blood on the cement.

This was the spot, Leisha had told Tal, where Scott Dunn's head rested when he was in bed.

Carefully, Lewis cut away portions of the Sheetrock containing the dark droplets scattered over the walls, put them in bags and sealed them. The ID Section protocol dictated that everything that might have evidential importance be collected, carefully placed in boxes and bags, sealed and labeled, signed by the officers present, ready to be delivered to the appropriate departments. In this case, everything except the duct tape would be taken to the Texas Department of Public Safety crime lab. The Lubbock Police Department had its own facility for examining fingerprints, but it had no forensic laboratory where other crime scene evidence, such as bloodstains, could be tested. The DPS had a crime laboratory in Lubbock, a few blocks from the police building. Evidence usually was sent there for testing. In some cases, the local lab forwarded evidence on to the State DPS Lab in Austin or to the FBI lab.

Lewis would take the duct tape back to the police department's ID office and check it for fingerprints. Any other evidence he could obtain, such as fibers or hairs, would be turned over to the DPS lab.

While the ID officer was gathering the items, a woman came to the door and introduced herself as the apartment manager, Gail Rose. When English explained what they were doing, she nodded. "I thought something peculiar was going on, with Leisha driving Scott's car all the time. It's none of my business, of course, but Scott was always out there working on his car, which was parked right next to their apartment. Then suddenly, she's driving it and it's all torn up and I didn't see Scott anymore. I thought they might have had a fight or something."

English nodded. "I noticed the car. You say it's torn apart?"

"Let me show you," Gail offered.

He followed her outside to where the yellow Camaro was parked perpendicular to the building, in an area that contained spaces for about six cars. Looking inside, English understood what Gail meant. The back seat had been removed, the passenger seat was tilted a little to one side and the dashboard was missing. Unattached wires were protruding through the firewall. He remembered that Jim

Dunn had told him Scott was transferring the motor and parts from this car to another Camaro with a better body. Apparently the work had already begun. He was surprised the car was operable.

Back inside the apartment, English showed Gail the stains in the living room and in the bedroom. She looked stunned. "That carpet was not stained or patched when Scott and Leisha moved in," she said firmly.

In the meantime, White had called the DPS crime lab and talked with Jim Thomas, a chemist and the supervising criminalist at the lab, which analyzed crime scene evidence in a ninety-county area. Evidence received at this laboratory covered a variety of substances: blood evidence for DNA and serological examination, hair and fibers, glass, shoe prints, tire tracks, controlled substances and various types of trace evidence that might be involved in a criminal investigation.

Although Thomas was the lab supervisor, he also was involved in analyzing certain types of evidence and giving testimony about his analyses. On occasion the chemist responded when an officer requested assistance in the collection of evidence at crime scenes.

White apologized for asking Thomas to stay late on a Friday afternoon and asked if he would stand by to look at samples the detective wanted to bring him. Thomas agreed. White called his LPD supervisor, Sergeant Randy McGuire, and asked him to come to the apartment. When McGuire arrived, English told Leisha, "We really need to ask you to come with us to the department. We'll need to talk more." Leisha agreed. McGuire and English drove Leisha downtown to the police department for further questioning.

White hurried to the DPS crime laboratory and waited while Thomas conducted a preliminary test for blood on a portion of the wooden carpet-tack strip, used as a nailing strip, that White had pried from the wall in Scott Dunn's bedroom. The method Thomas used was a presumptive test with Tetraethyl Benzedrine. Thomas' test revealed that blood was present on the wooden strip. There was one big question that had to be answered before the detectives proceeded. "Is it human blood?" White asked Thomas.

"I can't tell you right now," Thomas said. "The test to determine if this is human blood will take a while, but I'll call you when we run more tests."

White nodded. "I'll be at the office. Call when you know something."

Tal English and Leisha Hamilton were waiting in English's office when White returned. At 6:48 PM Friday, June 7, English read Hamilton her rights. She said she understood them.

Despite the unanswered question of whether it was human blood, White informed Leisha that the samples that had been found in the apartment were, indeed, blood. He asked her to let the police secure the apartment until a more complete examination of the premises could be done. Leisha nodded, gave White the key to the apartment and signed a consent to search it.

At that point, White called ID Sergeant Tomas Esparza, supervisor of the Identification Department, who had gone home for the day. White asked him to come back to the police department. When Esparza arrived, English explained the situation to him. Esparza said, "I'll get with the DPS lab technicians and ID Officer Lewis and perform a complete examination of the apartment."

English and White continued with their interrogation of Leisha Hamilton. Almost word for word, Leisha recited the same story of Scott Dunn's disappearance that she had told earlier to English. She claimed not to have seen the stained area of the carpet and did not have any explanation about the carpet that was cut from under the couch.

She said that when she came home on May 16 and Scott was not there, an afghan that was kept in the bedroom was spread out on the floor where Scott had been sleeping that morning. The bedding was missing. Leisha said she thought Scott had moved out, taking the missing items with him.

"Was he always so orderly?" English asked.

Leisha said it was not like Scott to be neat and spreading the afghan out so carefully was not typical of something he would do. She was not curious enough, however, to look under the afghan to see if there was a reason why it had been spread out.

Leisha also said she did not really believe Scott would leave any of his property behind, because he was too greedy. At that point she again gave detectives a detailed list of items she said were missing from the apartment: a blue laundry basket containing seven pairs of jeans; seven T-shirts, black, with ProSound printed on them in pink; ten pairs of socks and eight to ten pairs of underwear. Also, she said, the bedclothes, consisting of a solid blue king-size flat sheet, a blue-gray comforter, a light blue thermal blanket, three pillows—two were standard size and one was smaller—the small one had a blue-gray pillowcase; one pair of gray western boots, size twelve; one pair of Reebok air pumps, white, blue and orange in color; a second pair of tennis shoes, white with black trim; three towels with white and yellow stripes running lengthwise; one brown towel with a design in the middle.

Scott's brown leather wallet, containing about eight dollars, also was missing, she said.

Talking about her relationship with Tim Smith, Leisha said that she had gone out with him a few times and then tried to get rid of him, but he would not leave her alone. He had followed her several times when she went out with Scott. She said Scott and Tim did not like each other. Then, on being asked where Tim Smith lived, Leisha admitted, "In the same apartment complex where I live."

Although the investigators were still awaiting proof that the blood they had taken from the apartment was human, they asked Leisha, "Would be willing to stay somewhere else for a day or two, so that Esparza and an expert from the DPS can conduct Lumalight and Luminol testing on the bloodstains in the apartment?" She agreed. They also told her they wanted her to come back to the

Police Department the next day, Saturday, and give a formal statement about what she knew.

Once again, she agreed, saying she could find another place to
stay that night. "Can someone take me back to the apartment and let
me get clothes and makeup?" White and English took her home;
Sergeant Esparza followed them. After Leisha had gotten what she
needed and left, the three investigators walked around the outside of
the apartment, noting a chain link fence around the tiny back yard,
which only consisted of a small patio.

Esparza shook his head. "Anyone, especially if it's in the wee
hours of the morning, dark of night, when there's nobody else
around, could walk out the front door of that apartment lugging a
body, walk past this small fenced section and not be seen."

English nodded. "And the parking area is so close. Someone
could have had a car parked here and it wouldn't be one yard from
the front door."

"Yeah," White grunted. English glanced at his partner. Whatever
was on White's mind, he wasn't talking. English said nothing more.
He now felt there was a good chance that Scott Dunn had been brutally attacked in this apartment.

chapter three

Human Blood

Tal English dreaded going to work Saturday morning. He would have to call Jim Dunn and bring him up to date. He hated to tell the worried father that bloodstains had been found in his son's apartment. Perhaps he could wait until the test results came back from the DPS lab showing whether the stains were human blood. If they were, he would have to tell Dunn that he was probably right to be concerned about the safety of his son.

That morning English was barely settled at his desk when Sergeant Esparza buttonholed him. Esparza had already talked to the DPS chemist, Jim Thomas. The chemist had ascertained that the samples were human blood type O. Esparza was going to conduct Lumalight and Luminol tests at Leisha's apartment to determine the amount of blood that had been splashed around and find out if any efforts had been made to wash it away.

Even if blood has been wiped off an area such as a wall or has been cleaned from a piece of carpet, baseboard or ceiling, Luminol is so sensitive that it will show if blood has ever been present. Reputedly, Luminol is sensitive to blood up to one part in five million. Therefore, diluted traces that may still be present will be revealed by Luminol. In fact Luminol responds best to older blood stains.

Thomas had agreed to help Esparza with the test. They were going to meet later that day to photograph the room where the blood had been found.

When Esparza left his office, English sat for a few moments thinking about the case. Then he reminded himself to make the telephone call he had been so filled with anxiety about. He had to find out if Scott Dunn's blood type was O and the only way to do that was to call Jim Dunn.

Barbara Dunn answered the telephone and told English that Jim had gone into Philadelphia for a breakfast meeting, but would be at home a little later. Without thinking, English blurted out the news that blood had been found in Leisha's apartment and the lab tests that showed it to be human blood.

In shock, Barbara could barely speak. She told English that she would have Jim call as soon as he got home. English berated himself for being so insensitive. He shouldn't have told her about the blood. He could simply have asked her to have Jim call when he got home. He could have waited so that he himself could have broken the bad news to Jim Dunn. But there was a sense of urgency now, he consoled himself.

Because of it, English and White set out to discover everything they could about Scott Dunn's disappearance. They decided they would go back to the Regency Apartments and canvass the neighbors.

Since they began during business hours, they received no answer to their knocking at most of the apartments. The few people at home said they hadn't heard or seen anything unusual around 4B recently. White and English decided to resume the canvass later.

The two investigators wanted to know everything they could about Leisha Hamilton, so they next went to the restaurant where she was employed. The manager obligingly showed them Leisha's work record, which confirmed Leisha's statement that she was at work from 6:00 AM until 2:00 PM, on Thursday, May 16, the day she said Scott Dunn disappeared.

English and White returned to the police department to keep their appointment with Hamilton, who had agreed to come in that morning and sign a formal statement. A short time later, Leisha arrived, accompanied by a lanky, dark-haired young man whom she introduced as a friend, Burt Todd, a cook at the restaurant where she worked.

Again, English, George White and Leisha gathered in English's office and once again, English read her Miranda rights and asked if she understood them. Leisha said she did.

"My full name is Leisha Gwen Hamilton and I am twenty-eight years old." She gave them the name of her current employer and stated that her nearest relative was her father.

"I have known Scott Dunn since June 1990. We had been living at 5818 - 24th, Apartment B4, since March 4, 1991."

The remainder of her statement essentially repeated the story she had first told Jim Dunn and later Tal English. She mentioned that Scott had stayed all night at Max Gianoli's house Monday night and all day Tuesday, May 14, because he was sick. Tuesday was her day off. "I cleaned house and am sure the carpet under the couch had not been disturbed at that time."

Leisha went into great detail about that Tuesday evening. She said Scott had called her from Max's house and said he needed her to come and get him, because he was still sick. He also asked her to get him some medicine. "I went to the store and got the medicine; then I went to Max's to get Scott. When I got there, I had to dress Scott, then when we got home, I had to undress him. We stayed home the rest of the night. Scott had a high fever and could hardly walk or talk. I asked him why he had waited so long to call me. He told me he was too sick to make it to the phone. He was so hot, he asked me to turn the air conditioning on. Then I did some ironing. He got hungry and wanted to eat. He didn't want anything we had, so I went to the store and got him something."

Leisha said she remembered exactly how much money she took from Scott's wallet to get food—seven dollars—and he had eight dollars left in the wallet. "I brought home a dollar and some change and left it on the counter. Then I cooked a meal for him."

She said she also had gotten a thermometer at the store and when she got home she took Scott's temperature. It was 102.6 degrees.

"Then I went to bed in my room and Scott slept in the living room on the couch because he didn't want me to catch what he had."

Her capacity for detail continued in her account of the following day, May 15. "I went to work. Scott stayed home and did not leave the house as far as I know. When I got home after work, he was lying on the couch, complaining of a sore throat. I fixed him some tea and he complained, because there was no sugar in it. So I put honey and lemon in it. I made some soup for him. Later, when he got hungry, I went to the store and got him some brown gravy to go with some hamburger meat so he could eat it. I also got him some medicine for his throat.

"Then I went back home, cooked up the hamburger meat and we ate. For a while, we sat around and watched TV and talked; then I took a shower and went to bed. I was lying in the bed when I heard Mike Roberts come over and I could hear them talking. Mike was still there when I went to sleep."

Leisha said that when she woke up the next morning, Scott was in bed with her. She got up and got ready for work. According to Leisha, it was about 5:15 or 5:30 when she got ready to leave, and she woke Scott. He said that he didn't need to get up, that Mike was coming to pick him up. Leisha left and went on to work.

"I got home from work about 2:30 PM," her statement continued. "The front door was locked. I went into the bedroom and saw the afghan lying on the floor, where the pallet usually lay. It was spread out as if someone had made up a bed underneath it and the afghan was the bedspread. I could tell that there weren't any sheets and stuff under it. I lifted up the end of the afghan where the feet would have been when we were in bed and saw that there was nothing under it. I saw that the sheets and pillows were gone and so was the waterbed liner."

Leisha said that next, she went into the other bedroom, which she referred to as Scott's bedroom, and saw that a basket of his clothes was gone. The box that his shoes were in was gone. All of his shoes were gone. She said she noticed that his belt was still there, though.

"I checked the box containing about fifty dollars worth of change that I kept in my closet and it was still there. I also checked the coffee can in the kitchen where I kept change and the change was still there."

After that, Leisha said, she called Max at ProSound and asked him if Scott was at work. Max said he wasn't. He said Mike had gone to the house that morning and had gotten no answer when he knocked at the door calling Scott's name.

"I told Max about the stuff being gone. I made Max swear to me that Scott was not there. I thought that Scott had just packed his shit and left."

At that point in her statement, Leisha's memory became somewhat fuzzy. She didn't remember what she had done after she talked to Max. She didn't recall whether she went to her favorite club. All she remembered was going to bed Thursday night and getting up Friday morning. But her memory apparently cleared as she recited what happened after that.

"Friday, I went to work and came home. When I came home, the front door was open. I am very careful about locking the front door. I went on in the house and looked around to see if Scott was there. He wasn't. I looked in the spare bedroom where the back door was and saw the wood had been kicked off and it was busted in. I looked around and saw the stuff for Scott's radio controlled boat and the other clothes basket was gone. I had put the boat, my radio and all the money in the trunk of my car, so that if Scott came back, he could not get them and would have to come to me and explain what was going on.

"I called Max and asked him if he had seen or heard from Scott that day. I told him what had happened. I made him swear that he didn't know what was going on. I talked to Mike and made him swear to me that he didn't know what was going on."

Then she went down to the office of the apartment complex and told the manager about the back door, because there was no way to secure it. The assistant manager told Leisha to call the police and make a report. She also told Leisha they would need an estimate and directed her to find the maintenance man and ask him to look at the door.

"I found him and he gave me an estimate and locked the door up." Leisha said. "He was still there when the police arrived. I made the report."

At this point Leisha seemed so eager to talk that English didn't need to ask questions. It was as if she were reading from a script.

She continued. "On Monday, the twentieth, I went and got Scott's car at his workplace. Max was talking about towing it. At first I didn't go get the car, because I didn't know I had the keys. I was cleaning the house on the twenty-eighth and noticed the carpet under the couch was missing.

"I have also noticed several times that things were moved around while I was gone. The ashtray was moved, the chairs were moved out from under the table and the table mats were moved. I thought that someone had been in my apartment, but it was just small stuff, so I wasn't sure.

"This last Sunday I knew someone had been in my apartment because the key to Max's apartment, a letter and a comic card from Dairy Queen were all missing. I thought Scott had been there, because he would recognize the red key to Max's apartment."

Leisha told the detectives she had called both of Scott's parents a few times about the missing man. She said that she had not noticed the bloodstained carpet in the bedroom until English and White showed it to her.

Leisha Hamilton's statement was typed up afterwards and she signed it and dated it—June 8, 1991.

Next White asked Leisha if she would take a polygraph test and she agreed. An appointment was set for her to come in the following week. As she prepared to leave, Leisha told the detectives that Tim Smith continued to bother her and was leaving notes on her car and on her apartment door.

All the time Leisha had been talking, Burt Todd had sat quietly listening. But now as Leisha and he prepared to leave, English asked Todd if he would be willing to answer some questions for them. Todd agreed and stayed.

Todd told them that he was twenty-two years old and that he lived east of Lubbock, in a small community of weekend homes, along with some permanent residents. He said that he first met Leisha Hamilton when she went to work at the restaurant where he worked.

"A strange guy named Tim would hang around while Leisha was there," Todd said, "but Leisha was living with a different guy named Scott. Then one day Leisha came to work and said Scott had moved out."

"Right after that, I asked Leisha if she would go to a party with me." Pressed for the exact date, Todd thought it was on either the thirteenth or the twentieth of May. Although he wasn't sure of the date, he was certain it was after Leisha told him Scott had left. The party was at the home of one of his friends. Leisha drove over in the yellow Camaro that belonged to Scott. After the party, Leisha said that her taillights were out and asked Burt to follow her to her apartment. They got to her apartment about three or four o'clock in the morning. Todd and Leisha crashed on the couch in the living room. Todd said he had never seen Scott.

After Leisha and Todd had left, English remained at the conference table, feeling tired and frustrated. Nothing in either statement provided any new leads to the whereabouts of Scott Dunn—or Scott

Dunn's body. They felt Todd had only repeated what Leisha had told him, the same things she had told the detectives. The only new item of interest was Todd's report that he had spent the night with Leisha soon after Scott's disappearance. If Todd was sure it was a Monday, and he seemed to be, and if he was sure it was after Leisha told him Scott had left, then it would most likely have been Monday, May 20, five days after Scott's disappearance, the day she had gone to Scott's workplace and picked up his Camaro, Yellow Thunder.

English shook his head. Even in his line of work, people sometimes amazed him. Leisha's live-in boyfriend disappeared on a Thursday while she was at work. That night, according to her first conversation with Jim Dunn, another boyfriend, Tim Smith, had spent the night with her. Then on Monday, four days later, she had gone out with yet a third man, who had spent the night with her. What kind of relationship had Leisha Hamilton and Scott Dunn had, anyway? And did it have anything to do with Scott's disappearance? Whatever had happened in that small bedroom almost a month earlier, English's gut feeling was that it had been bloody and heinous.

While English and White were questioning Leisha Hamilton and Burt Todd, Sgt. Tomas Esparza and Cpl. Lewis drove to Hamilton's apartment, where they met Jim Thomas. Thomas made an initial examination of the scene and made a sketch of the area, noting traces of blood around the edge of the cut carpet in the north bedroom and on the carpet padding. He also noted some blood on the concrete underneath the padding. Thomas did some preliminary tests on the blood on the baseboard and the concrete slab, which showed positive for blood. He made note of numerous small droplets on one wall of the bedroom and on the ceiling above these spots. One small stain was on the windowsill, but it tested negative in a presumptive test for blood.

After he had finished examining the bedroom, Thomas tested several stains in the living room area to see if there was any blood, but everything in that room tested negative. There were no stains worth testing in the bathroom—nothing that, to Thomas's trained eye, indicated the presence of blood.

While Thomas was examining the scene, Lewis took some photographs of the carpeted area, even though he had photographed the scene the previous day. On this day he took all the regular photographs they needed and then he would take laser photos, because once they sprayed the walls with the liquid Luminol the stains would deteriorate and wash from their original consistency and position. He also had to make sure he had collected all the blood samples that would be needed, because the Luminol would destroy any chance of determining the blood type or DNA.

When Lewis had finished photographing the area, the detectives covered the windows with black plastic, plunging the room into total darkness. Lewis loaded a camera with 1600-speed black-and-white film and mounted it on a tripod, so he could leave the shutter open for the laser photos. The laser was a portable high intensity light that could be directed along the area the investigators wanted to search. They would wear special goggles to see what the light source was revealing. When they were ready to turn out the lights and direct the laser toward the stains, the light would cause the stains to glow and the fast shutter speed would be able to capture whatever was on the walls, ceiling and floor of the room. The shutter would be left open for about ten seconds, then Lewis would close it and move on to the next frame.

Under the laser light, the investigators could see some streaking on the walls, as if someone had tried to wash the walls. The light also revealed a set of fingerprints on the wall, only a few inches above the baseboard. No ridged detail could be seen, so the prints were useless to the investigators. Nevertheless, Lewis took photographs of them.

When the laser photography process was completed, Jim Thomas began to spray the wall with Luminol. Again, the room was in total darkness and the camera was on a tripod, using the same film speed and shutter speed. The three men stared in wonder at the sight before them. Their excitement at what they saw was short-lived, however, tempered by the sobering realization that it indicated that someone had been horribly wounded—had probably died—in this room.

"The whole room lit up," Esparza told English later. "It was unbelievable. It looked like there had been a bloodbath in that room. I mean, it was on the ceiling; it was on the walls; it was in the carpeting, on the doorknobs, everywhere."

The photographs had the appearance of an impressionist painting, done in velvet black and starshine white. The amount of blood on the walls was difficult to determine, but every swipe of the soapy cloth that had been used in attempting to clean the walls was visible—wide swaths of brilliant white, overlapping each other on a canvas of inky black. Bloody, soapy stains were visible up to a height of about five feet or more and extended horizontally for an equal distance along each wall.

Looking at the photographs the following morning, English and White agreed that the scene pointed to a murder—but they had no body and no suspect. Police statistics indicate that those closest to a murder victim usually have the strongest motive, means and opportunity to commit the crime. At this point, Leisha Hamilton topped their list of suspects. They could see already that the relationship between Scott and Leisha was anything but smooth. Leisha had at least two other boyfriends. Who knew how many more men she had relationships with? There was also the information from Scott's father that Scott had said he was engaged to another girl, who was in college in Mississippi. English made a mental note to get in touch with the Registrar's office at the college and see if he could locate the girl. Although the co-ed might not be enrolled in summer school, the university should have a home address and telephone number for her.

The relationship between Scott and Leisha was complicated. Though the detectives concluded that it probably was filled with tension, possibly jealousy and anger, they could see no motive for

Leisha to kill Scott. What did she have to gain by killing him? She certainly wouldn't be living alone if he left her, unless she chose to do so. Men were lined up at her door, apparently just waiting for her to let them in. One of those men, according to Leisha, was Tim Smith.

"Maybe we'd better go talk to Smith," English suggested.

White nodded. "I'll drive."

At the apartment complex, White parked in front of Number 229, where they had been told Tim Smith lived. They knocked on the door and there was no answer. English peered in through a small window and saw that the apartment was empty. An assistant manager told them that Tim had moved to Apartment 107 in the same complex. The new apartment was a two-bedroom unit. "Tim said he needed more room. He intended to provide a place for Leisha Hamilton and her daughter to live," the manager said.

This was the first the detectives had heard about Leisha's having a daughter. They exchanged puzzled glances.

At Apartment 107, Tim Smith invited the detectives into the small living room. English explained to Smith that they were looking for Scott Dunn, talking to people who knew the missing man, and they wanted to ask Smith some questions. Smith nodded— rather reluctantly, English thought. While they were talking, English noticed a roll of gray duct tape lying on its side on a bookshelf. English experienced a quick surge of adrenaline. This could be their first solid clue to what happened to Scott Dunn! He said nothing at the time, intending to ask Smith about it before they left.

"Mind if we search your apartment?" White asked.

Smith hesitated, glanced around the room, then wandered from room to room, as if he were making sure there was nothing to be found. Finally, he nodded to White. "Okay. Look around."

White offered him the Consent-to-Search form and Smith signed it. English still didn't mention the tape. Only the three of them were in the apartment. It would be safe where it was.

In one of the bedrooms, White found a cardboard moving box that still had a few items in it. It had been sealed with gray duct tape. White knelt and pulled off a piece. "I'm going to take this tape. See what the lab guys make of it."

"Did you notice the duct tape in the living room?" English asked.

White glanced up and shook his head.

"It's on the shelf."

"No!"

English grinned. "Right out in plain sight."

"Let's take a look." White got to his feet and the two men went back into the living room. English glanced at the bookshelf. The tape was no longer there. English gave Smith a steady, smoldering look. "We need that tape."

"What tape? I don't know what you're talking about," Smith said.

"I saw some tape up there, on that shelf. It was lying flat, on the sticky side. You moved that tape. There's nobody else here."

Without a word, Smith walked over to the shelf, took some books from the shelf below the one where English had seen the roll of duct tape, pulled the tape out and handed it to English.

By this time English's heart was almost pumping out of his chest. Staring at Tim Smith, English felt was involved in Scott Dunn's murder. Why else would he have hidden the tape?

After marking the duct tape as evidence, English and White asked Tim Smith for permission to search his car. Smith signed the Consent-to-Search form for his car, but the detectives found nothing that connected the car to Scott. Nevertheless, English asked Tim to accompany the detectives to the police department for questioning and he agreed. They also took several items from the apartment—a few towels, a pair of boots that appeared to have a stain of some kind on the soles, some old rags and T-shirts. All were grimy and soiled. English harbored a small hope that these items might have been used the night Scott disappeared. The detectives were not too optimistic, however, because they were investigating an event that had happened more than three weeks earlier. There had been more than enough time to dispose of any bloodstained clothing or cloths that might have been used to clean up Scott Dunn's blood.

After English read Tim Smith the Miranda warning, the interview went on for hours. Smith's response to every question seemed to the detectives to take forever, as if he were deliberating, figuring out an acceptable answer. When he did respond, he was hesitant and evasive, failing to give a direct answer to any question.

Smith denied over and over again that he knew anything about Scott Dunn's disappearance. He admitted, however, that he had been pursuing Leisha. He said they had been involved for several weeks, but now she was telling him their affair was over. He went on to say he couldn't accept that.

"I love her and I want her back," he insisted.

English asked Smith if he would be willing to take a polygraph examination and Smith agreed. At that point, without taking a formal statement, the detectives allowed Smith to leave, advising him that they would schedule a polygraph and let him know the date and time.

A weary English felt a faint whispering gnawing at the back of his mind as Smith left. He was all but certain this man walking the streets knew and probably had been part of what had happened to Scott Dunn.

Monday morning, when Jim Dunn called to see if the detectives had made any progress over the weekend, English told him the investigation was gaining momentum and that other detectives would be working with him. "George White will do the legwork necessary to trace Scott's movements and his relationships during the last weeks before he disappeared. At the same time Detectives Walt Crimmins and Billy Hudgeons will re-canvass the neighborhood around the Regency Apartments and follow up on any leads they unearth."

Missing person cases, English knew, grow colder with each passing day. English worried that too much time had passed already for detectives to find anyone who might remember a crucial detail. Nevertheless, the effort had to be made.

Leisha Hamilton came to police headquarters to take her polygraph examination that day. The examiner, Kenneth Ackors, explained that it was an evidentiary polygraph, given not because she was a suspect, but to determine if she had any knowledge that would help the police find out what had happened to Scott Dunn. An evidentiary polygraph examination differs from what the police call a specific issue polygraph in that the examiner asks more general questions of the witness. Leisha assured Ackors she understood. Ackors did not ask Leisha Hamilton point blank, "Did you kill Scott Dunn?" Instead, he asked questions such as "Do you know for sure the last time anyone saw Scott Dunn? Do you know for sure where Scott is now? Do you know for sure whether anyone has hurt Scott Dunn or caused him pain? Do you know for sure when the carpet was cut from under the couch?"

Thereafter Leisha always vowed that she passed the polygraph test, although she admitted to reporters later that her answer had appeared deceptive on one question: whether or not she knew where Scott Dunn was now.

After the examination, Leisha gave English some of the notes that Tim Smith had written her. After she left, he read the letters with a mixture of elation and sadness. Elation, because the letters strengthened Tim's motive for harming Scott. Sadness, because they revealed an insecure, lonely man who was obsessively in love with a woman who obviously was playing cruel games with him. Leisha apparently wanted relationships with both men. The resulting triangle was constructed on explosive elements—Smith's avowed love, a convenient living arrangement for Leisha and Scott and sexual control for Leisha Hamilton. Smith's letters indicated he was willing to go to great lengths to make it possible to be with her. The letters showed Smith had a powerful motive for wanting Scott Dunn removed from the triangle.

Leisha had indicated to English that she had begun seeing Tim around the time of Scott's disappearance, but the letters told another story. Some of the notes were undated, but one was a long letter dated almost three weeks before Scott's disappearance. It implied that Tim and Leisha were involved in an ongoing affair. From Tim's words, English formed an impression of a naive young man who had fallen in love with an experienced woman who knew how to manipulate men and enjoyed it.

"Dear Leisha," the note began. *"I'm sorry to have to say this, but I'm tired of being made to look like a dumbass fool!…You sleep with him,"* the letter continued, *"which makes me feel you are cheating on me, while I remain faithful to you. I am not going to cheat on you, but…*

"You seem to think this is some kind of waiting game. Well, the waiting is over for me because I am fed up with being made out to look like some stupid idiot born yesterday. I love you, but if you turn your back on me, then I will do my best to stay away from you and leave you to do whatever in hell it is you want to do. I will walk out of your life and plan on staying out of it for good. My heart cannot take any more indecision from you.

"…It is either me or him, I hope you don't make the wrong decision, but if you do, you do, and you most likely will. I will somehow have to deal with it in the best manner I know how. I love you more than you may ever know, but I will stay away if it kills me, if that is the decision you make. There are no more excuses. We can work things out.

"I have a lot of friends who can help me if I need them to because I have done a lot for them and you could say they owe me. A place for you and your daughter to stay is <u>no</u> problem. <u>You don't have to stay where you are!</u> The time to change your life for the better is <u>NOW! Please hear me!</u> I <u>love</u> you very much and there is nothing I wouldn't do to make your life better and more fulfilled. You are my Sunshine. You make me want to live life to the

fullest. You are very beautiful to me. <u>I don't care if you don't believe me</u>, *because it is true! This decision will change our lives for the better or the* *worse. Please make the right one! Love, Tim.*

"P.S. *I don't mean to sound like an ass about this but it is just time to* *take our emotions off this insane roller coaster ride and stabilize our feelings* *about one another. I realize I probably love you more than you love me, but* *if he wasn't around, I know that you would love me as much as I love you* *...You have <u>five</u> days counting today and Thursday to decide what to do. I* *am thru playing games! I love you too much to continue dangling on the edge* *of hope. I need to know, one way or the other. Love, Tim.*"

As English held the letter, his mind raced. Even though the lovesick man had given her an ultimatum—choose between Scott and himself—Leisha had refused to do so. So though Leisha made no choice, Tim continued to declare his love for her.

English put the letter down and picked up a card, which apparently had accompanied flowers. It carried a Mother's Day greeting. It simply said, *"The Woman I Love! Please accept my apology."* It was signed, *"Tim."*

Another undated note on a green 3x5 card read: *"Dear Green* *Eyes. I will always love you...If you would just accept God into your heart,* *you would change. I know it would work between us if we would trust each* *other. I don't hold it against you whatever you did with Burt. You are very* *special to me and I hope I get another chance to show you that I can trust* *you and stay off your back. With the greatest love. Tim (Superman)"*

English turned this card over in his fingers, pondering. It must have been written after Scott's disappearance, because Burt Todd had indicated that he and Leisha had not begun seeing each other until after May 16. How many other men were there in Leisha Hamilton's life?

As the relationship deteriorated, the tone of the notes changed dramatically. An undated card read: *"<u>Don't worry</u>. There won't be any-* *more flowers from me. You have turned into something ugly since I met you.* *You are letting things turn you into an ugly Bitch. It is very unfortunate,* *because you are, or were, a very beautiful woman at one time. I wish you would change back into that woman I know you can be. Don't throw everything away…I still love you. Tim."*

English picked up a pink card, undated, that continued in the same vein: *"Don't worry, there won't be anymore notes, calls or anything else. These are my last words to you. I can't believe you would think evil of me because you know me better than that. You owe me an apology when this is all over with. A big apology. I still love you and I don't know why. I should be extremely angry with you for the way you have been thinking."*

This must be a recent card, English concluded, written when Tim Smith found out that Leisha had been telling people she thought he had "done something to Scott."

A card dated June 8, English noted, said, *"Goodbye, Green Eyes. You broke my heart in two and don't care. I gave you all my love, my heart, and my soul, yet you threw it all away. I have loved you beyond words. We need each other, yet you don't see it. I wanted you to be the Yellow Rose of Texas for me, but you would not. I bought you a rose the other day, but you were gone. All they had today was a yellow carnation. As you have thrown my love away in your heart anyways, I want you to trash the carnation to symbolize your disgust of my love for you."*

The last card, also dated June 8, reinforced the sense that Tim Smith was filled with despair over the deterioration of his relationship with Leisha. *"It's ironic,"* Tim wrote, *"you seem to hate the one who loves you the most. All I ever wanted was to do things with you, be with you, and spend as much time with you as I could. And for this, you despise me?"*

English sat, hunched over his desk, fingering the small collection of vari-colored cards, wishing he had pushed Tim Smith a little harder when he had the opportunity. He consoled himself with the thought that Tim was scheduled to come in for a polygraph test in a few days and he would be able to question him further. Maybe then Smith would tell the investigators what had happened to Scott Dunn.

chapter four

Search for a Body

It was time—past time—English knew, to move the investigation into high gear. Impetus to do just that was provided when Jim Dunn called to relay the information that Scott had type O positive blood, the same type that had been found in that small bedroom.

English and White already had checked with Leisha Hamilton's employer and had discovered that she had been at work on her regular shift May 16. Now they decided to contact Tim Smith's employer. The manager was cooperative, agreeing to show them Tim's work records for the day in question. The time sheets revealed that Smith had not gone to work Thursday, May 16. Tim had told the manager his brother had been involved in a traffic accident. The other party involved in the accident was suing his brother and Smith's entire family, Tim said, so he had to go to help his brother.

Then English and White drove back out to the Regency Apartments and asked the manager if they could see Tim Smith's old apartment. They wanted to know if the carpet in that apartment was the same as Leisha's—gray and green, which was also the same as the carpet fibers found on the duct tape the investigators had found in

Smith's new apartment. The carpet in Tim's old apartment proved to be tan, brown and white, the same as that in his new apartment.

When the detectives returned to the police building, English spoke with Officer Gary Smith, who had taken the criminal mischief report that Leisha had made concerning the door that had been kicked in. He told them that when he went to the apartment, a blanket of some type was lying in the northeast bedroom. Leisha told him that this is where they slept. He did not notice the carpet missing under the couch. He couldn't remember if there were sheets on the couch.

White tracked down Tim's brother, who was at work in another town in Texas. White identified himself and Smith agreed to talk with the investigator. Smith said he had not been involved in an auto accident and that White could check his time card for May 15 and May 16 and see that he had been at work. He told White that on June 15, however, he had driven to Lubbock and helped Tim move to his new apartment.

When White asked the young man if Tim talked about any of his friends, he said Tim talked about a girl he was seeing. Tim seemed to like her a lot, but hadn't mentioned her name.

English then located Tim Smith's father, who lived in a small community near Lubbock. Tim had lived there with his family after high school. The elder Smith said to English that his son had told him that he had taken off from work because he was sick on May 16, the day Scott Dunn disappeared.

Meanwhile, White was checking into Leisha Hamilton's background. Since Leisha had told him she had been living in Albuquerque the previous fall, White called the Albuquerque, New Mexico, police department and talked to Detective Torres. White asked Torres to check their department and see if they had information on Leisha Hamilton, Scott Dunn or Tim Smith. Torres, after a little research, said he found information only on Hamilton. She had been convicted of theft and forgery and was currently on probation. He said she gave the names of a brother and her father, both residents of Texas. Another name she gave was of her husband, whose whereabouts were, Leisha would later tell White, currently unknown.

Later that day, White got a telephone tip from a man who lived about three blocks from Scott Dunn's apartment. The man, Ralph Jones, said it was his habit to take a walk early in the morning alongside the west perimeter of the Regency Apartments, which was only a hundred feet or so from B4, where Scott and Leisha lived. Jones said that one morning, he couldn't remember for sure if it was May 16, but it was around that time, he walked past the alley that abutted the parking lot north of B4, as he did on most mornings. In the alley, probably less than thirty feet from the door to B4, was a Dumpster. That morning, several cats had surrounded the Dumpster and were making noises, trying to get inside it. He had never seen this happen before, so he went over to the Dumpster, threw a handful of pebbles at the cats to scatter them away and opened the lid. According to Jones, the Dumpster was not quite full and he could see a large sheet of plastic and some rolled-up carpet that looked dirty and stained. He couldn't tell what color the carpet was because he could see only the backing and he thought it was brown. He wasn't sure what color the plastic was, either, but it might have been blue or green.

Detectives Walt Crimmins and Billy Hudgeons re-canvassed the apartments around Leisha's, but learned little new information. However, they did uncover tidbits that confirmed reports others had given them about Tim Smith. Several neighbors thought Leisha was seeing Tim Smith without Scott Dunn's knowledge. Smith often was seen walking around the complex parking areas, acting as if he were checking to see if the yellow Camaro was gone. The neighbors said Tim acted strange when he was out and about, always behaving as if he were watching someone.

Since Mike Roberts, who had worked with Scott Dunn, was the last person, other than Leisha, who saw Scott alive, English arranged for the man to come to the police building and give a statement. After stating his full name and giving his address and place of employment, he told the detectives he had come to Lubbock from Washington to live with his father. He said he had known Scott Dunn about three and a half months and that Scott had helped him get his job.

The remainder of Roberts's statement followed the story he had told detectives earlier. He said he had been working late on the van that they were getting ready for the Crank It Up Contest. Mike stopped by Scott's apartment on his way home. He knocked on the door, but there was no answer. The door was unlocked, so he went in to find Scott asleep on the couch. He shook Scott's shoulder to wake him up. They talked for an hour or so about what to do to the van. Scott asked him to stay the night, but Mike refused. He had gone back the next morning to get Scott for work, but had received no answer.

"I assumed Leisha had taken him to work," Roberts said. "When I got to work, no one was there and Max showed up about a half hour later."

Roberts said that since Scott's disappearance, Leisha had talked to him about Scott a few times, but mostly she talked to Max.

Another exercise in futility, English thought. Nothing they were doing, no one they were questioning, had given them one iota of information about what had really happened to Scott.

Crimmins, Hudgeons, White and English met to compare notes and decide on the next step in the investigation. English told Hudgeons and Crimmins, "I've gotten the information we've been waiting for from Jim Dunn; Scott's blood was type O positive, the same as that found in the apartment." He felt that Scott's blood had been spilled in the apartment; the challenge was proving his conviction.

"I know we haven't had the occasion to use reversed DNA testing much," Hudgeons said, "but why don't we try and see what we come up with? If we had blood samples from Scott's parents, couldn't tests tell us if the blood we found belonged to their child?"

"Good point," English agreed and began to research the issue.

His research led him to Dr. Arthur Eisenberg of the University of North Texas Health Sciences Center in Fort Worth, Texas. Dr. Eisenberg was a DNA expert with an international reputation. He was an associate professor in the pathology department at North Texas and director of the DNA laboratory there; he had been part of a group of scientists who developed the field of human identification using DNA testing. Eisenberg also had helped develop a company that was set up to use DNA for medical diagnostics in the field of cancer-based testing. In 1989, the State of Texas had established the laboratory at the University of North Texas Health Sciences Center for DNA testing for use in forensics and medical diagnostics, and to work with the state Attorney General's office in establishing paternity. The Texas Office of the Attorney General is responsible for child support enforcement, distribution of welfare benefits and the establishment of paternity in those cases where the father—or mother—is not paying the required child support.

When Hudgeons asked Dr. Eisenberg about the possibility of using reversed DNA testing in the Dunn case, the scientist explained to Hudgeons that the term "reversed paternity" is used in cases like theirs, when an unknown biological sample is available and the biologist is attempting to establish the identity of the person who contributed that biological sample. If he had blood from Scott's natural parents and the LPD sent him samples from the crime scene, a comparison could determine if the sample belonged to an offspring of those parents, Dr. Eisenberg assured Hudgeons.

Now English had to make two painful telephone calls, to Scott's father and mother, asking them to go to their local police labs and have blood samples drawn so they could be sent to Dr. Eisenberg. English told them he would make arrangements with their local police departments to ensure the unbroken chain of custody of the blood samples until they were mailed to Dr. Eisenberg. From those containers of blood and the samples sent to him from the Lubbock Police Department, the molecular biologist would attempt to ascertain whether the bloodstains came from Scott Dunn.

English felt strongly that Dr. Eisenberg's DNA tests would show English's theories to be true. He was also sure that Tim Smith somehow was connected to the bloodstains in Scott's bedroom, but he needed some tangible evidence. He called Gaylon Lewis in the Identification Section and asked him if he had finished his examination of the duct tape that had been used to patch the bloodstained carpet.

Lewis told him he had finished the examination of the carpet and the duct tape and had found no fingerprints. He had, however, found some hairs adhering to the tape. Since the LPD facility had no technology to make hair comparisons, Lewis put the hairs in a bag, sealed it and signed it.

The following day, Wednesday, June 12, Leisha Hamilton showed up unannounced at police headquarters. She told English that Tim Smith had made a statement she thought was strange. He had told Rachel Borthe, the assistant apartment manager at Regency, that if he had never met Leisha, Scott probably would still be around.

English called Borthe and asked her about any conversations she might have had with Smith. She verified what Leisha had said. "Tim said something else interesting as well," she said. "Tim and I had been talking about what could have happened to Scott Dunn. I asked, 'What would someone do with a body if they wanted to get rid of it?'

"'They might put it in the landfill,' Tim answered. 'The trash has to go somewhere.'"

Then, said Borthe, Tim was silent for a moment, as if pondering her question further. Finally, he said, "Or, they could chop it up and throw it in the lake. You know, they do that in drug shows all the time."

English felt a cold certainty: Tim's first response was the instinctive one, probably the truthful one. The body could have been put in the Dumpster that was only a few feet away from Leisha's apartment door and then dumped into the landfill. Tim's statement about the lake could have been made to throw Rachel Borthe off the track, to make her think he was merely speculating.

English was certain that Tim Smith could answer many of the questions he had about Scott's disappearance. He was looking forward to interviewing Smith again when he came for his polygraph test, which was scheduled for that afternoon.

Smith did not show up for the polygraph, however. Instead, he called English and told him that he had hired an attorney, who had advised him not to take a polygraph test and not to speak to the detectives unless the lawyer was present.

English sat in his office, re-reading his notes, berating himself for not leaning a little more heavily on Tim Smith Sunday night, when they had first questioned him. At that time Tim had declined the offer of an attorney, but he had displayed behavior that had seemed suspicious to English.

They *had* to find Scott's body, English thought. In his mind he explored the possibilities, asking himself if he were in Smith's place and needed a place to hide a 6' 2", 170-pound man, where would he go? More than likely, Smith would choose a site with which he was familiar, perhaps the area around the community where Smith had once lived with his family for several years. It was far enough out in the country to support farmland, along with some pastureland covered with thorns, a few trees and some dry washes that filled up when West Texas got its meager rainfall, but stayed dusty and weedy most of the year.

The Lubbock Landfill, where the city residents and businesses dumped their refuse, was in the same general vicinity as the airport and the area where Tim had lived. English had a strong hunch that was the place to search for Scott Dunn's body.

On the other hand, English had learned from two different sources that Tim Smith was fascinated by airplanes. Leisha had said Smith liked to drive out to the airport and watch the planes landing

and taking off. Smith's father had told investigators his son had taken
flying lessons at Wheat Aviation, located on the western edge of
Lubbock. This piqued English's curiosity. Wheat Aviation was surrounded by rough, brushy terrain. It would be possible to dispose of
a body there fairly easily and it might not be found for months, or
even years. Or never.

A third possibility, if Tim Smith was responsible for Scott Dunn's
disappearance, was the mile after mile of scrub grass, brush and shallow gullies that surrounded the community where his father had
lived. The ground was hard, but a shallow grave could have been dug
with a little work and there was enough dried vegetation and brush
to cover it. If one didn't care if the body was found eventually, it
could have been tossed in one of the gullies with dried limbs and
grass tossed over it. Even then, it might not be found until winter-
time, when the wild grasses and weeds died.

The only thing to do was initiate a search, walk the area around
Wheat Aviation and around Smith's father's home and talk to the
City Sanitation Department about the possibility of searching the
landfill for Scott Dunn's body.

Friday morning, a week after the discovery of blood stains in
Leisha Hamilton's apartment, Tal English, Billy Hudgeons, Walt
Crimmins, Randy McGuire and Texas Ranger Jay Peoples went to
Wheat Aviation. The five men divided the area into grids and walked
through the tall grass, thorny weeds and shallow ditches. Finally,
sweaty, tired and frustrated after a morning in the ninety-degree
weather, the group had found nothing indicating a recent burial or
other method of disposing of a body.

English was discouraged, but determined not to give up. After a
quick lunch, the group of searchers drove across town to East
Municipal Drive. The area where the Smiths had resided was rugged,
with a great deal of vegetation. The men combed that area, just as
they had the Wheat Aviation area, but discovered nothing remotely
resembling a grave.

While they were in the area, English stopped at the private company that collected garbage from businesses and dumped the refuse into the city landfill. English was introduced to Johnny Quintavilla, a supervisor who could give him information about the routes and schedules for the company's trucks. Quintavilla said his company collected garbage from Dumpsters on both sides of the alley behind the Regency Apartments.

"Can you tell me if a Dumpster from the Regency Apartments was picked up on May 16?" English asked.

"The Dumpsters in that area fill up quickly because of the large numbers of people in the complexes," Qunitavilla told him. "We pick up the Dumpsters on Mondays and Fridays, so a pick-up should have been made in the early morning of Friday, May 17."

Perhaps, English thought, Scott Dunn's body had been discarded in the Dumpster a few feet from his own front door. If the murder had occurred after Leisha got home Thursday evening, she and Smith might have felt safe disposing of the body in the Dumpster, knowing it would be only a few hours before the garbage was collected.

Back at the police building, English contacted Lee Ramirez, the superintendent for solid waste management for the City of Lubbock, and asked if he could locate the area where refuse from Regency Apartments was dumped. The superintendent assured the detective he could and offered to drive out to the landfill with English and show him the spot.

The two men drove to the landfill and met the site supervisor, John Alamanza, there. The supervisor showed Ramirez and English the approximate area where garbage from the Regency complex was dumped on May 17. The area was approximately seventy-five feet by thirty feet and was about fifteen feet deep. Alamanza told them that another layer of refuse would be dumped there in about two weeks.

Alamanza told English it would be possible to conduct a search of the area for a body, but it would require heavy equipment to dig up compacted refuse. English and Ramirez headed back for town and English wondered how he could justify to his superiors the expense of digging up a rather large portion of the city landfill. When he got back to the office, however, his attention was directed elsewhere.

While English had been out trudging through ankle-high grass, over dried rubboard washes and grass burrs, a Crime Line tip had come in from a police informant that a man named Doug Holden had once threatened to kill Scott Dunn. According to the inform-ant, Holden was an insurance salesman who moonlighted selling cocaine. The informant said Holden had believed that Dunn had rat-ted on him to the Drug Enforcement Agency. Holden was described as a white male, about twenty-five years old, muscular build, red hair, with almost an albino complexion.

Following up on this tip led English to a conversation with Lubbock Sheriff's Deputy Billy Tims, who said he had received the same information from a confidential informant. Tims's informant reported that Holden had said he was going to kidnap Dunn and then kill him.

English thanked the county deputy. He appreciated the help, but at that point, he could not correlate Holden's alleged threat with the other evidence the LPD had obtained. Too much time had passed since the incident between Scott and Holden.

On June 17, Leisha Hamilton called Tal English once again. He thought ruefully that she was calling him almost as much as Jim Dunn. Scott's father called every morning and English filled him in on everything he could about the progress of the investigation.

Leisha, on the other hand, seemed to find some new evidence to bring to the detective every day. In this case she told English that she had seen Tim Smith waiting for her in the restaurant parking lot when she got off work the day before. She hadn't wanted to talk to him, she said, so she asked one of the cooks from the restaurant to walk with her to her car. Leisha confided that Tim had told her he wanted to talk to her, but she had refused. When she arrived at home, though, he was standing near her apartment and again said he wanted to talk to her. "I told him to leave me alone and went into my apartment."

She also told English she had remembered something else about the days just prior to Scott's disappearance. She said that on the Tuesday night, before she had brought Scott home from Max Gianoli's, Tim had followed her to the grocery store when she went to get food and medicine. He had asked her to come home with him, but she had refused, telling him that Scott was sick and she had to stay home and take care of him. "That night," Leisha said, "Tim called the apartment several times, but I refused to talk to him."

The following day, when she had gone again to the store to get more food for Scott, Tim had followed her again, asking her to go to his apartment. Again she had refused.

English made notes of what she told him, wondering if she had conveniently forgotten to tell him this earlier or if she was simply stepping up a campaign to blame Smith for Scott's death.

For several days, English had been anxiously waiting for the Registrar's office at Mississippi State University to return his call concerning Jessica Tate, the girl Scott had told his father he'd gotten engaged to. Finally, it came and he learned that Jessica's records contained her mother's telephone number and that of her sister, both of whom now were living in Texas. English called Jessica immediately and, as the conversation went on, the investigation took a new direction.

Jessica Tate told English she had met Scott Dunn when she went to the store where he worked to buy a stereo system for her car. At that time she was eighteen years old and a senior in high school. Scott was twenty-two. She lacked only two courses to graduate, so she went to class for those two periods each day and worked part-time at a supermarket. Her mother and stepfather had given her a new car and she decided to use some of her earnings to get a better stereo system for it.

"I was frugal enough to try to talk Scott down on the price," Jessica told English. "We negotiated for a while. Finally, he said he would come down on the price if I would go out with him."

She didn't take him up on his proposition for several days, but she kept going back to the store to talk to him. "The weather was warm, so he didn't wear a shirt when he was working in one of the cars and he had a nice tan. He was cute.

"And he was funny, really funny," she said. "I just liked being around him. Finally, I told him I would go on a date with him and all through spring and summer, we were together a lot. "He treated me like a queen and he was very, very romantic. He would sing to me and do other things no other man had ever done for me.

"He was just sweet," she said. Scott also was very polite and respectful to her parents, who liked him and did not object to Jessica's dating him, although he was several years older than she.

During the summer, their days were rather unstructured, she said. Jessica still was working a few hours a week and Scott worked on a contract basis, so they had free daytime hours to cruise in Scott's yellow Camaro, "Yellow Thunder," she called it, or go to the park. If Scott had to work, sometimes Jessica would go to the shop and talk to him while he worked. Other times, she said, they would go to his house and watch television or movies.

The Simpsons was Scott's favorite television show, Jessica said, and they often watched it together. There was one couple with whom they spent a great deal of time. The woman was neat and they had a lot of fun, but the man made Scott mad. Scott didn't like the way the man treated his wife. He was violent and abusive and Scott couldn't stand that.

Scott also taught Jessica to play pool, she said. He was an excellent player and loved the game. Jessica said that they both had other interests and led busy lives, so they were not together all the time, but they did see a lot of each other.

English asked Jessica if she knew Leisha, but Jessica had not heard of Leisha Hamilton until shortly before Scott disappeared.

Jessica's stepfather was an alumnus of Mississippi State University and it was because of him that she had applied to that university and had been accepted. When she told Scott she was going away to college, he had not been happy about it. In fact, he had asked her to marry him. She had told him she intended to go away to college, no matter what he thought. Scott wasn't happy with her decision and they became estranged.

However, they had seen each other briefly the next Christmas, when she came home on holiday break, and Scott had told her that Max Gianoli was planning to open a new store in Lubbock and he would be moving there.

In mid-March, Jessica called Scott at work to tell him she was planning to come home for spring break and stay with her sister. The weekend she was to arrive coincided with the annual Rattlesnake Round-up, held in Sweetwater, Texas. Scott asked her to meet him there and they would spend the weekend together.

"We fell in love all over again," Jessica said. "I couldn't resist him. He looked at me with those sweet puppy dog eyes and asked me to take him back and he sang romantic songs to me and I said yes."

A carnival atmosphere had prevailed, complete with amusement park rides and entertainment, in addition to the rattlesnake hunt. "After I went back to school, we talked on the phone all the time," Jessica said. "Then one day just before the school term was over, I called him and a woman answered the phone.

"I couldn't believe it. I was so shocked. And when I asked her who she was, she said she was Scott's wife."

"You can't be Scott's wife," Jessica answered. "I'm Scott's wife and I want to talk to him."

"I don't know who you are or what you are talking about," the woman said. "I'm telling you, I'm Scott Dunn's wife."

Jessica slammed down the phone. Who was this woman? She couldn't be married to Scott. Jessica was certain of that.

The next day, when Scott called Jessica, she told him about the woman who had answered his telephone, claiming to be his wife. He assured her that he was *not* married to Leisha and that he was moving out of that apartment. He told Jessica there was nothing to worry about. Jessica told English, "He just went on and on about how much he loved me and that we were going to get married and he described the ring he was having made for me." Because she was in love, and because she wanted to believe him, Jessica accepted his explanation. Scott told her he really wanted to see her as soon as she got home from Mississippi, which would be the first week in May.

Jessica called Scott when she arrived at her sister's and told him she would be there for a while. He asked her if she would go to Pennsylvania with him in August, to meet his family. Delighted at the prospect, she agreed.

Scott also told her that he had to make a business trip that week and would have a layover at DFW airport. He asked her if she would meet him at the airport. He said he had only one more payment to make on her ring and would bring it with him when he came. She agreed to meet him. He told her he would call her back and let her know the exact day, time and flight number. She never heard from him again.

A day or two afterward, Jessica said, Leisha Hamilton had called her. "It was really weird. I already thought she was strange, because of what Scott had told me about her. She wanted to know if I had heard from Scott. She said he had left and had taken all his things and she thought he might have gone to Fort Worth because I was there."

Jessica confirmed what others had told English about the way Scott felt about his possessions. She said he loved Yellow Thunder so much that he would never let anyone else drive it. In fact, she said, *she* had never driven it and she could not believe he would have gone away somewhere and left it behind. Nor, she said, would he have left his tools. He would not even let other people *use* his tools, she said, unless the person was a "really, really good friend."

English went over and over in his mind all that he knew, trying to integrate the statement Jessica had given into the information the police already possessed. At this point he felt that Tim Smith was a promising suspect for several reasons. He had the opportunity and he had the motive. English believed that the roll of duct tape found in Smith's apartment would, when tested, put him at the scene of the attack on Scott. He was anxious for the DPS crime lab to finish testing the tape and the green carpet fibers that had been stuck to the tape. He felt strongly that the evidence would show that those carpet fibers had come from Scott Dunn's apartment. That would give the police solid, scientific evidence that Smith was at the scene.

Smith also had a motive for wanting to harm Scott—his obsession with Leisha and his belief that with Scott out of the way, Leisha would be all his. Smith also knew that Scott was sick and could have known that Scott was home alone after Leisha went to work the morning of May 16, because he obsessively watched Leisha's apartment.

The question in English's mind was how Leisha fit into the picture. He wondered how she could have lived in that apartment for two weeks without noticing the bloodstained, clumsily patched carpet in her bedroom. Had she been present when Scott was killed? If the attack on Scott occurred sometime after 1:00 AM, after Mike Roberts had left the apartment, then she had the opportunity either to kill Scott and persuade Tim to help her eliminate the evidence or to commit the killing with Tim. That made more sense to English. They could have killed Scott together and disposed of the body, then attempted to clean up the evidence. She knew more than she was telling; of that English was certain. The hole in that theory was lack of motive.

Until his talk with Jessica Tate, he hadn't been able to find a reason for Leisha to kill Scott. The things Jessica had told him could plug that hole. Combining Jessica's story with Leisha's, English began to form a picture of a stormy relationship between Scott and the two women. The resulting image provided Leisha with a strong motive for wanting to hurt—perhaps kill—Scott.

Before talking to Jessica, English had thought he had a pretty good picture of Scott Dunn, painted by Leisha Hamilton and Tim Smith and the people with whom he had worked: Scott appeared to be a young man who was immature, somewhat restless and a bit reckless. After talking with Jessica, the picture he had formed shifted. Where Jessica was concerned, Scott's true self shone forth. He had been considerate of her feelings, loving and devoted. Had Scott told Leisha he was in love with Jessica when she confronted him about Jessica's phone call? Had he told her it was over between them? How would Leisha have reacted to that announcement? English didn't think she would have taken the news gracefully.

As he thought about the things Jim Dunn and Jessica had told him about Scott, the detective realized that Scott had loved his family and this young girl who had agreed to marry him. Scott had hurt them sometimes, but English felt Scott never would have caused one moment's concern to any of them—at least not deliberately. No, the pain his disappearance had caused those he loved was inflicted by others. Of this English was now sure.

chapter five

A Father's Misgivings

Thinking back to the days between the Sunday night that Leisha Hamilton first called Jim Dunn and the Saturday Tal English called to tell him that, in his opinion, there had been some kind of violence in Leisha's apartment, Jim felt they had been the worst he had endured in his entire lifetime. Terrible questions about Scott had consumed him. Was Scott alive? Was he somewhere no one knew about, hurt, perhaps dying? Was he already dead? What had happened to his son? One minute, Jim would think that knowing definitely what had happened—anything, whether good or bad—would bring some relief to his heart and mind. Yet the next minute, he realized that not knowing was preferable in some ways. As long as there was no concrete proof that Scott was dead, Jim could hold onto some hope of seeing his son again.

However, that hope began to fade when he spoke to Tal and heard the emotion in the detective's voice. "I'm sorry to tell you this, Mr. Dunn. We believe someone got hurt real bad in Scott's apartment. Real bad." Tal paused for a moment, then hurried on. "We've uncovered a lot of blood in his bedroom."

Jim's world suddenly turned upside down. "I… is it… did the blood… where was the blood?" he finally managed to ask.

Tal explained. "Remember that piece of carpet Leisha told you about, cut out from under the couch? We found it in the bedroom, taped down in place of another piece of carpet that had been cut away. We found the blood underneath… an awful lot of blood. The carpet pad was soaked. We took samples for identification. They tell us it was type O."

Jim's heart sank. Immediately he realized that knowing was going to be infinitely worse than not knowing.

Tal had begun to tell Jim about the photography and the Luminol, but his words seemed to run together and Jim kept asking him to repeat. After a dozen interruptions, Tal was able to explain all the police had found in Scott's apartment. All the while he was talking, Jim kept wondering why Leisha had mentioned the suspicious piece of carpet to him or to the police. Why would she call attention to the crime scene if she was involved?

"What did Leisha say?" he finally asked.

Tal hesitated. "She said she didn't see it."

Suddenly Jim had strong feelings as to why she had told them about the missing carpet and about the break-in after Scott disappeared. She was covering her tracks and possibly trying to implicate someone else. "Surely you don't believe her," he exploded. "That doesn't make any sense at all."

"I know it doesn't," Tal admitted. "But I guess it's conceivable that she might not have seen the carpet, if she really didn't use the room after Scott left. And there's not much we can do about it right now, especially since the final tests haven't been done. We don't even know conclusively that it's Scott's blood."

Whose would it be if not Scott's? Jim wondered. Still, he was glad to clutch that small straw of hope. "How will you find out if it's Scott's blood?"

Tal's voice became even more sober. "You and Scott's mother will need to go to a police laboratory and give blood samples. The samples will be forwarded to a laboratory in Fort Worth, where they will be tested for genetic matching. The process takes a couple of weeks."

Jim was glad to be able to do something to help in the investigation. Waiting for others to do the work and then let him know what they had done was not his style. He had to be involved.

Tal had told him the local police would contact him about the blood test, so Jim was expecting the call when Detective Morrison of Lower Makefield Township in Yardley, Pennsylvania, telephoned to set up an appointment for the test. Morrison said he would escort Jim to Lower Bucks Hospital in order to have blood drawn. Jim agreed and hurried to police headquarters.

Throughout that week, Jim thought of little except Scott, and it seemed that Scott was all he and Barbara talked about. Every morning was dulled by the heavy weight in Jim's heart. It took all the energy he had just to get out of bed and struggle to call the Lubbock Police Department. Each day he talked to either Tal English or George White. After they talked, more serious questions tormented him. They didn't tell him that Scott was dead. They didn't have to. It was hard for Jim to fathom that Scott could still be alive. Nevertheless, he wasn't going to voice what they all were thinking. Not yet.

The question that tormented him was, what had happened to Scott? What had they done with his son? Already he was thinking in the plural—they—at least two people. It seemed inconceivable that one person working alone could have attacked Scott. Scott was young and strong, a real fighter.

The second question that spun around inside Jim's mind was what were the police doing to find Scott? Tal said they were working on several leads, but he didn't say precisely what they were doing or what progress they were making.

Tal and George were always sympathetic and polite and Jim thought they were keeping him informed as much as they could. But it wasn't enough. He wanted to retrace the footsteps of those unknown officers who had canvassed the city, looking for Scott. He wanted to ask the questions himself. Had anyone seen or heard anything on May 15 that had been unusual or suspicious?

Although he worked every day, it was rudimentary, keeping his body doing what it had to. All he thought about was what had happened to Scott. By the end of the week, Jim knew he couldn't stand to stay on the sidelines any longer. He had to go to Lubbock. In cases such as this, he reasoned, it was better for the police to relate to the victim's family directly, rather than just as voices over the telephone. He determined that he would approach the police soberly, reasonably and without undue emotion, because he didn't want to be written off as just another hysterical parent. Barbara agreed with him and would go also, so Jim called Derry Harding, another old college friend, now an attorney in Lubbock, and asked him if he could set up a meeting with the police for Monday, June 17.

At Lubbock International Airport, Jim and Barbara rented a car and drove toward town. Heat waves shimmered across the wide highway and over the fields of knee-high cotton. Their route took them through a dusty industrial area and then down University Avenue, past Texas Tech University. Jim pointed out the building where the School of Agricultural Sciences had named him Distinguished Alumnus.

In that moment, Jim knew he would never feel the same about his home town. In the decades since he had left Lubbock, he had traveled in forty-eight of the fifty states and lived in many of them. Throughout those years, he had thought often about how special Lubbock was. He had believed it would be wonderful to come back to Lubbock and spend the rest of his life where he had such good memories.

But not now. Not since this happened. Scott's death here destroyed all his wonderful feelings about the place where he grew up and where he got his inspiration. He still couldn't imagine that something like this could happen in Lubbock—and certainly not that it was happening to his family.

Jim turned east on Broadway and in his rearview mirror he watched Texas Tech University recede in the distance. He couldn't help comparing his present bitter state of mind to the enthusiasm he had felt on that long-ago graduation day—a day when the world was wide open to him and life was limitless.

Jim and Barbara checked into a downtown hotel. After a quick dinner and little conversation, they went to bed. The next morning, they were up early and had some time to waste before their appointment at the police department. They decided to drive to ProSound Electronics. This decision was made on impulse, so they didn't call Max Gianoli to let him know they were on their way. Although Max had called them almost daily, they had not told him they were coming. Jim wondered how he would react when they showed up. Would he be surprised? Would he offer condolences? Would he talk to them about what he really thought had happened to Scott?

The electronics store was at the end of a small strip mall. It was clear that Max needed every parking space his location provided. The little shop was bustling. Jim wedged the car into the crowded parking lot and noticed two men conversing near the driveway. He recognized one of them as Max Gianoli, having seen the store owner in the videotaped commercial Scott had sent home in April.

Gianoli stepped back as the other man got into his car and pulled away. Then he noticed the Dunns and waved as they got out of their rental car. "With a nice car like that," he said, nodding wisely, "I can see that you need a good stereo system."

Jim, a salesman himself, laughed in spite of himself, knowing Gianoli couldn't have recognized them. Instead, he thought he had snagged a potential customer.

"Well, not exactly," Jim said, offering his hand. "I'm Jim Dunn. This is my wife, Barbara."

"Hello." Gianoli shook hands with Jim, then with Barbara. "Come on in. I'll show you around." He turned and went inside the store, leaving Jim and Barbara looking at each other in confusion.

The man had looked distinctly uncomfortable, as if he wasn't sure what to say or do. The Dunns supposed that many people would feel this way. How do you act when someone you know might have been murdered? Still, it hurt them.

Gianoli was waiting behind the counter when Jim and Barbara entered the store. He gestured toward the showroom, a proud smile wreathing his face. "What do you think? Isn't this great? See, Scott built all these shelves."

He moved through the store, straightening boxes, and they followed him. "Yeah, that one gave us a little trouble," he said, bending down and pointing to a shelf. "See there, how he had to miter the corner, to get it to fit just right? He did a good job."

Jim's heart was pounding as he and Barbara followed Gianoli through a doorway into another room. Didn't he understand that they wanted to know what he thought about Scott's disappearance? Why didn't he say something? Instead Max stopped in front of a shelf displaying dozens of trophies.

"Recognize any of these?" Again, that proud smile. "Scott won most of these trophies in stereo competitions." He rattled off the details and named the awards, but Jim was having trouble paying attention. He knew Max wanted to make them feel better about Scott's achievements, but he couldn't get past the fact that Max wouldn't venture into the swampy territory of Scott's disappearance. He didn't indicate whether he thought Scott was or was not coming back for his trophies and other possessions.

Jim forced back the words he wanted to hurl at Max Gianoli, wanting to ask him: Do you know anything that could help us find out where Scott is? Wordlessly, he and Barbara followed Max from the showroom into the work bay area, where Max pointed out a handful of tools he said belonged to Scott. Jim knew Scott had a large collection of tools he had prized highly.

"Where are the rest of his tools?" Jim asked.

Gianoli glanced at him and shrugged. "I think Scott sold some so he could buy a stereo."

"A stereo for his car or for the apartment?"

Gianoli looked away. "I don't know. I never saw it."

Jim let it go.

One of Scott's prized possessions was still intact, however. Through the back window of the store, Jim could see the white Camaro, parked in the ProSound parking lot, a grand advertisement for the store's stereo business. It was still waiting for its new engine to be installed— a job that was destined never to be completed.

At last the tour was over, Max waved at a customer, then turned back to the Dunns. "How about a cup of coffee in my office?"

Without waiting for an answer, he led the way toward the back of the store. Finally, Jim thought with relief. Now they could really talk about Scott. At the door to his office, Max stopped short. "Oh, by the way, do you want to meet Mike Roberts?"

Jim hesitated, remembering what Leisha had told him about Mike Roberts. It was possible that he had been the last person to see Scott alive. Mike probably was the last person to talk to Scott, to laugh with him. Then, Jim thought, if Mike had stayed overnight, as Scott had asked him to do, Scott might not have been murdered. Jim shook his head. He wasn't ready to talk to Mike at this point. It simply was too painful.

Max shrugged uncomfortably and showed them into his office. Hastily, he cleared papers off his only spare chair so Barbara could sit.

Obviously trying to find another subject, he said, "Business has been great," and opened a package of Styrofoam coffee cups. "The boys have their hands full, keeping up with the installations. Scott was so fast, he could knock out five, six installations a day, no sweat, with everything else he was doing." Max smiled his shopkeeper smile as he filled the cup with coffee.

Jim cleared his throat. "That's one of the things I wanted to ask you about. I know you and Scott were doing well together. Why do you think he suggested to me that I come down and open up a father-son car stereo store?"

For an instant, Max was very still. Then he sat down behind his desk.

Jim could tell by Max's expression that he had hit a nerve.

"I don't know. I just figured it was a family thing, you being his father and all." He glanced at Barbara. "Would you like a doughnut?" Barbara declined and Max looked at Jim. "Well, that's about it. Would you like to see some other things Scott has done with the store?"

Jim stared at him in puzzled silence. What was wrong with Max? He must know they hadn't come all the way from Pennsylvania to make idle chitchat. Clearly, though, Max was anxious for them to leave. Jim could see the man was not going to talk about Scott's disappearance.

Rising, Jim announced, "We're expected at the police station. Perhaps later we'll come back and see those things." When they walked out of ProSound Electronics, Jim was wondering, did Gianoli know something, anything that he wasn't telling? Jim felt Max did, but perhaps that was because Jim was so desperate.

Derry Harding had cut through all the red tape necessary for Jim and Barbara to meet with police officials about Scott's case. At the police department, a secretary ushered them into a conference room. To Jim's surprise, it was full of people. Tal English introduced himself and shook Jim's hand. Then he introduced them to the men around the conference table: Sergeant Randy McGuire, Tal's immediate supervisor; George White; Walt Crimmins; Billy Hudgeons and a polygraph operator, John Mason.

It was Jim's intent to present a rational, determined, unemotional image. He knew the last thing these police officers wanted to deal with was a hysterical parent. This was confirmed by the demeanor of those at the table, who all sat stiffly with sober expressions on their faces.

Jim cleared his throat and began speaking. "Barbara and I want you to know that we appreciate everything you have done so far in looking for our son. He means a lot to us and I hate his having come to harm here. This is my hometown; I have a vested interest in Lubbock."

He glanced around the table and saw that the men were beginning to relax. McGuire and English nodded their heads. "I guess you know, this kind of thing could happen to your children, just as it did mine. It's a terrible thing, but we're prepared to help you in any way we can." He paused a moment and took a deep breath. He didn't need to collect his thoughts, because he'd been planning this speech ever since he and Barbara had decided to come to Lubbock. "We wanted you to see us face to face, to know us person to person, so that you can take a personal interest in finding out what terrible thing may have happened here."

Randy McGuire clearly was in command. "I think I can speak for everyone in this room when I say that you don't know how much we appreciate your approach," he said. His shoulders seemed to relax. "Most people scream at us that we're not doing enough or it's all our fault if the criminal isn't caught or anything else they can think of. Sometimes, dealing with the family is the worst part of this job. It's refreshing to find someone who's willing to look at the case from our point of view."

Jim sighed in relief, faint hope igniting. Maybe together, the police, with his help, could find Scott.

"Can you tell us what happened, as you know it?" McGuire asked.

Jim nodded and began telling him about his telephone conversations with Leisha Hamilton and Max Gianoli, as well as their visit to Gianoli that morning. When he finished, English and White asked him several questions, but it didn't seem that Jim told them anything they didn't know already. Then it was his turn to ask questions.

They described the case very much as Jim already knew it. He wondered out loud whether it would be all right to meet Leisha in person.

"I wish you would," Tal said. "With you, she might not be on her guard so much. She might make a slip and you would learn something important."

"Oh?" Jim said, surprised the investigator had agreed so readily, wondering what he meant.

George leaned forward. "Yes, I think that's a good idea. You're Scott's father and a private citizen. Perhaps with you asking the questions, she might admit something incriminating. If we were to do the same thing, it would be called entrapment and it would be thrown out of court. So if you find out anything helpful, we'd appreciate it if you would pass it along to us."

Barbara and Jim glanced at each other. They were both thinking the same thing: the police were having trouble getting the lead they needed to find out what had happened to Scott. "You mean we could get someone to confess and it would be all right?"

Tal smiled grimly. "It wouldn't be an official confession and could be denied. But you can do anything you want, as long as you don't break the law."

Jim immediately began examining this new angle, thinking ahead. He had never been exposed to the way law enforcement works, but he decided then and there that he would do all he could to further the investigation. There was no way he could have known at that moment how crucial this decision would become in keeping Scott's case alive. He would find out later that there would be many times when the police would decide to shelve the investigation because they felt they had reached a dead end, and his resolve alone would keep it going.

After the meeting ended, Jim and Barbara returned to the hotel. Jim immediately called Leisha at the restaurant where she worked, to make a date for dinner that evening. It was remarkably easy. Leisha didn't sound surprised to hear from them and she seemed pleased at the invitation. They agreed to meet at Huntley's, a steak house founded years earlier by one of the football players on Texas Tech's conference championship team that played in the late 1930s.

They got to the restaurant half an hour before their appointment with Leisha. Both Barbara and Jim were nervous. Although they were trying to keep their minds open, there was no escaping the fact that they were about to have dinner with the woman who might have been responsible for Scott's murder. They tried to calm themselves and prepare for this confrontation.

They didn't know what to expect. Barbara wondered out loud if Leisha might bring Tim Smith along. "What would we do if he came to the restaurant with Leisha and caused some trouble?"

"Let's don't even think about that," Jim said. So they talked about other things, to keep their minds off Leisha, but deep down all they could think of was: When would she show up? *Would* she show up?

Jim and Barbara were expecting the worst and getting more nervous by the minute when a tall, slim, striking young woman walked into the restaurant. She had flashing green eyes and long, straight, dark hair and carried herself with confidence that demanded attention. She spoke to the hostess, who pointed to their table. Jim and Barbara exchanged glances and smiles of relief. Leisha was alone and she looked more like a college preppie than a practiced seductress. She wore blue jeans and a cropped T-shirt.

Slipping into the booth across the table from them, she displayed none of the nervousness Barbara and Jim were experiencing. "I'm so glad to finally meet someone from the family." She smiled easily. "I always wondered what it would be like when I met you." She leaned forward, giving Jim a close look. "You don't look a bit like Scott. Scott was good-looking."

Jim tried to cover up his discomfort with a small laugh. Could anyone be that socially inept? Didn't this woman know her words were insulting? Or had she intended them to be?

The waitress came and Jim ordered a glass of wine, hoping Leisha would follow suit. Maybe some wine would relax her and she would open up a bit. Leisha shook her head, however, and asked for a glass of water. "I never drink anything but water after 6:00 PM," she said with that smile again.

Jim and Barbara knew this wasn't the truth. Leisha had admitted to the police that her favorite hangout was a club called West Coast.

By the time the food came, they had filled up half an hour with strained small talk. Leisha had ordered a small salad, but only picked at it. They ate in silence for a few minutes, while Jim was wondering how to broach the subject that was on everyone's mind. Finally, Jim took a sip of his wine and plunged ahead. "We were at the police station today and they were very cooperative."

Leisha nodded, leaned forward looking interested, but didn't speak.

"Um, if they have any theories, though, they didn't tell us." He was hoping Leisha might open up a little, but she said nothing. "Has anyone spoken to you about Scott?" he went on.

Leisha glanced around the restaurant, then touched a napkin to her mouth. "Well, people come up to me all the time at work. At first, most of them didn't realize that the missing person they were seeing in the news was Scott. But then when they saw his picture, they recognized him from seeing him around. Someone thought they saw him in the mall, but it might have been before he was missing. Other than that, no. That's about it."

"Have you talked to Max Gianoli?"

"Recently? No... no." She shook her head.

"And Mike Roberts?"

"No. No, I don't think so."

This is getting nowhere, Jim thought, discouraged. He tried another angle. "Leisha, how much of Scott's stuff is still at the apartment?"

"His things? Well, he left his pants, as I said, and a couple of sweaters, a pair of shoes, some papers. Not much of anything, really." She hesitated. "His boat."

The boat again. "Where is the boat, Leisha?" Jim asked.

Her eyes flashed, green and hard. "I put it in the trunk of my car, just in case he came back for it. I thought he did, too, that Friday when the door was kicked in."

"Where are Scott's keys?"

"Oh, I have them right here." She pulled some keys from her purse. Jim recognized the little pool cue that was attached to the chain and he knew they indeed were Scott's. He struggled to resist the impulse to snatch them from her hand. Then he saw that Leisha's eyes had filled with tears.

"I loved him so much," she said softly. "The weekend before he left, we went to play miniature golf together. See, I still have his scorecard." She rifled through her purse, finally pulling out a crumpled paper with Scott's handwriting on it. "Look, he signed it 'Ice Man,' because he liked to pretend that he was Vanilla Ice. He was always doing something like that."

Jim's heart raced. Scott had told his father that he was called Ice Man because of the way he used ice to improve the performance of his stereo speakers. Did Leisha not know this? How well had she really known Scott? He didn't challenge her on the issue, however. She looked at the crumpled paper as if it were a cherished possession and the tears began to roll down her cheeks.

Jim shook his head, baffled. From their telephone conversations in which she had talked so matter-of-factly about Scott, he hadn't expected this show of emotion.

"And the white car," she said, wiping her eyes. "He was going to paint it yellow and call it Yellow Thunder II. He was so excited about the car. He had so many plans. Even bought a new stereo to install first thing."

"Are you driving Scott's yellow car?" Jim asked.

"Not today, I didn't. I have my own car, but I do like driving Scott's car, because it reminds me of him."

"Leisha, that car is Scott's property. And you know that he never let anyone else drive it. I don't know that you or I or anyone else has any right to drive it right now. I don't think you should drive it anymore until he comes back." Jim knew there was little chance his son was coming back, but he wanted to hear what Leisha would say.

Her mouth hardened for a second, then relaxed into a sweet smile. "I know it's his property. But what if he's not found for four or five years?"

A cold chill crawled up Jim's spine. She knows! She knows Scott probably will never be found. "Well... well..." he stammered. "I guess we'll have a heck of a long wait."

Leisha looked down at her plate, picked up her fork and speared a tiny piece of lettuce. "I guess we will," she said.

"But Leisha, when this is all over and you help us find Scott, then... I'll give you the car."

Leisha nodded and smiled. She didn't seem to understand that this agreement implied that Scott needed finding and that she was the one—perhaps the only one—who could find him.

Jim decided to try another line of questioning. "What about this Tim guy?"

Leisha quit pushing her salad around on her plate and put her fork down. Her expression changed again. She had switched from happiness to anger to crying to sweetness so many times in this conversation that it was hard to know what she actually was thinking or feeling. She leaned back, lit a cigarette and her eyes narrowed.

"I can't get rid of Tim," she said, blowing smoke to the side. "It's kind of like a fatal attraction in reverse. I even heard that Tim passed up a good job offer in Waco, so he could stay here, just to be near me. I'm thinking of getting a restraining order to keep him away from me."

"Are you afraid of him, Leisha?" Barbara asked.

"Yes. I'm scared to death of him." In spite of her words, she neither looked nor sounded frightened.

Just then, the waitress came to take their plates. Leisha started fumbling with her purse, making excuses for ending the evening. Jim was ready to go too; dealing with Leisha had worn him out. Looking over at his wife, he could tell that Barbara was exhausted, as well. Jim paid the check and the three of them walked out of the restaurant together, exchanging goodbyes in the parking lot. Then Leisha walked away without a backward look. Had she bothered to glance over her shoulder, she might have been gratified to see that Barbara and Jim were watching her intently. Although they didn't want to arouse her suspicions, they wanted to see where she was going and if she was telling the truth about not driving Scott's car. They watched as she got into a brown sedan and drove out of the parking lot.

Getting into their own car, Jim just sat for a minute before he could even put the key in the ignition. A wave of exhaustion passed through his body. He hadn't realized how tense he had been about meeting Leisha until now. On the drive back to the hotel, he and Barbara discussed the meeting with Leisha, comparing notes on their thoughts and feelings about what she had said and the way she had acted.

Back in their room at the hotel, an equally weary Barbara took a quick shower and went straight to bed. Jim would have liked to do the same, but he couldn't tame the agonizing fear that had plagued him ever since Leisha had told him Scott was missing. He began writing down his account of the evening. He had taken notes from the beginning, keeping a record of all his conversations with everyone to whom he had spoken as events and news of Scott unfolded in the most disturbing ways. He still didn't have definite information on which to base any further inquiry or suspicions, but he felt that the police thought the leads on Scott's case were starting to fragment. If he didn't keep track of things, he might never again be able to pick up the threads.

After what the police had told him that morning, he realized he had to do more than sit by and wait for news about Scott while wringing his hands and agonizing over his son. Do more than flog himself over whether he had done everything he could to help Scott so this wouldn't have happened. Do more than berate himself for his faults—real or imagined—as a father. He remembered his vow to his children that he would always be there for them. But he hadn't been there when Scott needed him the most. On a rational level, he knew that he could not have prevented this awful thing from happening, but he kept questioning whether he couldn't have done more.

Now he vowed that he would never give up the fight to find his son, alive or dead. Though he prayed it would be the first, he felt in his heart it probably would be the latter. If it was, he told himself, he would find out who had done such a dastardly thing to his son. The person would be found and held accountable.

Jim opened his notebook to a blank page and started making a list—every person he could think of, every possible link, every friend, every relative, every stranger. He would talk to all of them, no matter how long it took. On the first line he wrote Leisha's mother's name and where she lived. Beneath that he added Leisha's father's name and address.

Sitting in a pool of lamplight at a little table that was uncomfortably small for such serious work, Jim wiped his eyes from time to time, blinking hard. Yet he didn't stop. Long after exhaustion threatened to overtake him, his pen scratched on. Long after he should have been in bed, Jim continued his list as if this frenetic work would somehow make the pain caused by his growing pessimism about his son's fate go away. It didn't.

chapter six

The Unspeakable Is Said

The next morning, right after breakfast, Jim and Barbara went back to the police station, eager to tell the detectives about their meeting with Leisha. In the conference room, the group had shrunk to three: Tal English, George White and Randy McGuire. They were dressed casually; the business suits of the previous day must have been worn specifically for their meeting with the Dunns. These men apparently were the core of the investigative team, however, and they obviously were committed to finding out what had happened to Scott. They listened intently as Jim reported on his meeting with Leisha the night before.

Randy McGuire seemed particularly interested in the discussion about Scott's car. He leaned back in his chair, rubbing his neck. "There's no doubt about it," he mused, as if to himself. "That car is the key to getting through to Leisha. Was she driving it?"

Jim shook his head. "Not last night. But I think she often does."

"Hmmmm." Randy sat staring off in the distance for a minute, then looked at Tal. "I think we need to grab that car."

Tal nodded. Then he began telling the Dunns about the investigation at Leisha's apartment, describing the steps he and George White had taken. Next, he rummaged through his briefcase and pulled out a thick yellow envelope. Jim watched Tal place the envelope on the table in front of him, then rest his hands on top of it as if protecting it. Jim's mind filled with dark questions about the contents. What horrible evidence rested under the detective's hands?

Jim would find out all too soon. Tal began to unwrap the little black cord from around the circular catch of the envelope. He removed a stack of pictures and laid them out in a row, in the manner of a dealer laying out a hand of cards. The series of pictures were all of one man—mug shots of a young blond man, about Scott's age. In fact, the man looked enough like Scott that Jim, startled, sat straight up.

"Tim Smith," Tal said simply.

Jim stared at the pictures, amazed. He had thought the sight of Tim, the man who had probably attacked his son, would enrage him. Looking at these pictures, however, he felt no rage, only puzzlement. Tim seemed so boyish and pitiful. Not the kind of person who belonged in a mug shot at all. He looked perfectly miserable. Jim shook his head slowly. Tim and Leisha both looked so innocuous that one would never guess they might share a deadly secret.

Tal took another bundle of photos from the briefcase. First, he glanced at George for approval. The older man nodded, closing his eyes briefly.

"I wasn't sure whether I should show you these," Tal said, "but I think you can handle it. I want you to brace yourselves. We feel these pictures tell an ugly story."

Jim had steeled himself both times before entering the police station, but no one could be prepared for what he saw next.

"These are pictures of the carpet," Tal said. "Where blood was soaked into the pad."

Jim took a quick glance, looked away taking a deep breath then a longer look. These pictures were far from what he had been imagining about the scene of the apartment. When Tal originally told him about the carpet that had been cut out of the living room and taped into place, he had expected that the person doing the job would try to fit the edges neatly together, then brush the carpet fibers in one direction so they would seem to match. Then there would be less evidence of a patching job. But no such care had been taken.

Outside of the jagged piece of carpet, the rug was splotched with more stains, about the size of footprints. There was no mistaking them: either someone had stepped in the blood and left these tracks or blood had soaked directly into places where someone had stood. To cover all the stained area, the new piece of carpet would have had to be much larger—more than one could remove from under a sofa. What Scott's attackers had been thinking when they left this mess was puzzling.

Jim stared at Tal, trying to hide his horror. "And Leisha said she never saw this?"

Tal frowned. "There was an afghan thrown over the spot. The only way she could miss that would be if the afghan was not moved after the day Scott disappeared. But it was too neatly placed for that. Just walking across the afghan would disturb it."

"You don't believe her?" Jim's heart was racing as he waited for the detective's answer. How could Tal believe her? Jim didn't believe her and he had seen only photographs. Tal had actually seen this carpet.

No one spoke for a minute. Then George broke the silence. "No, we don't believe her. But we have no way to prove she's lying."

Jim took the photograph in his hand and pressed it reflexively against his forehead, his eyes closed. A feeling of darkness overwhelmed him. Until this moment, he had been willing to give Leisha at least the shadow of a doubt, even though his belief in her story had been slipping steadily. Now all his fears for his son flooded his mind. He couldn't help thinking Leisha had been part of the savage plot. How could she not have been? And how could she continue to live in the same house with all that blood?

After leaving the police department, Jim and Barbara drove aim-lessly for a while before returning to their hotel. When they entered their room an hour or so later, the telephone was ringing. Jim picked up the receiver and said hello.

Leisha Hamilton's voice screamed at him. "You promised! Tell them they can't have the car! They're here right now and they're tak-ing Scott's car away from me. Tell them they can't have it!"

As much as he wanted to scream back at her *What did you do to my son?* Jim knew he had to calm Leisha down so the police could do their job. "It's all right," Jim soothed. In the background, he could hear several voices talking at once, "Hold on, Leisha. Who's there?"

"Tal English, for one. He's right at the door."

"Let me talk to him, Leisha."

There was silence and Jim could almost hear her making mental calculations. "No," she finally decided. "I don't think so."

"All right, Leisha," Jim said. "Let me make some calls."

As soon as Leisha hung up, he dialed the police station. He explained that Leisha Hamilton had called him and George and Tal were at her place and he needed to speak to them. The operator patched him through to George's car phone. George said he was in the car in front of Leisha's apartment, watching the scene. He sound-ed somewhat amused and pleasantly satisfied. "It's quite gratifying, Jim. She's throwing a regular fit. Kind of makes you wonder why that car is so all-fired important."

"I've been wondering that myself," Jim said. "What do you want me to tell her?"

George hesitated for a moment before speaking. "Why don't you tell her that we need the car at the police station, so we can give it a thorough going-over. Let's see what kind of reaction we get."

Immediately Jim called Leisha back.

"What did you find out?" she demanded.

"They tell me they need the car at the police station, so they can do a thorough search for evidence," he answered.

"What kind of evidence would they find in Scott's car? He isn't in there!" she shouted, sounding completely out of control. Jim could hear Leisha yelling at someone in the background. Then she got back on the phone. "Tell them they can't have it."

"I can't do that. It's not your car. It's not my car. It's Scott's car and if the police need it, they have the right to take it."

"No! I won't let them have it!"

"Leisha, you have to let them take the car. If they say they need it, it's out of my hands and it's out of your hands, too."

There was a long silence; then Leisha slammed the phone down. A short while later when he called Jim, Tal told him that Leisha had stormed outside, still shouting at the police, but they ignored her, hooking the car up to the tow truck. Then they drove away, pulling Yellow Thunder behind them, while Leisha stood on her doorstep, glaring at them, both fists clenched.

Jim opened his notebook to the list of names he had compiled the night before and started a barrage of telephone calls. First, he called Leisha's mother. He stumbled through an apologetic introduction, assuring her that his only interest was in finding Scott and every of bit information, no matter how insignificant it seemed to her, might be important. At first she was appropriately sympathetic, but when Jim began asking questions about her daughter, the mother's attitude quickly changed.

"Mr. Dunn," she said curtly, "I understand how you must feel. I have two daughters and a son of my own and Lord knows, Leisha isn't an angel. You don't know what kind of trouble your children can get into and you certainly can't control them after they turn twenty-one. I know for a fact that Leisha had another boyfriend. I can't see why that's any of our business. Leisha told me that Scott was jealous, very jealous. I imagine they got into a few fights about it. Scott could get awful smart when he wanted to and it's just possible that his smart mouth got him into trouble. But I'll do what I can. I'll ask Leisha what she knows, but I can't imagine hearing anything she hasn't already told the police."

"All right," Jim said. "I want to say just one thing: I think Leisha knows what happened to Scott. If she comes forward now, at this early stage and helps us find Scott, I'll do what I can to help her. Tell her that for me, if you will."

"I don't know what you expect her to do," Leisha's mother snapped.

"She could take another polygraph test, for starters. A different type of test, with different questions. I know she refused a second test."

"She took that lie detector test and she passed it. How many do you want her to take?"

"As many as necessary. If she has nothing to hide, it shouldn't matter."

"It matters very much, Mr. Dunn. I don't think you realize what an awful experience it could be. I don't blame her for refusing. One polygraph test should be enough."

Jim could tell Leisha's mother was getting hostile, so he backed off and thanked her for her time. He couldn't believe her words that Scott had actually been jealous of Leisha, especially since he and Jessica were getting engaged. Was Leisha lying to her mother? Or had her mother not wanted to tell him anything that could be used against her daughter?

Wiping sweat from his forehead, he called Leisha's father. Though a bit less hostile, he didn't seem to know anything.

After these two calls, it was four o'clock. Jim fell on the bed, exhausted. Lack of sleep and the stress he felt trying to draw out those he hoped could shed any shred of light on Scott's disappearance were taking their toll. Still he couldn't fall asleep. He decided he would go to bed early that evening and start again the next morning with a clear head.

Somehow the day inched by. That night at eleven when the telephone rang, Jim was in a nightmarish sleep. Once again it was Leisha.

"Mr. Dunn," she began hesitantly. "I've been thinking about Scott's disappearance a lot and I think I can guess what happened."

He wondered what really had prompted this call. What had changed her attitude? Was it the incident with the car? "What do you think?" he said slowly.

"I think Tim killed Scott."

Jim felt like he'd been hit in the stomach. There. It finally was said. For the first time, Leisha admitted that Scott might be dead. That Scott might have been killed. And that she knew who might have done it. Jim felt a curious mixture of excitement, dread and apprehension. Why was she telling him this?

"Don't you think you should tell your theory to the police?"

She was silent for a moment, then she said. "I suppose so. I'd rather talk to Tal, though; George is always trying to trip me up."

Jim was silent. "I think we should go to the police station tonight. Tell them what you know, so you can get it over with."

"Tonight?" She sounded doubtful, but Jim insisted, afraid she would change her mind if she didn't talk to the detectives immediately.

"Why don't we go now, Leisha? I'll get hold of the detectives and meet you at the station. How about midnight?"

She thought it over briefly. "All right. I'll be there." He hung up.

Jim called George and Tal, who agreed that it was vitally important to talk to Leisha while she was in her present frame of mind. Ignoring his exhaustion, Jim pulled on some jeans and a shirt. Barbara had awakened when the phone rang and she insisted on going with him. He couldn't remember much about the ride to the police station. His mind was filled with a myriad of different scenarios that Leisha might unfold for them—all of them ending with the unspeakable being voiced—the murder of his son. There were dozens of unanswered questions and Jim knew they had a long night ahead of them. *If* Leisha actually showed up.

In fact when he and Barbara got to the station, Leisha was already there, making small talk with Tal and George. Someone had brought in doughnuts and coffee. Maybe Leisha had brought them, her way of showing cooperation so she could get Scott's car back, Jim thought.

George started the interview by telling Leisha that if she wanted to talk to them, she would need to call her lawyer, Rick Wardroup, because he did not want her to speak to the police without his being present. Leisha said that she did not want to wake him up and that she was willing to talk. George read Leisha her Miranda warning at 12:13 AM. "Okay, Leisha, we understand that you have something to tell us. I'd like for you to tell us what you know in your own words."

Leisha looked at him with mistrust for a moment, then seemed to relax. "I don't know exactly what happened. But I think that Tim Smith had something to do with all this. You see, on Thursday, the day Scott disappeared, when I came home from work, Tim came right over to my apartment. He acted really nervous, you know, like he was afraid I would see something."

George tapped his fingers on the table, impatiently. "Go on."

"I think he's after me. I mean, this guy is a real kook. He follows me around everywhere. I think he's capable of murdering Scott. They had a couple of fights."

"About you?" Tal asked.

"Well, yes. Scott was really jealous of Tim."

"Did he have any reason to be?" asked George.

"I went out with Tim a couple of times. Nothing serious."

Jim groaned inwardly. Who was she trying to kid? Everyone in the room knew she had been having an affair with Tim. But they let it pass.

"I see." George looked steadily at her. "Did you see anything that might lead you to believe that Tim killed Scott?"

She appeared to be deep in thought. "Well, not exactly."

Tal stepped in. "Leisha, where were you the night Scott disappeared?"

"You mean that Thursday night?"

Tal nodded.

"Well…" Leisha put a finger to her lips. "I don't exactly remember."

Suddenly exasperated, Jim broke in. "Leisha, you told me Tim spent that night at your apartment."

She turned toward him with such a piercing, angry look in her green eyes that he shrank back involuntarily. That look would haunt him for a long, long time; her eyes were like two green, glowing coals. "No. I did not tell you that Tim stayed with me Thursday night. I told you that he spent Friday night at the apartment. Not Thursday. And I slept on the sofa when he was there."

"So you don't remember what you did Thursday night?" Tal pressed her, obviously not believing her words. "Did you go out?"

She shook her head. "I don't think so. I can't really remember."

Tal wouldn't let it go, but he spoke to her in soothing tones. "Leisha, it's very important that we know what you were doing Thursday night. Please try to remember."

"Oh?" She looked at him quizzically. "Well, maybe I'll remember."

Hours passed while the conversation continued in the same vein. Jim could not believe that so much time could be wasted. Tal and George asked the same questions so many different ways that Jim lost track of the conversation. Still, Leisha didn't budge from her story. She kept saying she just didn't remember. To Jim her insistence was bizarre, considering that she had remembered every small detail of the two preceding nights when she said Scott was sick.

She glared at Tal. "Why don't you go and get Tim? He would break if you questioned him the way you're grilling me."

The detectives refused to let her change the subject, however. They didn't get angry but kept asking her about her own actions. At one point, George even suggested that they might be able to cut her a deal if she came clean. But Leisha kept insisting that she just didn't know anything for sure.

Finally, at 4:30 AM, they faced the fact that they were at a stand-off. Leisha was the only one in the room who still looked fresh. In fact, it seemed to Jim that she was enjoying being in the spotlight. But Tal and George were through. So was he. This was enough for one night.

Barbara drove to the hotel, because Jim was so bone-tired he could hardly move. He wasn't sure if his weariness stemmed from the long day or the great disappointment of the meeting with Leisha, which had resolved nothing. They had seemed close to finding out what had happened to Scott. So close. *Perhaps,* Jim thought, *Tal and George could have pushed her harder.* On the other hand, he had seen and heard the whole thing and he couldn't think of any way to crack Leisha's armor, either.

On Friday a dejected Jim and Barbara headed back to Pennsylvania. They flew to Dallas, where they were to connect with a flight home. The plane to Philadelphia was delayed for four hours. At Dallas-Fort Worth Airport Jim paced the floor, impatient. He couldn't think of anything more he could have accomplished by staying in Lubbock, but he didn't want to go home and be so far away from the investigation, either. He decided to call Lubbock again.

Jim reached George White on his car phone and told him his flight was delayed. The investigator was glad to hear from him, almost chuckling with delight. "You're not going to believe what we're doing right now. Tal and I are watching Crimmins and Hudgeons arrest Tim Smith."

Jim's heart skipped a beat. "What…?"

"No," George interrupted. "It's not about Scott. While we were interviewing the neighbors, a woman identified Tim as the man who accosted her in the laundry room at the apartment complex. It happened a couple of months ago. She was doing her laundry when a man dashed into the room, put a pair of men's underwear over his face and exposed himself to her." George laughed. "Imagine that. Our star suspect is a pervert."

Jim was not amused. "So you're arresting him?"

"Oh, yes. We talked the woman into pressing charges so we can get him back to the police station. I don't know what's going to happen, Jim. As you know, he already has a lawyer."

"Do you think I should come back?"

"I'm not sure what to tell you." George paused, and Jim heard some talking in the background. "Jim, here's what I think you should do. How long is your delay?"

"Four hours."

"All right. Sit tight for now and call me back in a few hours."

Jim was all for grabbing the next plane back to Lubbock, but Barbara thought they should follow the detective's advice. They were exhausted and what could they do, anyway? Even so, Jim traded the tickets in for a later flight to Philadelphia, just in case. They sat in the lounge, trying to concentrate on the baseball game being broadcast on three television sets, but Jim couldn't help looking at his watch every few minutes. Finally, he couldn't take it any longer. He called George's car phone. No answer, but Jim tracked him down at the police station.

"Jim," he said. "I'm glad you called. There's no use coming back here. Tim's already been released on bail."

George explained that he and English had gone to serve a search warrant for Smith's car. There they'd found Crimmins and Hudgeons arresting Tim on the sex charge. A judge had issued the warrant allowing the detectives to have the car transported to the city impound area, where it would be examined for traces of blood and carpet fibers.

Unfortunately, the whole thing had ended in another dead end. English and White arrived at the impound ahead of the car and by the time it arrived, DPS lab technicians Jim Thomas and Cathy McCord had joined them. Thomas and McCord processed the blue car for evidence, but found nothing that would tie Tim Smith to Scott's murder. English and White left the lot, asking the identification officer to return the car to Smith.

chapter seven

Web of Lies

Jim continued his own inquiries as well as prodding the detectives every day, calling, inquiring about their progress. Meanwhile he continued his own search. During one conversation in late June, he told George he had received a telephone call from Max Gianoli. Gianoli said he had heard that a body had been pulled out of Saint Jo Lake, near San Angelo, a small city about a hundred and fifty miles from Lubbock. Jim wanted closure on the one hand, but on the other prayed it wasn't Scott, though by this time he was certain his son was dead. He asked if White knew anything about the report. White hadn't heard, but he promised Jim that he would follow up on the lead. After a few inquiries, White concluded the report was unfounded.

Gianoli also had told Jim that for a few days before Scott disappeared, he had been talking about moving out of Leisha's apartment. According to Max he still had a little time on his lease at the Fortieth Street apartment where the three of them had lived previously, and Scott had mentioned to Max that he might move in there. This was the first White had heard about a definite possibility that Scott had talked of moving out of Leisha's apartment and he made a note of it.

Jim also told White that in one conversation Leisha's mother said Leisha was married to a man in Columbus, Georgia. George took down the man's name and promised to check out this information.

The next day, Jim Dunn called White again, saying he had just talked to Pat Lane, the mechanic who was supposed to have helped Scott change out the motor in the yellow car before Scott disappeared. Lane told Jim that Leisha Hamilton had called him and asked about Scott. Lane asked Leisha where she got his phone number and Leisha told him she had gotten it from Scott's wallet. Jim said that he understood that Scott's wallet disappeared when Scott did.

White checked the file to refresh his memory. Sure enough, when he and English had interviewed Leisha Hamilton the first time, she had told them that Scott's wallet was missing. White decided to hear for himself what Pat Lane had to say, so he drove to the auto shop where the mechanic was working. Lane readily confirmed the information Jim had been given.

"Yeah, I've known Scott for about five years, but I didn't even know he was gone until Leisha called me," Lane said. "I had worked on the clutch in the yellow Camaro that Scott was driving and he asked me to help change the motor from the yellow car to the white one. Scott was going to give me the body of Yellow Thunder as payment for the work. Then a couple of days after that, Leisha called and asked me if I knew where Scott was. I was surprised she called, because I didn't know she had my number. I had given it to Scott the last time I talked to him, two days before."

The mechanic leaned against the Mustang he had been working on. "I asked Leisha where she got my phone number and she said she had gone through Scott's wallet and found it there."

Lane also said Leisha told him that Scott was missing, along with his keys and some clothes, but that she had his wallet.

Why had Leisha lied about not having Scott's wallet? Jim wondered when White told him about the meeting. Was she just a habitual liar who couldn't keep her stories straight or was there a more relevant reason—something to do with Scott's death?

Sergeant Randy McGuire had arranged with the city's solid waste department to conduct a search of the landfill area where the Dumpsters from the Regency Apartments would have been emptied on May 17. Early on June 29, McGuire, Esparza, White, Hudgeons, Crimmins and Lewis met the city sanitation people at the designated location. McGuire also had enlisted the aid of a dog handler whose animal was trained to locate decomposed human remains. For four hours, men operating heavy equipment bearing augers began the slow, torturous process, drilling holes about twenty-four inches in diameter to a depth of five feet. The searchers hoped the holes were spaced closely enough together that if a human body were buried in the area, they could locate it. As each hole was dug, one of the detectives sifted through the debris that was brought to the surface. The men were searching not only for a body, but also for traces of a waterbed mattress liner, pillows, towels and other items Leisha had said were missing from the apartment. After all the holes were dug, the dog and his handler walked the area, but nothing was found.

When English and White heard the results of the search, they were very disappointed. English, particularly, felt certain that Scott Dunn's body had been placed in the Dumpster near his apartment and subsequently dumped into the landfill. "In spite of the close proximity of the holes drilled at the dump, they still could have missed the body," English argued doggedly. Particularly, he went on, if it had been dismembered, which was a possibility that had been lurking in the back of his mind for a number of days.

Or, English theorized, Scott's killers might not have put it in the Dumpster nearest the apartment, but in one in another sector of town. If so, it could be a mile from the area they had searched. And if so, how had they transported it? Not in Tim's car. It was now obvious that Leisha's car must be examined by the forensic experts.

English mused about Jim Dunn, knowing that tomorrow the grieving father would call him again, with his own findings from those to whom he was speaking, wanting to know what the police were doing to find his son—and to get those who had taken Scott.

English wondered what he would tell Jim, for he still was focused on following Scott's trail of blood to the victim and his killers.

With Tim Smith still the strongest suspect, the police once more turned to the sparsely populated area where Smith had lived on East Municipal Drive. English and White had driven through the area once and had walked over a large portion of it, but there still were acres of barren land, covered in dead trees, wild grass and thorns that they had not explored. Now, English coordinated a widespread search of the area, using officers in cars, on foot and in a DPS helicopter. In addition to the area where Tim's family had lived, there were several abandoned home sites and uncultivated areas in this northeast corner of Lubbock County.

A few hundred yards northeast of the enclave, derelict outbuildings and shabby pens for cows and hogs huddled next to a cluster of ramshackle houses that still were inhabited. English and White made their way from house to house, walking cautiously, trying not to breathe too deeply of the putrid odors. Most of the people they found either refused to talk or had nothing to offer. They said they hadn't seen or heard anything suspicious. After days of searching the area, the detectives admitted defeat. They had found nothing relating to Scott Dunn.

With no new leads and no ideas of where to search next, English tried to work on other cases. One afternoon Mitch Fletcher, an LPD patrol officer, sought him out in his office.

"I don't know what to make of this," Fletcher said, "but I thought I better report it."

"What's that?" English asked.

"I was standing outside my apartment when a woman came up to me. She said she needed to ask me some questions, off the record. She identified herself as Mrs. Smith and said Tim Smith was her son. I never saw her before, didn't know who she was and I had never heard of anybody named Tim Smith. This Smith woman explained that her son was the main suspect in the missing persons case, or murder case, involving Roger Scott Dunn. Mrs. Smith said she didn't know if Tim killed Dunn, but she didn't think he raped anyone."

Fletcher told her he didn't know what she was talking about. She explained about the charge that had been filed a few days earlier accusing her son of sexual assault and said she thought Tim had been framed, either by the police or by the other main suspect, Leisha Hamilton. Fletcher shrugged and hooked a hip over the corner of Tal's desk. "She said she could see her son losing it and killing someone, but that he didn't even date much, so she didn't think he would rape anyone.

"Now get this. Next, his mother told me she thought someone was after her. No one had approached her, but she had seen cars with dark-tinted windows in the parking lot. She was afraid someone would retaliate against her and her daughter because of what her son might have done.

"I checked around, found out about the Dunn case and here I am, for what it's worth."

Tal thanked the patrolman for coming in, at the same time admitting he didn't know how the information could help him with the Dunn investigation. After a discussion with George, the two detectives decided they wanted to meet her and hear for themselves what she said about her son. Before they could reach her, however, Mrs. Smith showed up at the Detective Division and repeated her story to English. She thought some woman friends of Leisha Hamilton were stalking her.

Mrs. Smith reiterated that she thought Tim had been framed on the sexual assault and then told the detective that she wasn't sure but admitted that with the right provocation she could imagine Tim becoming violent.

Talking to Tim's mother confirmed the detective's suspicions about her son. However, she seemed in an emotional state and English wondered how reliable her statement was.

Early in July, Dr. Eisenberg, the Fort Worth biologist who was performing the DNA testing on the blood samples, reported to English. The news confirmed their worst fears. After completing four probes of DNA testing, the blood sample recovered from Leisha Hamilton's apartment had a 99+ percent probability of being the blood of an offspring of James Dunn. Dr. Eisenberg said he was in the process of doing two more probes that had not been completed as yet. He assured English that he would send a DNA laboratory report to the LPD. English sadly notified Scott's parents. Jim Dunn, who had steeled himself for the news, was nonetheless heartbroken.

At that point, all of Scott's belongings were still in Leisha Hamilton's apartment, as far as English knew. Although there was little chance of finding anything new, he decided to bring them into the LPD property room and go through them again, to see if he could turn up anything which might be a clue to where Scott's body was hidden. Hudgeons went with English to pick up the property, which consisted of six posters and nine boxes of miscellaneous personal items belonging to Scott.

The detectives also went to Scott's workplace and asked for Scott's tools. They were given two toolboxes filled with an assortment. All of Scott Dunn's remaining possessions went to the police property room. A thorough examination of the items revealed nothing new. Nevertheless, he would hold them. If they didn't provide evidence in the case, they would be turned over to Jim Dunn.

Scott Williams of the DPS crime lab called Tal a few days later. Williams's specialty was the area of drug analysis and trace evidence. He had made the comparison between the duct tape found in Tim Smith's apartment and that used on the bloodstained carpet in Leisha Hamilton's bedroom.

"We looked at all the different physical properties of all the different components of the duct tape, including the adhesive, the fabric material and the backing," Williams told English. He explained that there are several different types of manufacturers of duct tape and they can use different types of adhesives and different additions to the adhesive to make it more plastic or more rubbery. They can use different types of fiber and different thicknesses of fibers. The same is true of the tape's backing. Manufacturers may use different thicknesses and different materials. They can stamp it with the their own marking. On the fabric material they can have different numbers of strands depending on how much strength they want in the fiber. Basically, each type of tape has different applications; the manufacturer determines what type of application the consumer might be interested in.

Even though each manufacturer can make different types of duct tape that, from a distance, all look very similar, they are different. The difference can be determined by counting the number of fiber strands per inch, and the fibers themselves are different. Some of them have an embossed design on the tape. Probably the most noticeable difference is the adhesive.

The roll of duct tape detectives had taken from Tim Smith's apartment was microscopically indistinguishable from the tape on the carpet in Scott's bedroom, Williams told Tal. They had the same number of fibers, the same adhesive—all the characteristics were the same.

The picture of Tim Smith as the prime suspect in Scott's killing had been emerging steadily in the detective's mind. The lab report on the duct tape brought that picture sharply into focus. But where did Leisha fit in?

With Tim and Leisha, it could have gone two ways, English decided. Leisha could have been furious, because she had learned about Jessica. Maybe Scott had told her that he planned to marry Jessica. Max Gianoli had suggested that Scott might have been planning to move back into the Fortieth Street apartment where the three of them had lived. If Scott told Leisha he was moving out, that could have made her even more jealous and angry. So, she was feel-

ing the wrath of a woman scorned, plus, Scott would be moving out
and she was going to be stuck with paying for the apartment and the
bills herself. That could have been too much for her.

Tal had spent a good deal of time determining that Tim Smith
was jealous of Scott because of Scott's relationship with Leisha. His
notes to Leisha clearly indicated that Tim was convinced that if Scott
were out of the picture, he would have Leisha all to himself.

So both were suspects. The duct tape connected Tim to the violence in Scott's bedroom. And Leisha had to have known about the
blood in the bedroom. Plus, she had lied about some crucial points,
such as whether Scott's wallet was missing and whether Tim was
with her on the night of Scott's disappearance. English's belief that
Leisha knew what happened to Scott solidified. Had she killed him
and gotten Tim to help remove the evidence? Or had Tim actually
done the killing and had she covered up for him? Or—the most
likely possibility in English's mind—had the two of them worked
together to eliminate Scott Dunn? How would they be able to prove
which was true, since there was no body? And the most important
question was, how would they ever be able to prove a murder had
taken place?

chapter eight

Desperate Measures

As June turned into July without the police finding Scott's body, Jim was a man possessed, wanting desperately to find out what had happened to his son. Although he talked to the police every day and he was informed of the avenues of investigation they were following, he didn't think enough was being done. He knew they thought the investigation would go nowhere unless they found Scott's body and he continually was pushing them.

Meanwhile he continued his telephone barrage, talking to anyone who had the slightest connection to Scott or Leisha. Leisha called him. She told him she had some news, but she didn't know how good it was. "I don't know if anyone's told you about this or not, but I just spoke to my attorney and he said it was true. For some reason they have leads…they believe Scott's body is at the landfill."

Jim didn't mention that Tal had told him about the previous week's fruitless search of the landfill and the adjoining prairie that surrounded the enclave where Tim Smith's family had lived. "I appreciate your telling me about it, Leisha. I'll follow up."

"Okay. Also, I have another question. I just got off the phone with my attorney. He called, because I guess your attorney called him and said he wanted a hold put on Scott's car and possessions. But at the same time, it was also my understanding that you would have no objection to their releasing the car back to me."

She stopped and Jim could hear her rapid breathing as she waited for him to answer. If he let her have the car back, the police would lose the only real bargaining chip they had with her. He had to think fast. "The police…can't release the car."

"The car…okay, I don't mean to sound like a smart ass or anything, but the car was ready to be released last Monday, because I called…"

Jim interrupted. "Are you sure? They told me they hadn't released the car and they weren't planning to release it."

Silence. Then, "Okay, well, somehow words are getting crossed, because Detective English told me personally that they were done with the car. That if you or Scott's mom were here they would release the car to you. He said that if I had a letter from you stating that you had no objections, they would release it to me."

Damn! Was Tal on a different planet? What was he thinking? Jim wondered.

"Detective English told me that *himself*," she insisted. "And now, my attorney tells me that your attorney said no, that you did not want the police to release the car to me."

Jim tried to keep his exasperation from showing. "I don't understand this, Leisha. You have a car. Why do you want Scott's car?"

"Because that car was more Scott than anything else. When I walked out and saw that car, I saw Scott. When I came home in the afternoons and saw that car, I saw Scott. I don't want the car to sell it. When I had the car I didn't hardly drive it at all. Granted, it wasn't running for a couple of weeks, but I could have gone out and jump-started it and it would have run."

"But Leisha, from what you've told me, it sounded like your relationship with Scott was in really bad shape."

"It wasn't in that bad a shape. We had—"

Jim interrupted, "Your mother told me that you and Scott were going out with different people."

"We did for a while, yes. I'm not going to deny it. That's how I got involved with Tim. But that had quit."

"It hadn't quit! You told me yourself that you were with Tim the night Scott disappeared."

"No, I did not. I said I didn't remember where I was the night he disappeared."

"Before you told me that, you said that Tim was with you that night."

"That afternoon. Not that night. Tim came over that afternoon. And I also told you that during the last two months, I've been trying to get Tim to leave me alone. Well, you know, my first impression when I came home and saw everything gone was that Scott had left me." Her voice dropped. "That was my first impression. But I told you either of the two places I was at. I know for a fact that I was either here or at my favorite club, so I know that for a fact. I can't guarantee that I went out and I can't guarantee that I didn't. But if I did go out, that's where I went." She hesitated for a long time. "So I don't know. I'm sure I was probably in shock over it all, because I don't think Scott would have just left me. I really don't."

"Then why was he going to move out?" Jim asked

"Move? Scott wasn't going to move." Silence. "Not that I know of. Did he tell you he was moving?"

"Max Gianoli told me that Scott was going to move back into the apartment on Fortieth Street."

"Max told you that Scott was moving out? I don't believe it. Max's never said anything about that to me, but I'm going to call him and ask him."

"He said it was just a matter of time, that your relationship was pretty well over before Scott disappeared."

"I'll call Max and ask him what he meant about that. But what about the car?"

"I don't think Scott would want you or anyone driving his car, and *it is still* his car."

"That's right." Now she was defiant. "It *is* still his car. And if he didn't want anyone driving it, why did he leave…?" She backtracked hurriedly. "We don't know if he left the keys here voluntarily." She was silent for a moment. "Okay, let me ask you this: if my attorney files a motion to have the car released, are you going to have your attorney block the motion?"

My God! "File a motion to—do *what*?"

"To have the car released. They're done…"

Jim interrupted angrily. "On what basis could you do that? That's Scott's car."

"Because it was left in my possession."

"No, no, no! It was left in Max's possession and you went down to the store and got it off of his employee parking lot."

"Okay, but the keys were in my possession."

"The keys. That's ridiculous. I'm going to ask you again. On what basis are you going to claim title to the car?"

"Wel-l-l…I really don't know that I have a basis. He just said that he would file a motion to have it released back to me."

"Tell me this, Leisha. Did that car belong to you or did it belong to Scott?"

"It belonged to Scott." She sighed heavily, clearly frustrated with the way the conversation was going. "Look, if it comes right down to it, I don't actually need the car. I want the car. There's two categories in life: there's the want and there's the need. I don't need it. I want it. I want to feel Scott when I go out in the morning. I want to feel him when I come home."

Her words did not convince Jim of her affection for Scott. She had given the clear impression that she cared more about the car than she did about Scott. She must have some stronger, more compelling reason to want Yellow Thunder so badly. What was that reason? Did the car have something to do with Scott's disappearance? How could it have? It was parked at Scott's place of employment when Scott was killed. Jim shook his head. He was going to have to further investigate this.

"As far as the car goes, Leisha, I think we had better leave it with the police for right now. I know you don't agree with that but…"

"No!" she interrupted sharply. "I'll be perfectly honest with you. I will have the attorney try to go ahead. I mean, I know you don't want it released, but I'm going to go ahead and have him try."

The conversation continued in the same vein for several minutes. Jim didn't tell her he was determined that she would never get it, because he still saw the car as a bargaining chip and he didn't want her to know that her position was hopeless. Finally, he changed the subject. "I've heard you already have another boyfriend."

"What?" She sounded truly surprised. "I have another boyfriend? I don't know who is telling you that, but they have the wrong information."

"I talked with your father and he told me that you went to Coleman with another man."

In an exasperated tone, she informed him that yes, she had gone to Coleman with Burt Todd, but insisted that Burt was not her boyfriend.

"Then what is he?"

"He is a damned good friend. He's been here when I needed him, when there was nobody else here." She sounded as if she was about to cry. "See, you have your wife to support you; I don't have anybody. I didn't have anybody for a long damn time. Burt was there to listen to me when I needed someone, because there ain't no one else in this damn town that gives a shit.

"Burt is a damned nice person. Damned nice. He's helped me through some rough times. And yeah, he went to Coleman with me, because he didn't want me to go all that way by myself."

Jim knew that Coleman was a small town about two hundred miles from Lubbock. It wasn't as if she were going to the moon alone, Jim thought. She had gone to Albuquerque by herself, a distance much farther.

"Look, I'm not going to argue," she said. "This has been a rough week. I've run into a lot of Scott's friends and…maybe this is just a bad time for us to talk, because I'm really upset right now. I know it's rough on you because he's your son. But I face his friends every day and I face my friends every day."

Jim blurted out. "It seems to me that the hardest part would be living in that apartment full of blood. I don't know how you do that."

"It's… all gone, except for the ceiling. It's gone as much as I can get it gone. There's still a little bit on the floor, but I've got it covered. But you want to know a good reason why I'm staying here? I can't break my lease and I really can't afford to move right this minute. And the first couple of weeks I stayed here because there was so much of Scott here. But, see, there's nothing of Scott's here now. Except some blood."

Jim couldn't take any more; abruptly, he told Leisha he had to get off the phone.

"Okay, but I have one more question. It's about the car. When my attorney called me today, he said that he needed both yours and Scott's mom's consent. So I did call his mom and left a message with her secretary. I don't know if she's called back." Leisha was hurrying, her words tumbling over each other. "Now I know how you feel about it, but she might have already called them and told them it was okay. I don't know if they are going to need both or they only need one."

Jim took a deep breath and spoke as calmly as he could. "I'm telling you right now. That car is going to stay right there at the police impound lot. As I said, if we come through the whole thing and you've cooperated fully, then I'll see that you get the car."

He hung up then, feeling more tired than he could remember ever being. Leisha didn't need the car. She wanted it for some reason. Maybe now that he had spoken so sternly to her, she would let the issue go. He hoped so, because he was totally exhausted and he needed time to look into this conversation.

In a few days, however, Leisha called again, armed with new information. She first said she had just called to check in, that nothing much was going on. Then she said her attorney had told her the police were ready to release the car. "They just need your okay," she said. "My attorney is going to try to contact your attorney. My attorney said there is no reason for the police to keep it. He called the district attorney and the district attorney said if they do not need it for anything else, it could be released."

What did the district attorney have to do with this? As far as Jim knew, the police were a long way from being able to present a case to the D.A.'s office.

"And so my attorney called Detective English and he said yes, they are done with the car and yes, they will release it to me when they get your okay."

It was as if their earlier conversation had never taken place. Jim didn't say anything, just waited her out. She paused a moment, then continued. "If you don't want me to have the car, I wish you'd tell me."

"Look, Leisha, our deal was that you were going to cooperate until this thing is through. Then, at that point and time, you can have the car."

"I am cooperating, okay? I'm putting my life in danger right now, trying to find Scott."

"I don't know what you mean by that."

"I just am. The detectives have cautioned me very sharply about what I'm doing and my dad's not too happy with what I'm doing, but I'm doing what needs to be done and I have been doing it and I will keep doing it."

She would not say precisely what she was doing, but Jim had his suspicion: nothing. She was trying to gain his sympathy, but she had not succeeded. If she thought her manipulations would sway him, she was destined to be disappointed. Her dogged insistence on getting the car only served to make her seem more suspect. Her words were flying in the face of common sense and she was so intent on getting the car that she didn't see how bad her actions appeared. Or maybe she didn't care. No one was buying her story about wanting a memento of Scott, but Jim had heard of killers who wanted a souvenir or personal trophy from their victims. Is that what Leisha wanted?

She seemed to have forgotten that the issue at hand was not the car, but finding Scott, which Jim had come to believe at this point meant locating his body.

Though Jim kept on prodding, July passed and the police seemed no nearer to finding Scott or apprehending his murderers. They were in possession of the evidence; they had Leisha Hamilton and Tim Smith under observation. What more could they discover? Tal had said they had enough "goods" on Smith to try him for assault, but not for murder. Because of his hairs on the duct tape and the carpet scrapings, they could prove he had been in the room where Scott's blood had pooled on the carpet and spattered on the walls. Since they had no body, however, the police felt they hadn't enough evidence to charge him with murder.

The good news they told him was that they had seven years before the statute of limitations ran out on the assault charge. This gave them a long time to keep investigating the murder before they would be forced to settle for a lesser indictment. And there is no statute of limitations for murder. Jim tried to be patient, but he was filled with frustration.

To him, as important as it was to punish Scott's murderer or murderers, of equal importance was finding Scott's body. What more could be done? The police had dug up the landfill, at God knows what cost to the taxpayers. They had used dogs to scour miles of scrubby, brushy land, much of it overgrown with weeds so thick you would need a machete to penetrate it. Finding a body in all that underbrush was unlikely, to say the least. Still, bodies did turn up in such areas from time to time. Somehow, if Scott were out there, there must be a way to find him.

Then Jim read a story in the newspaper about a psychic who worked with police in cases concerning missing persons or murder. At first, Jim brushed aside the thought, more willing to rely on solid police investigation than on something so ephemeral as psychic phenomena. So far, though, the police had nothing to show for their efforts. When he mentioned the article to Barbara, she told him one of her cousins knew a psychic who also worked with police. Now he was intrigued. When Barbara's cousin mentioned Scott's disappearance to Alice Connors, the psychic, Alice suggested that Jim contact her.

Jim gave the idea a great deal of thought, having no trust at all in psychic phenomena. That he was even thinking about enlisting her services indicated his desperation. Finally, he called Alice. After all, he theorized, what did he have to lose? He was nervous at first, but Alice put him at ease, then she astonished him, because she immediately got a reading on Leisha Hamilton.

"She's a young lady, mid-twenties, with long, dark hair," Alice said. "Am I right?"

"Yes," Jim answered, stunned.

"Tall and thin, nice looking but a little untrustworthy. Is this Scott's girlfriend?"

"Yes," Jim said eagerly. "The girl he was living with."

Alice hesitated for a long time. "I can see Scott's body...in a ravine. Let me see. There's a gully, a kind of rolling hillside depression. Not mountainous, but hilly. The gully goes down into a ravine—a kind of dry creek bed or something. I see a railroad track, a barbed-wire fence going along the side of a road. Off the road a ways. And then there's a butte. Yes, definitely. A low-lying butte that sticks up toward the end of this."

Jim knew exactly where she was talking about; the place he was visualizing was farther east of Lubbock than any site where the police had been looking for Scott's body. This was the area where the geography of the flat plains of far west Texas gives way to low, rolling hillocks. The line of demarcation, the bluff that she was referring to was called the Caprock.

"Yes," he said, excited. "But there are only a few locations where the railroad tracks run adjacent to any roads or would cross a ravine like this."

"There is some low-income housing near this area," Alice went on. "It's possible that Scott might be found by kids playing in the area."

They talked about this for a time, then Alice blurted, "Bud! They call you Bud."

Jim was amazed. She was right. When he was four years old, before his name had been changed from Walter Lee to James Henry Dunn III, the name of his uncle who had died during World War II, he had told his grandparents, "I don't like my name. I don't want to be called Walter Lee. From now on, just call me 'Bud'." And from that day forward, his granddad had called him Bud. But it had been years since anyone except one of his cousins had called him that, and no one outside his immediate family knew about the nickname. There was no way Alice could have known.

"And you've had a very serious operation," Alice added.

Again he was surprised. He had cancer surgery twenty years earlier. Although it was possible that Alice might have found out about it in some way, it was highly unlikely. It had happened years before he had met Barbara, even before he moved east. At that moment he was ready to accept that some people might be gifted with a highly developed sixth sense which most of us have not recognized. This realization would start him on a surprising journey.

Alice told Jim that Leisha didn't carry out the actual murder, but that she was actively involved in the set-up, that she orchestrated the whole thing. In a general way, Alice described the bedroom and the circumstances surrounding the murder.

Money was involved somehow, she said, less decisive than she had previously been. She didn't know exactly how it figured into the equation.

"If I went down there," Jim mused, "do you think I could locate this place you're talking about? The state police have searched with a helicopter already, but I'm not sure how much territory they covered. They may not have gone as far as the Caprock. I could probably get them to try again."

He could tell that Alice was considering her answer carefully. "If you think you know some site that matches my description—yes, it's possible that you might find him. I can kind of be there with you, in spirit. I can travel astrally."

His silence must have told her he didn't have a clue to what she was talking about. What in hell was astral travel?

"I mean, I can transport myself through the air to other places," she said.

Jim was skeptical about that statement, but he was convinced of her psychic abilities enough that he started making plans to go back to Lubbock and search for Scott's body. At that point, he had tried everything else he could think of.

In August, Jim and Barbara flew back to Lubbock. He was a little surprised to find that the police were responsive to his inquiries when he started asking about whether they'd searched particular areas that he had he thought might be possibilities after his talk with Alice.

When he told Tal about Alice, he discovered the LPD had dealt with psychics before and they were amenable to trying it again, although they emphasized that there was a huge risk that nothing would be learned. When Jim described the region he wanted to search, the detectives mentioned some other spots that fit the description, areas of which he had not been aware.

For the next three days, Tal English and George White accompanied Barbara and Jim as they scoured several areas. They went to five or six spots near the railroad tracks and discovered an area that matched Alice's description almost perfectly. The only discrepancy was the housing project she had described. The area was about twenty-five miles from Leisha's apartment, on the road that led southeast of Lubbock, half a mile off the highway. There was a big ravine overgrown with mesquite trees and underbrush, a gully that broke into a cliff a couple of hundred feet high, a barbed-wire fence and railroad tracks. And the butte.

The next day, Jim went back to the same spot and while he was looking over the area, he was filled with the sensation that yes, something was there. For hours he walked back and forth in the hot sun, examining the ground as carefully as he could. The terrain was rugged, full of briars and bramble bushes, and the wild summer growth was so thick that much of the brush was impenetrable. Considering that the murder had taken place in the spring, it certainly was possible that a body had remained hidden in this place and would be invisible until winter.

About fifty to seventy-five yards from the highway, about halfway to the gully, Jim spotted a long strip of duct tape. A chill ran up his spine and he almost expected the tape to be wrapped around a waterbed mattress liner. However, from the looks of it, this duct tape had been there a long time, much longer than Scott had been gone.

The day before the Dunns were to return to Philadelphia, Jim went back to that same area a third time; this time his cousin, Diann Dillingham, accompanied him. Diann said she experienced the feeling he'd had, that something was there if they could only find it. She started searching through the brush like a hunting dog. Watching her, Jim's stomach clenched. He felt she would find something. After a few hours, though, she had found nothing. Discouraged, Jim called Alice Connors from their hotel room that night.

"You didn't find anything today?" she asked, sounding disappointed.

"No, we didn't."

"I was with you in the helicopter," she said.

Jim sighed, frustrated and hugely disappointed; reality intervened. Although initially they had arranged to search the area in a helicopter, the plans had fallen through. There was no helicopter; hence, there was no astral presence.

Although the psychic episode had proven a washout, Jim was not ready to give up the idea that a psychic could help. An acquaintance had told him of a psychic who had promising credentials. Alex Rogers had been instrumental in finding a missing person for the Oklahoma police and he had contributed to several other cases. In fact, Rogers claimed to have found twelve bodies for various police departments during the past ten years. Jim contacted the police, who gave him a positive report on the psychic. In addition, the news media had done an in-depth story on the case, in which Rogers described his methods.

"I can't tell exactly where a body can be found," the psychic explained. "I can see certain geographic characteristics in the vicinity of the body, but I may not know exactly where that location is. I could search through an area that I know about, which looks right and feels right, and totally miss the real location that looks just like it, simply because I'm not aware of its existence."

In the Oklahoma case, he did manage to find a body because he knew to look for a piece of clothing, which turned out to be the only thing visible under a heap of branches that hid the body in a stream.

Alex Rogers's credentials were impressive, so before they left Lubbock, Jim and Barbara went through Scott's belongings at the police station, selected a few items of clothing and sent them to Rogers in Dallas. When Alex received the clothing, he immediately did a reading and taped it for Jim. He described Leisha and Scott, as well as a few circumstances surrounding the murder. His description of the actual murder was similar to Alice's, but his impression of where the body lay was totally different. Alex thought Scott could be found near some trees, under some brush, near a pile of trash, within eight miles of the apartment. He, like Alice, thought there might be some money involved in the murder somehow.

In September, Alex Rogers agreed to go to Lubbock and look for Scott's body, with the condition that the media be told about the search. This was disturbing to Jim, because it sounded too opportunistic. Was Rogers interested in finding Scott or was he more interested in enhancing his reputation? Nevertheless, Jim contacted Tal English at the LPD again. Again they agreed to cooperate. One television station obligingly ran a piece on Rogers's visit to Lubbock to investigate Scott's disappearance. Alex seemed sure he could find Scott's body and he asked Jim to obtain maps of certain areas in the region.

On September 8, Alex Rogers arrived in Lubbock and went into lengthy meetings with police investigators. This visit was designed primarily to set the groundwork and he would give the police his initial feelings about the case. He ventured that Scott's body was down a country road, near the church/school where Tim Smith had lived as a teenager. Alex visualized what had happened in Leisha's apartment and then "saw" the area where he thought Scott's body lay. It had been raining for several days, however, and the road was so wet, the police couldn't get a vehicle down it. Frustrated, Alex planned to visit the area again in two weeks.

Rogers went back to Lubbock on October 1. This time he accompanied the police as they searched the area he had "seen" earlier. From his hotel room that night, he called Jim and gave his version of what he thought had happened to Scott.

"The way this thing went down, to me… is that Scott and Leisha have had some problems. He's sleeping there on the couch and Mike comes over—the door's unlocked—Mike wakes Scott up and they talk. Scott tries to talk Mike into spending the night, but Mike says no, he doesn't have any clean clothes to change into and he'll see Scott in the morning."

Jim interrupted his narration. "You talked to Mike?"

"Yes. So now Mike leaves and Scott's there on the couch in his underwear. And he gets up, he goes to the bathroom. And when he goes to the bathroom, he discovers that Leisha's not in the apartment. And the reason she's not in the apartment is because while he's asleep over there close to the front door, she slips out that back door to the patio. Then she slipped over that fence—not a hard thing to do."

This did not ring true to Jim, but he suppressed his frustration. "The fence is not that high?"

"No. It's easy to get up on, because there's wooden slats on the inside you can climb like a ladder. And the car's parked right next to the fence, so it's not hard to get back over it again, either. Then she's gone out the back door and gone down to visit Tim Smith. And Scott finds out about that and is somewhat upset.

"So he locks that door," Rogers went on. "He goes around over there to that window that opens onto that parking lot. The window is normally left open an inch or two, but he closes and locks it. He goes around to the front door that was open and unlocked, and he locks it.

"Some sort of confrontation ensues when Leisha comes back home. He won't let her in. She leaves again, goes back to Tim Smith's place. A little time goes by…" Alex paused for a few seconds. "And I think Tim Smith comes back and tries to get in that back door… can't get in that back door. Something takes place there and that back door is kicked open and some confrontation then ensues. And Tim Smith kills Scott with a knife."

Jim was silent for a minute, not sure what to think. "Well… that's about as logical and makes as much sense as anything anybody has come up with. Could you actually see some of this, Alex?"

"Hm." With the briefest of acknowledgments, Alex went on as though Jim had not interrupted. "They put Scott in the waterbed mattress liner…"

"Oh, now, Leisha's involved in this, too?"

"She's involved to the extent that she was there when it took place. Enough to know who did it."

"Did they tell you she passed the lie detector test?"

"Well, that doesn't necessarily mean that she's telling the truth. Lie detectors are not infallible. I looked at the questions she was asked and given the way the questions were asked, she could have passed it psychologically. Knowing her own mind, she didn't cause the death of Scott, she's not responsible for Scott's death, she was just there when it happened and she may actually not really know where Scott is. Because I think they took him and put him in that mattress liner, put some duct tape and stuff on it. I think they then worked on cleaning up the mess—and there was a lot of mess—and moving the carpet and doing other things."

"So you think she was involved with the carpet?" Jim asked.

"Yes, and the clean-up. And I think this bundle of stuff was then put into her car—wouldn't fit in Tim Smith's. And I think the next morning, Tim drove her to work and let her off at work and then went on from there to dispose of Scott.

"Then Mike shows up at the apartment, the door's locked and there's nobody in there. The door's almost never locked, so if it's locked, Tim must have locked the door and left. Remember, a little after twelve the night before, Mike just walked in the front door, unlocked, walked over and put his hand on Scott to wake him up. So the next morning, he tries to get in, pounds on the door, hollers at Scott, goes around to the window on the side, which is always left open a crack, so he could holler in. But he can't lift it open because it's locked."

"There's no screen on that window?" Jim asked.

"No. I understand that sometimes they run an extension cord out the window, for a battery charger or something."

Alex was quiet for a second. "So... that's what I think has happened. We've got this Tim Smith, who's a religious fanatic; Leisha can push his buttons, manipulate him."

"You mean, to do something to Scott?" Jim asked.

"Well, not necessarily to do something *to Scott,* but to do something *for her.* She's trying to land in a good spot—you know, her relationship with Scott is deteriorating quick. She's not really in love with him. She's a very experienced woman who knows how to manipulate men. In the past, she's had some success manipulating Scott, but now she's not having any success at all. But she has a lot of success manipulating Tim, because he is inexperienced.

"Leisha starts crying and acting upset and putting on her song and dance about what a terrible person Scott is. Tim totally freaks out and comes storming down to the apartment and kicks open the door and jumps on old Scott, full of righteous indignation.

"Then Tim has to decide what to do with Scott. Now the spot I picked is out there is close to the church camp. It's an old, aban-

doned place where there's some buildings and stuff, very overgrown.
The spot I found is down the road a mile or two from the church."

"Is this the same area they searched with helicopters?" Jim asked.

"They've flown over that area, yes. And we actually walked in
that area and looked in the buildings, but they haven't done much of
anything else. I looked in some trash piles and stuff, but you're talking about places that were overgrown back in May—when in places
the weeds were six inches high. Now they are six feet high."

"But you definitely had the feeling that he's there." Jim was insis-
tent.

"Well, Jim, I feel pretty good that we're barking up the right tree.
And the police are checking around to see if the church camp owns
any other pieces of property in another location—maybe close to
the spot I picked out. Still, I'm going back out to do some more
work on this spot. It's a rough spot to search. There's a field out there
behind where I'm looking and I want to see if there's any trash pile
or pile of old boards or tin and stuff from off an old roof."

Alex promised to take as much time as he needed to find the
body. Jim had no choice but to put his faith in this lead. It was all he
had. After all, Alex was the only one who had ventured any explanation of what might have happened. And it made as much sense as any
theory the police had offered.

Although Alex said he planned to go back to Lubbock and
search for Scott's body, he never returned. Deflated, Jim gave up on
psychics, convinced that they could not really help.

When Jim and Barbara had visited Lubbock in August, the
police assured them Scott's murder would be solved by Christmas.
But now it was mid-November. Jim called the Lubbock County
District Attorney, Travis Ware, and the hopelessness of the investigation became evident. As in any jury trial, the prosecutor's commitment was imperative. To bring a case to the grand jury, the prosecution's argument must be convincing. To win a conviction beyond the
shadow of a doubt, the argument must be irrefutable. Travis Ware,

who had a reputation for trying only those cases that were slam dunks, had no such confidence in this case.

"I don't know what you expect these men to do," Ware snapped, when Jim voiced his frustration at all the setbacks and lack of progress the police had made. "These detectives have probably suffered more than you did, with all the hours they have sunk into this case. It has been extremely difficult for them."

Jim couldn't believe what he was hearing! How could Ware possibly compare the detectives' feelings to his, when their involvement was merely professional and Jim had lost his son?

"Listen," Ware went on. "Without a body, there is no case. I will not go any further until we have proof there was a murder."

The district attorney had spoken and his decision was final. At long last, Jim understood what Tal and George could not tell him without breaching professional ethics, that they needed a commitment from the district attorney. Finding the body was everything. A case without a body would never be tried.

The weeks passed. Christmas was fast approaching and it seemed that the critical moment for action had passed. Jim was determined not to give up, but he didn't know what to do next. Hope seemed as fragile as the glass ornaments they hung on the Christmas tree. But Jim believed where hope failed, the human will could take its place. Somehow, he would have to figure out a way to get the investigation moving again. But how? A Christmas tinged with sadness faded into a dreary new year and Jim was thankful for the heavy demands at work. Still, Scott was never far from his thoughts nor was his determination to find his son somehow and bring his killers to justice.

chapter nine

Crime Fighter,
Last Resort

Over and over Jim reviewed the details the police and he knew about his son's disappearance and his notes from those to whom he talked. Meanwhile, when he had a free moment, Tal English was reviewing his file on Scott repeatedly as well. Just as it did Jim's, the case haunted Tal English's dreams. Jim would wake up in the middle of the night, asking himself, "What are they doing? What is the next step? They don't have a case, because they don't have a body. How can I keep my word to my son to be there for him?"

Tips still came into police headquarters. One of them looked promising, at first. This one involved a telephone call to a crisis hotline from a young woman who appeared very upset. She said her name was Beth Parks and she was married to Alan, a twenty-one year-old man who was an ex-marine and an alcoholic, who got very violent. She and her husband knew a man named Scott, who was the missing person the people had been looking for.

Beth said Alan had been bragging to her that he knew the location of Scott's body and told her Scott was buried ten miles south of Shallowater. She either could not or would not be more specific about the location. Beth was certain that Alan and his brothers had something to do with Scott's murder, because they were gone the night Scott disappeared and did not come home until 4:30 AM. She was extremely afraid of Alan and was afraid to go to the police with this information.

The following morning, Tal English and Walt Crimmins interviewed the woman, who said Scott had lived across the street from her, in his great-grandfather's house, and they had always been friends. She lost touch with him, however, when he moved to Abilene. Then, not long before Scott disappeared, she had met him accidentally in a fast food restaurant in Lubbock. They started talking and before she knew it, she was telling him about her relationship with Alan and how abusive Alan was and that she was afraid of him.

"Scott said he knew what I was going through and he wanted to help me," she said. He gave her his telephone number at his work and suggested that she call him. She said she and Scott had kept in touch, that she could talk to him about their problems. She insisted theirs was not a romantic or sexual relationship; they were just good friends. Scott had told her he would help her get out of her abusive relationship, that he would take her to the home of one of his friends who lived at Buffalo Lake. He told her he would help her plan for her future, what to do about Alan and her children. And they would find a way to keep Alan away from her. To English's surprise, Beth said she had talked to Scott on May 12, the Sunday before he disappeared on Thursday.

After she started hearing about Scott's disappearance, Beth suspected Alan and his brother might have had some knowledge of it. She had tried to quiz him about it on several occasions. Alan would not let her read the newspaper when it had a story about Scott Dunn in it. Once, when the two of them saw a story about Scott on the television news, Alan said he didn't think Scott was killed in his apartment. He said he thought he was probably beaten severely in his apartment and then killed wherever he was buried.

Beth asked Alan where he thought Scott was. Alan said he thought he was probably buried ten miles south of Shallowater. She had asked Alan if he had killed Scott and Alan said he hadn't. Beth told the detectives she did not think Alan would kill Scott, but she thought that his brothers were capable of it.

English didn't know what to make of Beth's story, but he definitely wanted to have a talk with her husband. It was a week, however, before they were able to bring him in to the Detective Division, where English and White conducted the interview

Parks insisted he had seen Scott Dunn only one time and had never spoken with him. He denied knowing anything about Scott's disappearance. English believed the man was telling the truth, that a drunken, jealous Parks might have made some remarks to Beth, but he thought Parks actually held Scott Dunn in such little regard that there was no reason to kill him.

During those long winter months, every lead in the Dunn case sputtered to a dead end and both Jim Dunn's and English's frustration grew. The only new information was that Leisha Hamilton and her daughter had moved into a home with Tim Smith. It seemed strange to Jim that after all she'd told him and the police that now she would live with Smith. More than ever, he was convinced that Leisha had been lying. She hadn't been afraid of Tim at all, because both she and Tim were involved in Scott's death and she thought she could control him through sex and drugs.

Other than that, the leads had dwindled down and the probability of solving the murder of Scott Dunn became more remote.

The shorter days of winter turned into long weeks and then into interminable months. Jim's heart grew heavier each time a lead fizzled. He didn't call the police every day, as he had in the beginning, when he had such high hopes that they would find his son. He called every week, however, and with each call, he grew steadily more discouraged. Nothing was happening. He knew they were following evidence as it arose, but they had other crimes to solve and Scott's disappearance had to take a backseat to their current cascload. Tal continued to be polite and considerate to Jim and they obligingly followed up on information he provided for them, but like Jim they were frustrated.

As the first anniversary of Scott's disappearance passed, Jim had to acknowledge, as District Attorney Travis Ware had pointed out, the problem was and always had been the lack of a body. They had strong suspicions about Leisha Hamilton and Tim Smith, but without Scott's body, without convincing evidence that a death had occurred, they were stymied. Jim knew they were doing everything they could, but they simply didn't know where to go in a murder case without a body.

As Jim worked to find Scott, he read and saw on television news stories about tragedies similar to his. He realized that it does the family no good to sit by silently and wait for the police to solve the crime. The family has the most compelling concern about the victim. The family has to live with their loss night and day for the rest of their lives.

Jim became convinced that the family must become the victim's advocate. That is why he worked constantly to uncover information that would help the police in their investigation. Now as the police turned to more pressing current concerns, he knew if Scott's killers were ever to be brought to justice he had to find the way to do it. He wracked his brain and searched, but he too was stymied. Until, in an effort to get more information, he and Barbara went on a road trip to Albuquerque, where Leisha had lived. In their hotel room in Albuquerque, Jim turned on the television and became enmeshed in the news program *48 Hours*. The episode was about the Vidocq Society. It was destined to change his life.

On the *48 Hours* episode, he learned that the Vidocq Society was named for Francois Eugene Vidocq. One of the most exceptional men of the nineteenth century, Vidocq had a profound impact on investigative procedures.

Vidocq himself had been a criminal before his unparalleled rise to the heights of law enforcement. Having made himself indispensable to the authorities as a jailhouse informant, he eventually attained his release from prison, then set out to revolutionize the police force of Paris. His inventions were as remarkable as his audacity; it was Vidocq who pioneered the practice of fingerprinting and the use of ballistics testing. Vidocq was the first person to start keeping records of a criminal's history, so that a pattern of crimes could be traced to an individual.

Eventually, Vidocq founded the *Sureté* in Paris—the French equivalent of the FBI. After his government service ended, he founded the first private detective agency in the world, thirteen years before the well-known Pinkerton agency opened.

In the late twentieth century, Vidocq's memory had been revived by a small group of crime fighters, whose original membership of eighty-two—one for each year of Vidocq's life—encompassed some of the most experienced experts on crime in the world. Founded in 1990, the society originally gave its members an opportunity to meet and exercise their minds by solving crimes that had proven elusive to the police.

According to the *48 Hours* report, the Vidocq Society met four times a year and ruminated over lunch, considering such cases as the 1935 Cleveland Torso Murder Case and the twenty-year-old kidnapping and murder of a young girl.

Soon it was discovered that their extraordinary talents would be useful to solve current as well as past unsolved crimes. Since members participate on their own time, they have to be extremely selective about the cases to which they are able to commit.

As Jim watched intently he learned that the Vidocq Society's membership included a wide range of experts, starting with co-founders William Fleisher, a U.S. Customs agent; Frank Bender, a forensic sculptor; and Richard Walter, a forensic psychologist at Michigan's maximum security prison in Jackson. Frank Bender specialized in creating three-dimensional busts, forming recognizable likenesses from only a skull. His sculptures had led to positive iden-tifications in missing persons cases. He could show how a person would have aged after the passage of time, such as in the celebrated case of John Emil List, missing for nineteen years after the murder of his family. Once the clay model of List was displayed on the televi-sion show, *America's Most Wanted*, the resemblance was so close to List's current appearance that he was arrested within a few days after the program aired.

Richard Walter specializes in profiling criminals, which at that point was a relatively new but highly successful branch of crime fighting. Profilers narrow down the field of suspects by studying the patterns and characteristics of crime scenes and determining the type of killer the police are seeking. Walter had spent the last fifteen years perfecting this new discipline, while establishing an extensive network of contacts, including some at Scotland Yard.

Excited by what he had seen, when Jim and Barbara returned home, after he talked to the police about Leisha and learned some interesting information, immediately Jim called Bill Fleisher. For all he knew, he was setting himself up for yet another polite refusal. By then he had developed a thick skin; it had become routine to call someone, tell them his story, then listen to a sincere, "I'll see what I can do," which usually was the end of it. But, he figured, he had to make them see, make them understand that this could be the only way to bring Scott's killers to justice.

Fleisher listened to Jim's earnest plea and offered to meet him at the police station in the Philadelphia suburb of Bensalem. He said he would arrange a meeting at the office of Frank Freil, the Bensalem police commissioner and another member of Vidocq.

Jim and Barbara drove to the Bensalem police station, hoping they finally had found the vehicle to help Scott. However, when they walked into the reception area, Jim shivered in the dispirited atmos-phere. The officer on duty faced him through plexiglass windows, through which he could see other officers in a loud-voiced confrontation with a pair of exotically clad women.

"What do you want?" the officer rumbled through the window.

Jim told the officer they wanted to see Bill Fleisher and he picked up the phone. After a moment, the officer unlocked the steel door and ushered them into the inner sanctum of the police building.

Frank Freil, thin-faced, with light blue eyes and gray hair, introduced himself in a strictly business, no nonsense tone. Then he introduced Bill Fleisher, who was wearing a gun on his hip and sitting below a sign saying "Be Sure You've Got Your Firearm With You."

Fleisher, a large man with a dark, gray-streaked beard, was an ex-Customs agent who obviously was comfortable with authority. They shook hands all around and, as they were being seated, Jim noticed that there were a half-dozen guns mounted on the wall, along with official-looking certificates surrounding a picture, which, he was soon to learn, was of Francois Vidocq.

To Jim's relief, and somewhat to his surprise, both men clearly were willing to listen. He forced himself to relax and tell Scott's story in a rational, logical manner. For the next two hours, he told them all about his son. Both investigators interrupted occasionally to ask questions. They both agreed that it was very difficult to prosecute without a body. But, they said, it was not impossible.

"Sure, the police want a body," Fleisher said. "It makes their job so much easier. But these days, they can identify DNA through the bones or the skull." He thought for a moment, slowly nodding his head as though conducting an internal dialogue. "Or, if we could get a forensic pathologist to look at the evidence, it might be possible to prove that enough blood had been shed that it would have been impossible to sustain life."

Jim practically leapt from his chair. This was the most encouraging statement about not letting his son's killer go free that he had heard in months. "Say that again!" he demanded.

"It's difficult, but not impossible, to gather enough evidence from the crime scene to determine that a murder has been committed. The blood already has been identified. Assuming the detectives did their job, all the evidence we need is in their report, whether or not they knew what to look for. They may not have had a pathologist look at the report."

Freil interrupted. "It's very important for you to reconstruct exactly what Leisha said in that first conversation. We know the day that Scott disappeared." He drew a chart on a piece of paper. "We know you told us she said the apartment was broken into the next day, but she didn't call you until Sunday."

Freil looked hard at Jim, as though he could draw the answers out of his brain. "So what happened to Friday and Saturday? What did she do on those days? Did anybody ever ask her?"

Jim shook his head. He didn't know. This was something he had never even considered.

"You need to try to reconstruct what she said," Freil continued. "Try to recall exactly what she said in those first few conversations. It's what people do in those first few hours after a murder that becomes vitally important."

Jim mentally calculated the two-day gap in Leisha's activities, as she had recounted the story to him. After the alleged break-in, Leisha had Friday, Saturday and most of Sunday to build her story, because she hadn't called him until around midnight Sunday.

"Interesting," Fleisher interjected, "that she gets very hyper late at night. It's a high-stress time... it's a pattern."

Freil said, "We need to see if Texas has an Open Records Law, so we can get access to all the records. But talk to the mailman, the deliveryman, anyone who may have seen someone go in or out. They're not going to tell anything they may have seen unless you ask them directly."

The meeting gave Jim some exciting new insights and he was eager to talk to Tal English. As the Dunns were leaving, Fleisher said he would ask Richard Walter to give Jim a call. "Richard will have more to say about the case. Oh, yeah, he'll solve it."

Jim looked at Fleisher skeptically. He wasn't so sure about this Richard Walter, but he was willing to try anything, to work with anyone who had new ideas about how to bring Scott's killer to justice.

When Richard Walter arrived in Philadelphia the night before the quarterly meeting of the Vidocq Society, he found a message from Bill Fleisher waiting for him. Walter was tired and hungry and in no mood to talk to anyone. Since Fleisher was co-founder, with Walter and Frank Bender, of the Vidocq Society, he thought the message might be about the meeting the next day, so, reluctantly, he dialed Fleisher's number.

Fleisher told Walter about his meeting with Jim, Barbara Dunn and Frank Freil. "He's a nice guy," Fleisher said of Jim, "and it's a tragic thing. His son has been missing so long. The Dunns and the police feel certain the boy is dead, but there is no closure. I told him you were the one who could help him. Would you ring him up and have a chat with him?"

Walter groaned. "I really don't want to," he told Fleisher. At Fleisher's insistence, however, Walter made a reluctant promise to call Jim Dunn, although after he hung up, he argued with himself: *I'm hungry and I'm tired, and I don't want to do it.* Even when he wasn't hungry and tired, Walter was reluctant to talk to a victim's family. For the most part, there was very little consolation he could offer, and the family usually was too frantic to help him in his investigation. The worst of them were the well-intentioned, the hysterical folk, grasping at straws and often so desperate that they threw red herrings at him, just to give him any information at all.

Yes, but you're duty-bound to do it, the other part of his mind argued. *This is why you helped found Vidocq.*

Well, all right, he argued with himself. *I'll call and if he doesn't answer by the third ring, then he isn't at home. At least I will have done my part.*

Walter did not expect Jim Dunn to understand who he was or what his area of expertise was. Even when people were told that Walter was a forensic psychologist, they usually didn't know what to expect or have any sense of what he was going to say to them. Most people expected psychologists to respond to psychological issues rather than criminal ones.

Jim answered on the second ring and Walter introduced himself. Walter said. "I'm a psychologist whose basic expertise lies in profiling serial killers."

"Do you..." Jim hesitated. "see this as something along those lines?"

"Not necessarily. But from the little Bill Fleisher told me, I suspect my skills might be of some use to your son's case."

For a moment, Jim seemed somewhat suspicious. He seemed shocked that Walter would call him at all. Walter sensed that Jim thought he was getting the runaround—that Bill Fleisher had sloughed him off to this so-called expert, who would give him some pat answer and be on his way.

"Profiling is an added skill to police work," Walter told him. "It is an extraordinary luxury. One cannot expect police departments to have that level of technology at their disposal. At best, there are five qualified profilers in the world and to get access to one is not that easy. We tend, from other people's point of view, to make magic out of disorganized bits and pieces of a crime."

The two continued to talk. After a few minutes, Walter still was hesitant about agreeing to take on Jim's case, but he had been impressed with the grieving father's resolute determination and his amazing calm. He knew instinctively that Jim was a man who was trying to think rationally—almost too much so—rather than succumb to panic. He thought that a meeting between the two would help him decide one way or another if he could help Jim. The two men agreed to meet at Walter's hotel at eight o'clock the following morning.

The hotel lobby was crowded when Jim walked in the next morning. Walter was just stepping off the elevator and Jim spotted him immediately. Almost at the same moment, Walter saw Jim and, without having ever seen each other before, they recognized each other instantly.

The two men shook hands and sat down on the couch, each, though very different, liking what he saw. Walter's face seemed ready to break into a smile, although one could not be sure whether the expression was amused or sardonic. He moved and sat with an economy of motion and his way of peering at one with a stern, forbidding gaze was startling. Jim would find out later that Richard Walter loves giving people "the look," which frequently elicits information they hadn't intended to give him.

Jim, on the other hand, was in perpetual motion, using his hands to talk. Neither man could explain it, but an immediate bond was formed between the two that would create the basis of an enduring friendship.

"Would you like to come up to the room and show me what you have?" Walter asked, gesturing to the heavy briefcase Jim was carrying. "I can order some coffee brought up."

When they were seated at a small table in Walter's hotel room, the psychologist glanced at Jim over his glasses. "All right. Tell me what you have. Tell me about the case."

Opening his briefcase, Jim pulled out his carefully prepared notes and tapes he had made of telephone conversations with Leisha, Max Gianoli and others, and records of the searches he had initiated, as well as possible theories. Watching Jim set up his papers—much like a sales presentation—Walter recognized that he was seeing a weary but determined man, a man who had been struggling to keep his emotions separate from his reasoning. He was worried that Jim Dunn's studied detachment could be injurious to his mental health, because sooner or later, the backlash was bound to come. This was one of the first things with which Walter would have to deal; he wanted to reduce Jim's hurt by giving him a sense of emotional placement. Only then could Jim know that it was all right to hate the cause of his tragedy, all right to focus his anger.

As Jim's story of Scott's disappearance unfolded, Walter listened to Jim tell him everything he knew. Then Jim spoke about Leisha Hamilton and Walter called a halt. Already, he felt strongly this was a case of murder. And he could see that Leisha Hamilton was playing Jim up one side and down the other. He also saw Jim's tremendous hurt, his agony, which had surfaced along with his presentation. He knew they were going to have a long, hard fight.

Richard Walter looked searchingly but compassionately at Jim. "Jim, don't you see what she's doing to you?" He lowered his voice so that Jim had to lean forward and strain to hear what the man was saying. "Leisha is running a number on you. She's squeezing you about the car. At the same time, these rather disturbing, unsocialized bits and pieces are coming out under the name of love, affection, caring, concern. But it's like she is showing you concern and kicking you at the same time."

Richard leaned forward, raising his voice again. "She's trying to make you her next victim. She not only killed the son, she's killing the father, too, and bragging about it. Oh, yes, she's pulling some strings here because of your love for Scott. She's saying 'Yes, see how much I loved him too, how much I'm doing for him?' You, the father, are too close to see the pattern of what she's doing. Without realizing it, you are going back and forth in your own approach to Leisha. At one moment, your attitude is condemning and in the very next moment you're talking about her in warm, friendly tones. You don't know what she is, so you don't know how to react to her.

"She is a good psychopath; that's what she is. And this is the biggest scheme she has ever played out. She is trying to shape you. She knew you would want to know where your son was, eventually. So she was willing to take the risk and lay the framework in hopes of deflecting your suspicion toward someone other than herself."

Richard lowered his head and looked at Jim over the tops of his glasses again. "Jim, aren't you tired of being the grieving father?"

Jim looked shocked; how could Richard ask such a question? "I thought that was what I was supposed to be."

Walter shook his head. "No! You're supposed to be goddamned mad! That bitch murdered your son and we have to go after her!"

For a long moment, the two men stared at each other in silence. Richard could almost see the weight lifting from the other man's shoulders, as if an evil spirit had been exorcized.

"Don't you hate her—even a little bit?"

Jim looked at his hands, then met Richard's eyes and the emotions he had been feeling and holding back for so long burst to the surface. "Hell, yes! I hate everything about her! But I keep thinking that as long as I can keep her talking, I may learn something about Scott's whereabouts. Maybe she'll slip up."

"She murdered your son," Richard said, giving him "the look." "You don't need to cut her any slack. She's not a sweet, innocent thing. We're going to make sure she comes to justice. It's all right to hate her. She's a vicious killer and none of her bullshit is going to change that."

Richard walked over to the balcony window and lit a cigarette. "Let's look at Leisha. Now I'm going to call a spade a spade and tell you that the way you described Leisha matches the description of a psychopath. Here, let's do a countdown of a psychopath's characteristics: superficial charm, egocentricity, grandiose sense of self-worth, predisposition to boredom, low frustration tolerance levels, pathological lying and deception, lack of sincerity, callousness, lack of empathy, parasitic lifestyle, short temper, sexual promiscuity, early behavior problems, lack of realistic long-term plans, impulsive, irresponsible behavior as a parent, frequent marital relationships, juvenile delinquency, full probation or parole, failure to accept responsibility for her own actions, many types of offenses, drug or alcohol abuse."

He gave Jim a long, level look. "Wouldn't you say Leisha fits many of these characteristics?"

Jim nodded. "No doubt about it. I was in Albuquerque last month—in fact, when I saw *48 Hours* and learned about Vidocq. While I was there, I talked to the local police about her. They were more than willing to help. In fact, they shared the information in their files on Leisha. That was when I learned that she had been jailed in Albuquerque for stealing from her employer. And there's more. Leisha had also been jailed for passing bad checks. She forged her own sister's name. Before that, she had spent time in a Florida prison. And you should have seen her when I made her angry. She turned on me with a look that would have burned a hole through you."

Richard took his glasses off. "Like this?" He narrowed his eyes and focused on Jim, piercing Jim with his glare.

Jim recoiled. "Exactly like that," he said.

"Yes." Richard nodded, putting his glasses back on. "It's one of their tricks, to put you on the defensive. Let me explain something to you, Jim. If we are going to do this, we are looking at two levels. On the personal level, there are issues of hurt and anger and frustration. That's to be expected. But on the level of Leisha, we have to be as cold and as direct and as businesslike, using your terminology, as possible. I play hard; I play straight and, to get where we need to be, we have to do that."

The conversation between Richard Walter and Jim Dunn continued for an hour longer, with Walter explaining why he thought Leisha was cold and calculating. He mentioned to Jim that she may very well have incorporated other people into her scenario. Walter saw Leisha as a Mata Hari sort of person, who, in a quixotic moment, had drawn others into her scheme. Therefore, he told Jim to stop calling her, that he needed to cut communication with her immediately. Walter explained to Jim that while he was trying to get information from Leisha, she was getting more information than he was.

"So, what are we going to do?" Jim asked.

Walter told him that the Vidocq Society could not become involved in the case unless he had the cooperation of the Lubbock Police Department. He would need access to their records, to lab reports and to witnesses and suspects. Jim needed to explain to Tal English that Jim had talked to Walter and he wanted them involved. Walter emphasized that the Vidocq Society charged nothing for its assistance and told Jim that he should explain that to English as well.

"Then it's up to the Lubbock Police Department to contact me," Richard said. "Until that happens, all we've done is have a conversation."

"They'll understand. They have to," Jim said passionately.

As the meeting ended, Richard watched the other man walk out of the hotel room, noting that Jim had a spring in his walk that had been lacking when he entered. Seeing the change in Jim Dunn that had occurred over the short course of a few hours gave Richard a keen sense of satisfaction. Richard had taken an immediate liking to Jim. He wanted to help him if he could. At that point, he didn't entertain any hope that he would actually find Scott Dunn. But the effort needed to be made and whoever had done away with the young man needed to be apprehended. Richard saw no reason why they could not achieve at least the latter goal. For Jim's sake, he vowed to do all he could to bring closure to Jim so that he could find peace, knowing his son's killers were no longer escaping.

chapter ten

Profiler on Scene

After his visit with Richard Walter of the Vidocq Society, Jim immediately called Tal English and told him the many insights Walter had disclosed about Scott's case and that, if Vidocq were to be involved in Scott's case, the Lubbock Police Department would have to request its participation. Tal seemed agreeable and said he would set the wheels in motion for Richard Walter to begin his investigation. Jim and Barbara flew to Lubbock once more and Jim asked Sergeant Randy McGuire to set up a meeting with district attorney Travis Ware.

McGuire shook his bald head. "Oh my God, Jim, I have seen Ware cut people right off at the knees when he feels they don't have a strong case. Believe me, you don't want to talk to Travis Ware."

"Yeah, Randy, I really do," Jim insisted.

Randy shrugged. "Okay. I'll call him up and see what I can do." He went into another office to make the call. A little later he came back, smiling grimly. "You have an appointment with the man at two o'clock."

Barbara and Jim arrived at the courthouse a little early, prepared for a long wait. From all Jim had heard about Ware, he figured the

CDA would want to take control of the visit immediately, and making them wait might impress them with his importance and the big favor he was doing for them by giving them a few minutes of his valuable time.

Jim was totally surprised, then, when Ware came out of his office immediately, his hand outstretched. "Mr. Dunn? I'm Travis Ware."

They shook hands and Ware led the Dunns through a warren of narrow hallways, small offices and workstations to his own office. For two hours they talked. Jim explained what he had done to further the investigation and told Ware how much he appreciated the work the Lubbock Police Department had done. He also mentioned that he understood their dilemma: without a body, they were at an extreme disadvantage. Then he told Ware about his desire to get Richard Walter and the Vidocq Society involved in the investigation.

Ware listened politely. When he nodded from time to time, Jim felt Ware was sympathetic to Dunn's point. In fact, when the meeting was over, Jim had the feeling that the district attorney's office would cooperate with Richard Walter when he became involved.

At that moment, Jim vowed to himself, though he couldn't bring his son back, he would not allow him to have died in vain. He believed when Richard had an opportunity to review the evidence and interview the witnesses himself, they were going to make some progress at last.

The first question Richard Walter asked Tal when they spoke was if the evidence from the crime scene had been examined by a forensic pathologist. When English told him it had not, except for the blood and DNA tests, Walter suggested that such an examination needed to be the next step. He felt a forensic pathologist might be able, from the blood-soaked carpet and the blood spatter patterns on the walls and ceiling, to determine that so much force had been used and so much blood had been spilled that it could cause someone's death.

English immediately contacted Dr. Sparks Veasey, Lubbock County pathologist. Veasey met with English and looked at the evidence. The result was disappointing. Reluctantly, Veasey told English that he did not feel there was enough information to say whether a person had died in this incident.

But Jim Dunn prayed Walter would not let the matter rest and he didn't. Richard Walter told English that he knew a forensic pathologist, Dr. Richard Shepherd, who worked for Guy's Hospital at the University of London and was a consultant to Scotland Yard. Walter said he would ask Dr. Shepherd to look over the evidence for the crime scene and see if he could make a determination on whether a victim could have survived such an attack.

From the evidence room, English obtained samples of carpet and padding that had come from Leisha Hamilton's apartment. From his own files he made copies of all the photographs taken at the crime scene, copies of all the laboratory reports on the evidence they had and all reports concerning the crime scene. English made sketches of the murder room, including its dimensions, and added them to the other material he had prepared. Then he mailed them to the British forensic expert.

It might be weeks or even months before he got Dr. Shepherd's report, but Jim Dunn went over his notes one at a time and continued his own investigation. He pushed the police to review any of their findings as well. Tal English scoured the Dunn case reports once more, even though he had practically memorized every page. He weighed re-interviewing the people who had known Scott and Leisha. Maybe some of them had remembered something they had not already told the police or maybe they could suggest other people who might have some information about either Scott or Leisha that might be helpful.

Dr. Shepherd's analysis of the crime scene evidence did not take as long as Jim Dunn and Tal English had anticipated. His letter came the first week of November. Dr. Shepherd wrote:

"...The pattern and distribution of the Luminol-positive staining of the south and east walls of the bedroom are consistent with spraying of blood from points low down and adjacent to each wall. In addition, there is evidence of wiping or cleaning up the blood on the wall surfaces. The presence of dried blood spots on the wall and door handle are also consistent with spraying of blood.

"While there may be several possible causes for this degree of spraying of blood, by far the most likely is repeated blunt trauma. The distribution of the spraying of blood is entirely consistent with the victim lying on the floor while the blows that resulted in this spraying were struck. It is possible that fragments of skull or brain may still be detected in the weave in the original pieces of carpet if it is still present. The pattern and degree of blood staining to the carpet shows not only spraying of blood, but also transfer of blood on feet or shoes around the area of carpet, which has been removed in toward the doorway.

"I note that blood staining of the underlay of the concrete floor was seen in addition to the coagulated blood adjacent to the tack rail. I have examined the portions of carpet and underlay you provided, and I note that the carpet has a loose weave on a rubberized base which permits easy movement of fluid through the carpet. The underlay has a plastic sheet surface which, if undamaged, is impermeable to fluids.

"It is quite probable therefore that a bloodstained object or pool of blood would result in blood permeating the carpet and reaching the upper plastic surface of the underlay. Where the plastic covering of the underlay was damaged, the blood could also permeate through to the floor beneath.

"It is not possible to attempt to estimate with any degree of accuracy the amount of blood that would have been shed to cause either the staining of the walls or the staining of the carpet or underlay. It is, however, possible to state that it is most unlikely that the amount of blood was less than 500 milliliters, approximately a pint, and it is much more likely to have been considerably more than that amount.

"The amount of blood lost during repeated blunt trauma injuries is not necessarily the prime factor in causing death, since it is possible to donate over 500 milliliters of blood without any ill effects. The prime cause of death in such cases is the degree of injury to the sensitive areas of the body, particularly the brain.

"Dr. Eisenberg concludes that the bloodstain from the tack strip and carpet padding are 958,680 times more likely to originate from the offspring of

James Dunn (than anyone else). The pattern and distribution of the bloodstains in the room are such that I must conclude that (1) they have not resulted from a natural disease process; (2) they are entirely consistent with the infliction of multiple blows from a blunt instrument or instruments; (3) they are entirely consistent with those blows being delivered with a force of sufficient strength to cause death; (4) that a child of James Dunn has suffered severe multiple blunt trauma injuries while in the corner of the south and east aspects of this room, and these injuries resulted in the death of that individual."

The report was signed, *"Richard Thorley Shepherd, B.SC., M.B., B.S., M. R. C. C. PATH., D.M.J., Senior lecturer and honorary consultant in forensic medicine. United Medical Schools of Guy's and St. Thomas's, Guy's Hospital, London."*

When Jim learned from Tal English the contents of Dr. Shepherd's letter, he was overwhelmed by a profound sadness. In his heart, he had felt for months that Scott had died in that small room, but now that his belief had been confirmed by science, he felt sick—heart sick, soul sick. Scott had been *murdered*—coldly, brutally, ruthlessly murdered. This understanding, as agonizing as it was, filled him with a new resolve. He *would*, somehow, find Scott's killers. He would not rest, and he would not let the investigators rest, until his son's killers were behind bars.

The first thing that had to be done, obviously, was to obtain some more laboratory examinations. Dr. Shepherd had suggested that bone fragments might be found in the blood-soaked carpet. English took the entire section of bloody carpet to the DPS laboratory, but it was three weeks before the report came back negative for bone fragments; however, technologist Cathy McCord said she found a great deal of a substance that appeared to be some type of cleaning agent.

English was sending everything he found to Richard Walter. Now Walter decided it was time for him to pay the Lubbock police investigators a visit. English met Richard Walter at Lubbock International Airport on December 7. The contrast between the two men could not have been greater. Walter was dressed in a conservative dark blue suit with a button-down collar and tie. English could tell that the older man was surprised to see an easy-going detective in a casual outfit and well-polished cowboy boots. They went back to the Detective Division and English introduced the psychologist to George White, Randy McGuire and some of the other detectives who had worked on the case from time to time.

Lubbock Avalanche-Journal reporter Grady Simmons had arranged to interview Walter when he arrived. The two met in the Detective Division. Walter, with the Vidocq Society's French tri-color pin on his lapel, confidently declared that the police would solve the case of Dunn's disappearance.

"Success," he said, "will be based on two things: A) The case merits success; and B) I don't like losing a case. I have a bulldog mentality, and what I want to hear are handcuffs, and I want to do it right."

He told Simmons that "Having no body is a relatively rare case. Here I believe we're talking about not *all* of the body. What they thought may have been the complete absence of a body may not be the case—people make mistakes."

Simmons asked if he was referring to Scott's blood that police had found in his apartment, and Walter responded, "Blood certainly is a connective tissue, isn't it? But I wouldn't limit it to that (blood) exclusively."

Walter told the reporter that he had consulted an "internationally known forensic pathologist with impeccable credentials and a brilliant mind." He was referring, of course, to Dr. Shepherd. The pathologist, Walter said, had reviewed the case and written a report that would be important.

"We're reassessing previous assumptions," Walter said. "It's premature to say we've laid out a prosecutable case, but if I were a suspect, I wouldn't feel comfortable—I wouldn't buy any green bananas."

Walter declined to reveal the profile he had developed in the case. "The most generic thing is to say these killers are nasty and clever enough to avoid detection for eighteen months," he said. "The best case is the one offered by suspects," he continued. "Errors of omission and commission. People always make mistakes, and *these killers* made mistakes."

After the interview Walter was ready to get down to business. He asked to see the entire file so he could review everything the LPD had on the case thus far. First, though, he wanted to go to the crime scene, drive by ProSound Electronics, drive around Lubbock and the various places the police had searched for Scott's body and get a feel for the city. Tal English drove Walter to the places he requested and described to him the background of each and the investigative process related to each site.

After spending several hours reviewing the police file, including laboratory reports and statements of witnesses, Walter asked if English could arrange for him to meet some of the criminalists at the DPS crime laboratory. English took him to the lab, carrying the Dunn file. Richard asked the supervisor, Jim Thomas, to review the Luminol photographs of the crime scene and some of the lab reports with him. Thomas agreed, describing the processes they used and how he reached his conclusions.

That night, after his meeting with Thomas, Walter called Jim to report on what he had found. "I think I can give an accurate profile of the person or persons who murdered Scott," he told him. I am going to write it out for Tal and I can make a copy for you."

"Do that," Jim said eagerly. "But give me the oral version now. I want to know what you think."

"Okay. Now, for a minute, let's look at the crime scene. Taking a broad overview, one could say there are two kinds of crime scenes—the organized and the disorganized. If organized, the crime follows certain patterns: There has been an attempt to hide or destroy the body; there has been an attempt to clean up the crime scene and destroy evidence; there is evidence of planning and foresight; there is a sequence of events; if it is a serial killer, there is a certain type of victim that is sought.

"There are also indications of post-crime behaviors: What do people do after the crime? Sometimes, the killers will interject themselves into the criminal investigation. They immediately establish an alibi, their work and drinking habits may change temporarily, their religious habits may change temporarily, their pattern is disturbed for a matter of days. So it becomes critical to look at what may have been unobserved behavior. The organized person will be bright—or try to be bright—at times with a rigid demeanor. Cold. Cunning.

"The disorganized killer is far more compulsive; he may leave the crime scene without giving thought to the mess. The crime more often is set off by anger or some sudden emotion. After the crime is over, it's over. This person is an emotional boiling pot. Things are always happening. He may have all these needs; he may just happen to be carrying a weapon that day and he sees a victim or blows up and 'acts out' the crime, then walks away. Where they live and how they organize themselves is significant."

He paused to allow the other man to ask any questions in case he was not following Walter's train of thoughts. Then, satisfied by the silence, the profiler went on. "Then, there is the mixed crime. One may go from *organized* to *disorganized,* but never from *disorganized* to *organized*. Now in this case, I'd say we are dealing with an organized crime. We have evidence of planning: There was the clean-up, the careful way the carpet was replaced. I'd say the preplanning may have backtracked a good week ahead. This only increases the maliciousness of the crime.

"Also, we can recognize organized planning from the absence as well as the presence of evidence—the missing carpet piece, the missing water bed mattress liner, the missing murder weapon. People make the mistake of thinking that when evidence is not there, there's a loss, but this is not necessarily so. Sometimes the absence of an object demonstrates that something significant has happened. For instance, when you walk into someone's room and their clothes are missing, you make certain deductions.

"Once we decide that we're dealing with an organized crime, we can make certain deductions. What may seem unconnected to you becomes very significant, if viewed from a certain perspective. Remember, sometimes one just has to ask the right questions, that's all."

Walter recapped the reasons why he thought Leisha Hamilton fit the pattern of a psychopath and he listed the characteristics. Then he explained, "The psychopath is wired differently from the rest of us, in the sense that they are ultra-sensitive to ego-powered needs. You can put them on a lie detector and ask them about the most grisly bits and pieces of what they have done, and if it's in their best interest to lie, they have no problem with it. Their blood pressure will not rise. You can't find any differentiation in their reaction, whereas you or I would be going wild.

"But if you challenge their power, *they* go wild. You look at Leisha, and you can see that everything going on with her is power based. See how she interjected herself into the investigation; that's not uncommon with psychopaths.

"When we look at her history and her relationship with Scott, we recognize that she absolutely cannot stand rejection… because that means she is not in control. She has a series of short-term relationships which are not monogamous because she needs… it's not so much an issue of conquering men as it is emasculating them. What we then come up to is this: Scott is a relatively strong-willed man himself, though I have never met a twenty-four-year-old who didn't think he could conquer the world. He sees this rather malevolent, vixenish woman whom one wouldn't mind having an affair with, but he wouldn't want to introduce her to his parents.

"Now he has Jessica and he's gathering strength. He doesn't need Leisha anymore. If anything is going to get you killed, it's to reject the psychopath and say 'I'm better than you are.'

"Besides the psychopathic aspect of rejection, Leisha viewed herself as the Mata Hari of love. *No one* rejects Leisha."

Walter's tone grew even more somber. "So, what do we have? She loses control of the situation; rejection is absolutely unforgivable. And now there is another woman in the picture, Jessica, who obviously means more to Scott than Leisha does. Leisha is going to get control back, no matter what it takes to do it. And if she has to involve some other people, as long as she's in control of the situation, it doesn't matter.

"If we look at her story, we see that it is not internally consistent across time. Though you may have a consistent story today, tomorrow and the next day the story will be different.

"That kind of person has an insatiable appetite for stimulation, even when they know better. Though they have the intellectual ability to see the big picture, that ego 'gotcha'—thinking the other persons are idiots and needing to prove it—gives the psychopath satisfaction to see they are duping the idiots. So they'll go ahead and involve themselves in the investigation, because they are certain the police would never suspect them.

"This move has two benefits: It gives the psychopath a kick—sort of prolonging the fantasy of staying in control. It also permits the psychopath—in this case, Leisha—to stay ahead of the investigation, so she doesn't get tripped up, and it also makes her look like the aggrieved woman, discarded when he ran off with someone else.

"I still think Leisha had an accomplice. First of all, it was just too easy to dupe Tim into helping her and perhaps pin the whole thing on him if she had to. She has already tried that, although unsuccessfully so far. Still, here we have this naive, ineffectual, pathetic man involved in possibly his first relationship and he's willing to do anything to please his new love because he is in lust, he is a primary suspect for aiding/abetting. This is enough to get him convicted of murder alongside Leisha, whether he's actually the one who committed the act or not."

After hanging up from his conversation with Jim, Walter met with English to inform the detective of his conclusions. He also provided English with a written version of his opinion.

Richard Walter's profile strengthened Jim Dunn's feeling that
Leisha and Tim had committed the murder. If Leisha really was the
psychopath Walter described, then her motive was apparent.
However, Walter provided no new leads or evidence.

Walter and Jim now felt police had enough to take the case to
Criminal District Attorney Travis Ware. English was skeptical and he
warned Walter that the relationship between the police department
and the D.A.'s office was somewhat strained because of an ongoing
controversy between the two agencies. Walter, on the other hand,
thought Ware's situation might make him more cooperative, give
him an opening to create some good will between his office, the
LPD and the public. English was not convinced, but felt they had
nothing to lose. So, with Sergeant Randy McGuire, Lieutenant Dean
Summerlin, and Captain Frank Wiley, head of Crimes Against
Persons, he took Walter to the courthouse to meet Ware.

Walking into Ware's office, Walter took note of the way the district attorney arranged the five visitors in a row of dark leather chairs
drawn around a high, glossy desk without a single item on it. Ware
was slim and well groomed, his white shirt starched, his expensive
gold watch worn loosely on his wrist so it showed under the cuff.
The profiler saw immediately that here was a man inordinately concerned with image.

Ware informed Walter that he had been educated in London, and
they discussed that city amiably for a few minutes. Walter told Ware
that he taught in England periodically and frequently consulted for
Scotland Yard.

Then Ware leaned back in his tall chair and put his right foot up
on the desk. "Well, it's your meeting," he said abruptly. "What do you
want?"

Walter, never short for words, told him exactly what he wanted—murder charges filed against Leisha Hamilton and Tim Smith.

Ware launched into a series of grisly stories about murders he
had prosecuted. Walter waited patiently, deciding the best move
would be to let Ware talk for a while.

"All you have is a missing person. You don't have a body. When you have a body or you have a case, come back to me," Ware concluded.

Walter gave Ware his infamous glare, over the tops of his glasses. "If you want a goddamned body, I'll give you one. It's right here, in Dr. Shepherd's report."

"What the hell are you talking about?" Ware demanded.

Walter explained who Dr. Richard Shepherd was, that Shepherd had examined the forensic evidence and determined that Scott Dunn could not have survived the attack on him.

"Well," Ware said, "I'm not sure what Texas law would say about this."

Walter grinned. "I just happen to have that section of Texas law here."

Ware's response was a grim smile. "I thought you might."

"In essence, Texas law says we have to have (a) a body, (b) part of a body or (c) a confession with corroborative evidence. We have (b)." Walter grinned triumphantly. "We have blood; blood is connective tissue; ergo, we have a part of a body."

Ware stared at the psychologist long and hard. Finally, he nodded. "All right. You have a murder."

Scott Dunn (left) and Jim Dunn the last time they were together

Scott working on the engine of Yellow Thunder

Leisha Hamilton

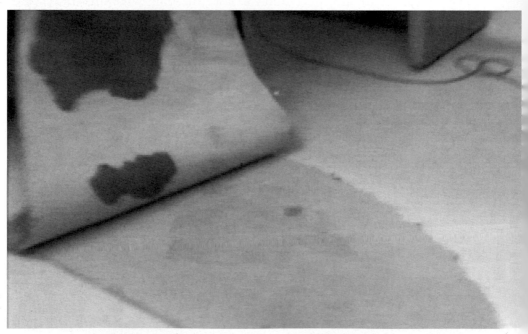

Carpet and carpet padding from Scott's bedroom

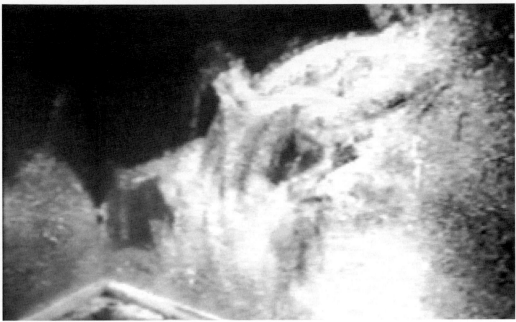

Luminol photograph showing blood on the wall of Scott's bedroom

Scott's Camaro at the impound lot

Jim Dunn (seated) with
Richard Walter

Lubbock County
Courthouse

Scott Dunn's empty grave

chapter eleven

Return to Lubbock

Another new year. It was 1993 and Jim felt more frustrated than ever. He'd had high hopes that Dr. Shepherd's report and Richard Walter's analysis would have created some momentum for the investigation. Nothing had happened, however, so he called Richard Walter to see if, by brainstorming, they could come up with a new angle, a different slant, anything to get the stalled investigation moving again. Walter proposed to Jim a return visit to Lubbock at the end of April and Jim welcomed the prospect. So did Tal English.

At that point, foremost on Walter's mind was whether Tim Smith's hair had been compared with the hairs that had been found on the tape used to patch the carpet in the killing room. Tal English had talked to Jim Thomas in the DPS crime lab about such a comparison, but Thomas had been skeptical: since it had not been done at the time of the murder, the passage of time causing the deterioration of the hair samples would render the comparison of no use.

Tal English persisted. At Walter's suggestion, English decided to run the idea by the FBI forensic analysts. The local agent, Bob Matthews, contacted the FBI crime lab. Their criminalists told him they were willing to try to make a comparison. First, though, English would have to get a sample of Smith's hair and that entailed getting a search warrant. English enlisted the help of Roger Pettiet, an investigator in the Criminal District Attorney's office, to help prepare the warrant. Meanwhile, Walter, who had arrived in Lubbock, wanted to interview the principals in the case personally.

English and Walter went first to the new ProSound Electronics store, which Gianoli had recently opened as a second outlet, and spoke with Max Gianoli. Gianoli seemed reluctant to talk to them, but answered Walter's questions, repeating the information he had given the police and Jim Dunn. Then Gianoli suggested that Walter might want to speak with Pat Taylor, who had worked with Scott, and who was still working at ProSound as manager of the original store.

Walter said they would get around to Taylor. At that point, however, he decided to put some pressure on Gianoli. "You know, Max, it's been suggested you know more than you're saying about the murder."

Walter just wanted to push Gianoli's buttons and observe his reaction. Gianoli became very nervous, very pressured and hostile, actually.

When the two investigators were back in the car, Walter mentioned that antagonism had been building between Scott and Max, as evidenced by the report of a fight between him and Scott shortly before Scott's disappearance. The police knew about the fight, but Gianoli had been able to explain it to their satisfaction.

"They were both very strong personalities," Walter told English, "and that environment was becoming extremely competitive and tense, not only between Max and Scott, but it included Mike Roberts as well, because Roberts evidently was annoyed that Max considered Scott his best installer—better than Roberts. Lots of jealousy in that shop," Walter mused.

The following morning, Roger Pettiet finished the warrant to obtain hair samples from Tim Smith. English, accompanied by Walter, went to Judge Tom Cannon to get it signed. Then they began

their search for Smith. Tim and Leisha were no longer living together and he had moved to an apartment in west Lubbock. There was
no response to their knocking on his door, so English taped his business card on it and they left.

Next the two men drove to Tim's mother's apartment. She did
not invite them in, but came outside and sat in the car with them;
she talked readily about Tim, although she said she had not seen him
recently.

She repeated the allegations she'd made earlier to English, that
people were following her. Walter could tell she was nervous and
having a difficult time staying focused on the subject at hand. She
kept wandering off on tangents. She did, however, tell them about
Tim as a child, that even as a little boy he was a perfectionist: One
time when he tried to learn to ride a bicycle, he fell over and then
he deliberately ran the bike up a tree. He had absolutely no patience
or self-control at all.

While Mrs. Smith was talking to the two detectives, her husband
came out of the apartment and wandered around the car, peering in
the windows with a menacing scowl on his face. Suddenly, she
appeared in a hurry to get out of the car. After she left, Walter told
English, "She gave me a sense of how her son thought and the things
that might motivate him to violence." Walter formed a profile of an
often punished, yet self-indulgent youngster who learned how to
survive by trickery, deceit and isolation. Walter mentioned that he
sensed that Tim had the attitude of "I want what I want when I want
it," and he had learned how to play the different games so that he
minimized the number of attacks on himself. So he basically grew
up with no restriction, Walter said; he grew up by avoidance.

"I don't like what I'm seeing," Walter said, "because when lust or
whatever else came into play, Tim would be without boundaries."

Since Tim was unavailable, Walter told English he wanted to have
a talk with Pat Taylor, so the two men went to the Thirty-fourth
Street location of ProSound Electronics. Taylor talked with them
readily. He told the investigators that he used to hang around with

Mike Roberts and Scott Dunn before Scott turned up missing. Taylor said that Mike Roberts's personality changed drastically after Scott's disappearance, that Mike became more violent and irritable. Mike was caught stealing some ProSound shirts and was fired. Taylor said that Roberts had started doing car burglaries after he got fired, but was not very successful. Not long afterward, he went back to Washington State. Taylor's words added fuel to the suspicion Walter already was feeling about Mike Roberts.

Just before 10:00 PM, English and Walter went back to Tim Smith's apartment. This time he was at home. English told Tim why they were there, that they had a warrant allowing them to collect hair samples from him and he would have to go with them to the Lubbock County Jail, where a nurse would get the samples. Tim seemed puzzled, but nonresistant. English read him his Miranda rights. He asked Tim if he understood his rights and the younger man said he did.

On the ride downtown, Tim talked to English and Walter, but did not tell them anything of any relevance. At the Lubbock County Jail, Walter and Tim waited in the hall outside the infirmary while Tal went to find the person in charge. Walter used those few minutes to push Smith a bit.

"Young man," he said, "don't you realize that Leisha Hamilton accused you of killing Scott Dunn? That's why you are here. We have to rule you out. Now, son, I'm going to tell you, if you want to save yourself, if you can to save yourself, then now is the time to come forward. It may be a bit dirty, or whatever else, but in point of fact, unless you tell us what we want to know, you're going to do time for murder. And this is real."

Walter watched Tim, who was shifting from foot to foot, fidgeting nervously, looking more and more anxious. For a long while, he said nothing, then with great frustration evident in his voice, he said, "But I can't turn against the others."

A jolt of energy surged through Walter. Others? What others? He looked sternly at Tim. "Tell me."

Tim immediately began backtracking. "It's not right," he said. "I'm a Christian."

"Not right for what?" Walter asked. "What's Christian about letting a woman—helping her get off for murder and you taking the rap for it? I don't understand that kind of Christianity."

Walter had boxed Tim in, but contrary to his boyish appearance, Tim proved tough, refusing to say anything else.

Tal English and the nurse on duty approached and led Tim to the infirmary. The nurse obtained twenty-five samples of pubic, body and head hair from Tim Smith. These samples were placed in plastic bags and sealed. English took custody of the samples. Then English and Walter took Tim back to his apartment.

The following day, English prepared a package that contained Smith's hair samples for the FBI laboratory. Earlier, the day after English and White discovered the roll of duct tape in Tim Smith's living room, English had asked Leisha Hamilton for a sample of her hair. She had run a brush through her long hair, then carefully pulled some hairs from the brush and gave them to English. At that time English had asked Leisha if there were a brush or a comb around that might contain Scott's hair. She had given him a blue plastic hairbrush, which English had sent to the police property room. English put the hair samples from Leisha and Tim and the hairbrush that had belonged to Scott into the package, along with the hair obtained from the duct tape used to fasten the carpet to the bloodstained floor in Leisha's bedroom and the roll of duct tape found in Tim Smith's living room.

When that task was finished, English and Walter decided to confront Leisha Hamilton at the restaurant where she worked. When Leisha saw them she looked annoyed. To avoid a scene in the place, they asked her to come out to the car and talk to them. She agreed. Seating Leisha in the back, the two men sat in front, half-turned, so they could face her.

Obviously striving to be charming and informal, now she chatted, as if this were a social visit. Walter had another agenda. He knew she had been blaming Scott's death on Tim Smith and Walter wanted her to nail Tim, then and there.

Walter moved this idea forward. "Leisha, I wish you would explain what is going on. I mean, I don't know of anybody else in America who does a murder and then cleans up the crime scene afterward. That is, unless it is done in their own home. And in this case, you're the only one who had access to that house. And you don't have an alibi for the murder."

"But I do have an alibi," she protested.

Walter's voice hardened. "You mean you know when he died? I thought you said you didn't know."

"I know when I found out he was missing," she said. "And I was at work when he left."

Walter gave her his "look" over the tops of his glasses. "Let me explain something to you. Scott Dunn is *not missing*. I don't want to hear the word 'missing,' okay? Scott Dunn was murdered. We've got that established and you're a suspect."

"Then I guess I don't have an alibi," she said.

Walter pounced. "You know, Leisha, I've noticed that your paramours always seem to be younger than yourself. And I realize that I'm old, I'm ugly and I'm tired. But looking at you, for all intents and purposes, I have to ask, what did these guys see in you?"

For a moment the car was filled with shocked silence. English looked as surprised as Leisha did. She said nothing for a few minutes. Walter had asked the question simply because he knew it was the last thing she would expect. She always wanted to be in control and with that question, Walter took control away from her.

Then she smiled, an artificial smile, and said, "Well, I don't know."

"Is it because of the sexual tricks you can offer them?" Walter asked.

She nodded curtly. "I guess so." Quickly she opened the car door and got out. "I've got to get back to work."

Walter and English watched her walk away. English shook his head. "Richard, why didn't you just call her a dog?"

Walter grinned. "I thought I did."

"But why?"

Walter explained. "I asked that question to see how she reacted to unexpected situations, to see how quick she was in her thinking and what her game was all about. And it worked. More than anything," he told English, "her game is all about power—power and control—and information is part of that power. I planted seeds of doubt, as well as direct information I wanted her to know, such as that she is a suspect. I wanted to create some anxiety and I think I succeeded. Maybe her story will be different next time."

English nodded. "Undoubtedly. But not necessarily the truth."

After seeing Leisha, English went to see Sergeant Bill Hubbard, who recently had replaced Tomas Esparza as identification supervisor when Esparza was promoted. He told Hubbard Pat Taylor's story about Mike Roberts having committed car burglaries. English had obtained copies of Roberts's fingerprints from the Pierce County Sheriff's office in Tacoma, Washington and Hubbard did a search on numerous vehicle during the period in question, comparing fingerprints from the crime scenes to those of Mike Roberts. No matches were found.

Before Walter left town, he informed Jim of his assessment of the people involved in the case, the exact assessment he had given Tal English. "This is a very organized crime—from top to bottom—from removing the body to replacing the carpet to devising a cover-up story. It took an organized mind to work this all out. And Tim Smith is just not an organized person. No way. He may have been the patsy, but someone else organized the crime.

"Look at Mike Roberts. It says in your files that he made a statement to Leisha and Burt Todd that 'It's probably just as well that this happened, because Scott had become a real asshole.' Does this imply that he was involved somehow? Do we really know that he visited

Scott the night he disappeared? We have only his word on that—
Leisha has told two stories about that. Once she said she heard him,
but in another version, she was supposedly asleep, remember, so she
might not be able to confirm that he was there at all. There is no
independent corroborative evidence that he's telling the truth.

"The only thing we know for sure is that no one besides our little circle of suspects actually saw Scott after Tuesday afternoon, when
the next-door neighbor noticed Leisha helping him into the apartment. The neighbor said he looked drunk, because Leisha was practically carrying him into the apartment. So, that leaves a lot more
days unaccounted for than we originally thought.

"And think about this: why did Max, who was supposed to be
Scott's friend, go off and leave him alone all day, when he was so sick
he couldn't get to the phone? Why wouldn't someone check on him
during the day—especially when they were working so hard to get
ready for this stereo competition?"

Walter had a theory: he conjectured that Crank It Up Contests
could be an excellent vehicle for illegal activity. Participants came
together from distant counties and sometimes even states. The cars,
basically boom boxes on wheels, could provide convenient hiding
places for contraband. Drugs could have been distributed.

Another theory involved a car burglary ring that flourished in
Lubbock at that time. A scam could have been perpetrated when
new stereos were installed. Soon afterward, someone might break
into the car, get the new stereo system, return it to inventory of the
store where it came from and, when the auto owner showed up with
his insurance check in hand, install a new system for him. Another
electronics store in Lubbock was already being investigated for such
illegal activity, so police were suspicious of it also going on at other
stores, like ProSound.

Or an employee of the store who knew the new stereos had
been installed could be stealing them and pawning them or selling
them privately. Either way, if Scott became suspicious and threatened

to blow the whistle, he could have initiated his own death. Walter wanted to check out Mike Roberts's movements that night.

Another theory of Walter's centered on Scott's condition. "It's possible," Walter ventured, "that, considering the symptoms, Scott might have been poisoned that Monday night. He felt hot, he couldn't stand the light, he couldn't stand any pressure on his body—clothes or anything like that—he was too weak to walk. All these are symptomatic of poisoning with organic phosphates—something like pesticide or herbicide. Then, in a weakened state, he would have been much easier to kill."

Walter felt they had to concentrate on Leisha's accomplice. It may not have been Tim but one of the others.

"Since Leisha thinks she's got an alibi, she feels safe to call attention to herself. She thinks she's smart enough to outwit everybody and she can play cat-and-mouse with the police. This massages her ego and keeps the spotlight on her. What we must do is make her feel insignificant—unimportant. This will drive her crazy and she may well make a mistake."

Jim was more impressed with Richard's analysis than English was. English respected Walter's assessment, but he had drawn another conclusion. He could see Leisha and Tim committing the crime together, but felt the others weren't the right targets. His experience in criminal investigations had led him to believe that the more people who are involved in a crime, the more likelihood there is that someone will talk. And no one had talked about the murder of Scott Dunn. To him, then, there were only two people involved—Leisha Hamilton and Tim Smith.

As Jim Dunn agonized, four months passed before the FBI crime lab sent its report on the hair samples English had submitted. Then Jim learned that the FBI lab concluded that one head hair taken from the duct tape located under the carpet exhibited the same microscopic characteristics as the hairs taken from Tim Smith's head and that it was consistent with having originated from Tim Smith.

The remaining hairs taken from the duct tape exhibited the same microscopic characteristics as hairs taken from Leisha Hamilton and were consistent with having originated from Leisha Hamilton. No hairs taken from that duct tape were consistent with those taken from Scott Dunn's hairbrush. Jim's agony grew.

Jim Dunn prodded both Richard Walter and Tal English regularly—weekly, at least. He felt strongly that any discussion among the three of them could trigger an idea or open a new avenue of exploration. They decided to ask the FBI to re-examine the forensic evidence in the case. Since hairs as well as carpet fibers had been removed from the roll of duct tape found in Tim Smith's apartment, English wanted those hairs compared with the hairs taken from Tim and Leisha and from Scott's hairbrush. That package went to the crime lab in November, but another four months went by before the analysis was completed.

The report on the items sent to the lab confirmed that the blood on the ceiling was human blood, but the type could not be determined. The results of the analysis on the hair samples showed that nine hairs were collected from the roll of duct tape found in Tim Smith's apartment. Of these, two hairs were microscopically similar to the hairs from the hairbrush of Scott Dunn. None showed any similarity to the hair samples from Leisha or Tim Smith.

"One step forward, two steps back," Jim Dunn vented to both Walter and English. Frustration mounted.

Finally, Jim got the news he had been waiting for—there were rumors that, at last, Criminal District Attorney Travis Ware was ready to move toward a grand jury investigation of Scott's murder.

chapter twelve

A Step toward Justice

After meeting with Richard Walter and officials from LPD's homicide division, Travis Ware discussed the Dunn case at length with his first assistant, Rebecca Atchley. The two prosecutors finally came to the conclusion that they would be justified in asking a grand jury to investigate the murder. Ware and Atchley were hoping that if all the people connected with the case were re-interviewed and subpoenaed to appear before the grand jury, new evidence might be uncovered or evidence already in the possession of the police might take on new significance.

Not only would Atchley be able to question the witnesses under oath, but the twelve members of the grand jury also could ask questions. One of those people might ask a question no one had asked before. Atchley also knew from her experience as a prosecutor that sometimes witnesses were more in awe of a grand jury than they were of police detectives and, knowing they were under oath, more inclined to tell the truth.

It was a slim hope, but it was the only glimmer of light Atchley had.

In July, Atchley contacted Jim Dunn. He was eager to share all
the information he had amassed over the past two years. By this time,
he had accumulated more than a dozen audiotapes of conversations
he'd had with almost everyone involved with Scott after he moved
to Lubbock. So once again, he plunged into the investigation and
over the next several months he outlined the case for Atchley, from
the day he learned that Scott was missing to that point. Dunn's notes
were so thorough she was impressed. He had at his fingertips an
amazing wealth of details, dates and impressions. As a parent herself,
Atchley empathized with Jim Dunn and found herself wanting to
help him find out what had happened to his son.

"Leisha has been able to manipulate everyone who has been
involved in this situation," Dunn warned her. "She is very good at
it."

"She hasn't ever come up against a woman and she definitely has
not had to come up against me," Rebecca Atchley assured him with
quiet authority.

Atchley had numerous conversations with Leisha Hamilton.
Some the prosecutor initiated; many were initiated by Leisha.
Atchley found that Leisha could be charming and persuasive when
she wanted to be. She gave the appearance of wanting to be cooperative, eager to give Atchley all the information she had.

Leisha spoke the right words, but as Atchley came to know her,
the prosecutor perceived Leisha as manipulative and determined to
control every situation she faced. The only time Leisha's cooperative
facade cracked was when she and Atchley talked about Jim Dunn.
Leisha was not at all sympathetic to him, in spite of the fact he had
lost his son. Instead, Leisha saw Jim as someone who was out to get
her.

Atchley saw during further meetings and conversations that
although Leisha changed her story in small ways several times, Leisha
herself did not believe she was lying. Leisha was unable to see her-

self as lying about anything. She always had a reason, a justification for every variance in her answers to Atchley's questions. Atchley felt that Leisha never saw any of her statements as lies.

While she was getting to know the real Leisha, Atchley asked Tal English, with the assistance of Roger Pettiet, an investigator from her office, to go over the ground the police had covered a dozen times before. They would find and question witnesses English had talked to over and over again. It was her hope that someone might have remembered an important bit of information that would shed some light on the case.

Atchley asked English to try and confirm the date that Tim Smith moved from Unit 229 to Unit 107 at the Regency Apartments. English and Pettiet went back to the all-too-familiar site and talked to the manager. She told them that ownership of the apartment had changed and that they did not have any records of when Tim switched apartments. However, she mentioned that Rachel Borthe, who had been an assistant manager then, still lived on the premises. The detectives found Rachel at home and she told them she was sure that Tim Smith moved to Apartment 107 *after* she heard about Scott Dunn being missing. Rachel said she had spoken to Tim on several occasions and that he scared her. She described him as a quiet person who always talked in a monotone. She thought he was a window peeper. The first time she met him, he was sitting on the fence located outside her apartment. Several people were gathered around the pool and she joined in the conversation. They started talking about what might have occurred in the Dunn case. Tim, who talked about the case quite frequently, said he thought he could solve the case, especially if he had as much information as the police did. He said he could not believe anyone would think Scott was not killed in the apartment. Tim insisted Scott was killed in the apartment and it was because of Scott's car and drugs. Rachel said she first talked with Tim quite a bit. She then became frightened by him and tried to distance herself from him, but he was always coming to her apartment wanting to come in and talk. He always told her about how he was a ladies' man and that he went out with a different girl every night, although she never saw girls or anyone else go to his apartment. He was always by himself. She figured him for a loner.

During the course of the summer investigation, English learned that Leisha was now living with a man named Karl Young. She had left her employment at the restaurant where she had worked while Scott was alive and currently was taking a course to become a licensed vocational nurse.

As Jim Dunn waited, watching days and weeks inch by and his son's killers go on with their lives while his mind remained fixated on all he'd lost, the re-investigation of the case dragged on. It was not until August 4, 1994, that Rebecca Atchley began presenting the case to a Lubbock County grand jury.

Jim and Barbara Dunn arrived in Lubbock a few days before the grand jury was scheduled. Jim spent several hours going over his testimony and discussing every facet of the case with Rebecca Atchley. At one point, Jim asked Rebecca if she was going to question Leisha Hamilton about Scott's remote control boat—the boat Leisha claimed had disappeared when Scott did.

Atchley reminded Jim that authorities had not turned up any evidence that the boat was related to Scott's murder.

"Then why is it missing?" Jim demanded. "What did she do with it? Why is it important to her? If you ask her about it on the stand, maybe, under oath, she'll talk about it. If she lies—well, that's perjury, isn't it? And if she is indicted for murder and it comes out at trial that she lied to the grand jury, that has to have a negative impact on a jury, don't you think?"

Atchley agreed and added the whereabouts of the boat to the list of questions she had for Leisha.

Tal English was one of the first witnesses to testify. Jim also testified as did Tim Smith, Max Gianoli, Mike Roberts, Richard Walter, Leisha's mother and Leisha herself. To everyone's surprise, she wore a maternity smock to the hearings. She said Karl Young was the father of the child she was carrying.

Leisha was questioned on the third day of testimony. She was asked about the remote-controlled boat that had belonged to Scott. She said she had given it to a friend, Dave Hayden, for safekeeping. The grand jury directed that a subpoena be issued to recover the boat and Leisha agreed to get it back.

At the lunch break that day, Rebecca Atchley, Roger Pettiet and Donny Carrasco, another investigator from the district attorney's office, went to the pump company where Hayden worked and asked him to go with them to get the boat. During the drive to his place, he told Atchley and the two investigators that he had just completed a telephone call from Leisha Hamilton.

"Leisha said she needed a big favor from me," Hayden said. "She said there were some people looking for the boat and she wanted to take the boat to my house and leave it there. She said she had told someone that the boat was there."

Hayden assumed she was talking about a small radio-controlled boat that she had talked about a couple of years before, but which he had never seen. Leisha said she would put the boat under the steps of his home and if anyone came looking for it, he was to tell them it was there. If anyone asked, he was to tell them that the boat had been there six months and that the reason it was under the porch was because he didn't have enough room in the house. She said, "Someone will be out to get the boat," and then she hung up. Hayden had barely replaced the phone when Rebecca Atchley walked into his office with the two investigators.

Later, when they arrived at his gated community, they saw Leisha outside. She appeared to be leaving. Dave suddenly remembered that he had placed a security watch on his home and no one could enter unless the guard at the gate obtained permission from him. He had forgotten to tell Leisha she couldn't get inside.

They watched as Leisha got in her car and drove eastbound on Nineteenth Street and concluded that she probably was headed back to the courthouse. To make sure she hadn't somehow placed the boat or gotten someone to put it under Hayden's porch, the investigators went to his home and looked. It was not there.

Then they hurried to catch up with Leisha, whom they surveyed from a safe distance. She stopped at the outside pay phone of a convenience store and made a phone call. When she resumed her trip, they followed her to the Lubbock County Courthouse. In the parking lot, Pettiet jumped out of his car and approached Leisha, demanding the boat. At first, she denied having it, then suddenly made an about-face, opened the trunk of her car and took out the small yellow boat.

"Here," she said. "I was bringing it to you."

Pettiet took custody of the boat and escorted Hayden to the D.A.'s office to make a statement. He called Tal English to tell him that he was taking the statement from Hayden and suggested that English might want to sit in on the session.

Hayden spoke animatedly. He said he had met Leisha Hamilton a month or two before Scott Dunn's disappearance, when they both worked at a southwest Lubbock restaurant. He never met Scott, but knew of him from things that Leisha had said. When Scott disappeared, Hayden said, Leisha told people she thought he had just left her and she didn't know where he had gone.

About two or three months later, Hayden said, he and Leisha started going out together or partying together at her house, even though her daughter was living with her. One night, they started to have sex in the early morning hours and Tim Smith walked into the bedroom. Leisha later told Hayden that Tim had a key, but she didn't know how he got it. She said that she had not given it to him.

"Leisha yelled at him and asked what he was doing in the house. He tried to answer her. He seemed upset, but not real mad. Leisha got out of bed and started talking to him. I don't remember exactly what was said. Tim grabbed her by the arms as if he were trying to keep her from hitting him. I saw Leisha's hand come up and slap or hit Tim. I think he asked her why she did that. She was telling him that he was not supposed to be there and she had not asked him to come over. She told him he was not supposed to have a key. She was finally able to get him to leave. After he left, she called the police and reported the incident. The police came a little while after she called. Tim Smith didn't really seem mad when he was there that night, but seemed hurt emotionally."

Hayden said he went out with Leisha a few times after that incident, but the relationship changed and they became friends rather than lovers. He worked on her car a few times after that and she would make dinner for him in exchange. "I kept in contact with her for a while. Today was the first time I had heard from Leisha in about six months."

Jim Dunn felt they were finally getting somewhere. However, the grand jury indicted Leisha on one count of aggravated perjury and one count of tampering with evidence, both stemming from her testimony about Scott's boat. It took no action, on the murder charge, though, which left authorities free to file charges against her in the future, if more evidence was discovered. Several days passed before the orders for the arrest of Leisha were ready to be served. To Tal English's surprise, Leisha called regularly, asking him if he was going to arrest her. He wracked his brain, trying to figure out what she was thinking. Was she daring him to arrest her? Or was she acting like the sociopath Richard Walter had diagnosed, feigning helpfulness in order to stay in the loop of the investigation? He came to no conclusions. There was no way to anticipate what Leisha might do next.

In a front page story in the *Lubbock Avalanche-Journal* courthouse reporter Max Gulick said, "A small radio-controlled speedboat that belonged to Roger Scott Dunn floats near the core of a mystery and at the center of two sealed indictments returned Wednesday against Dunn's former girlfriend, Leisha Gwen Hamilton."

Gulick wrote, "Authorities refused to discuss the boat's meaning to the case, but Criminal District Attorney Travis Ware said the little yellow speedboat is highly significant."

Ware refused to say why the boat was important to the investigation into Scott Dunn's death. As investigators would learn, after the boat had been examined for forensic evidence, fingerprinted and x-rayed, it had absolutely no bearing on the case—at least as far as they could determine.

Two weeks passed. Then Leisha was arrested and jailed on a total of $100,000 in bonds—$50,000 bond for each of the third-degree felony offenses.

The grand jury investigation had left Rebecca Atchley with more questions than answers. Undoubtedly, the physical evidence pointed to Leisha Hamilton and Tim Smith as the killers. Of one thing, however, Atchley was sure. Whether or not Leisha had actually bludgeoned Scott Dunn to death, she was certainly capable of such a crime.

On the same day that Leisha's court-appointed attorney filed writs seeking a bond reduction, she was arraigned in Justice of the Peace Tom Head's court on a probation violation from New Mexico. Atchley feared that if her bond were reduced, Leisha might leave town. The prosecutor was hopeful that the bond would not be reduced while they were waiting to see what New Mexico was going to do about Leisha. Five weeks later the New Mexico court wouldn't revoke her probation and during that time she remained in Lubbock County Jail. When New Mexico made its decision, Wardoup's request for lower bail was granted and she got out on bond.

The fact that the grand jury had left the case held both good news and bad news for Jim Dunn. The good news was that Leisha's time in jail might soften her up a bit, help her to realize what it would be like to be sent to prison for years, if she were convicted of Scott's murder. There was always the possibility that the district attorney might cut some sort of deal with her to minimize her time, if she confessed and told them what had happened to Scott's body.

The bad news was that the investigation might fizzle again.

Richard Walter did not share Jim's optimism. Walter told Jim that his training and expertise in forensic psychology and his exposure to Leisha led him to believe that Leisha was not afraid of prison. Her prior history indicated that jail cells were almost a second home to her. She knew the system and she would have no trouble coping with life there. Jim had to agree.

When Leisha was released from the Lubbock County lock-up, she returned to the home she shared with Karl Young and gave birth to a son. Her life seemed to go on as usual. There was one glitch, however, when she attempted to find new work. The State Board of Health refused to grant her a nursing license because of her criminal history.

chapter thirteen

Another Grand Jury

Despite Richard's pessimism, Jim was not going to allow his hopes to crash to the ground. However, after a few days at home, he became more discouraged and dejected than he had in months. He'd had such high hopes for an indictment. Rebecca Atchley had seemed confident that she would get an indictment. The evidence seemed to be enough to warrant an indictment. So what had happened? No one could come up with a reason for the grand jury's failure to act.

Jim pressed on. He called Rebecca Atchley and Tal English, who assured him that the case still was open. The grand jury had not issued a no-bill, which may have indicated they were not convinced of Leisha and Tim's innocence, only of the weakness of the evidence against them. Rebecca Atchley, no matter how much she might want to get Leisha and Tim to trial, would not be involved further, because her boss, Travis Ware, had been defeated in the Republican primary that spring. There would be a new district attorney in January and, more than likely, the new chief prosecutor would want to hire his own assistants, so Rebecca would be without a job.

Despite his earnest endeavors to gain closure, once again Jim found that the justice system had its own timetable whose major imperative seemed to be hurry up, please wait. Nothing happened on the Dunn case after the grand jury, except that Lubbock County had a new Criminal District Attorney. There was common speculation that he would consider this case too cold to revive. Then one day in January of 1995, Karl Young called Tal English. Young wanted to talk, he said, but he feared for his life. English agreed to meet Young at a small, east side coffee shop. The other man's nervousness was evident. He sat with his back to the wall and kept his head lowered as he spoke. His eyes darted from side to side and, occasionally, over Tal's shoulder, toward the front door of the little shop.

Young, the alleged father of Leisha's new child, told English he had moved in with Leisha after having met her at a south Lubbock nightclub. When she got out of jail after serving five weeks on the perjury charge, her personality had changed, Young said. Before her incarceration, she was very loving and understanding, but after she got out of jail, she got extremely angry in an instant over simple things. And other aspects of her behavior changed, as well.

"I remember one night, she watched this unsolved mystery movie about a husband who was missing and presumed dead. Now, Leisha didn't like to watch TV, but she watched every second of this movie." Young said.

Then, a few weeks later, Leisha again seemed hypnotized, this time by a talk show about the execution of a prisoner. "Usually, she went to bed before eleven o'clock," Young said, "but that night she stayed up until around one o'clock in the morning watching this show. She couldn't sleep after seeing the show and she had bad dreams."

"She hasn't slept well since that night," he confided, "and I think it's because her conscience is bothering her."

Young told English he was trying to find a way to get Leisha out of the home where they lived without losing his baby. He said he was also afraid of Leisha, that his own life might be in danger.

English asked Young what Leisha had told him about Scott. The story Young related sounded exactly like the story she had told English. At first, Young said, he believed her when she said she didn't know anything about Scott's death, but recently he had changed his mind. Now, he thought she probably killed Scott and got Tim Smith to do the cleanup. Leisha wouldn't talk about Scott or the case still hanging over her.

Young also told English that Leisha was very good with people; she knew how to play them and she did it well. As an example, he said, Leisha got a job with a marketing research company after she got out of jail and the first month she was there, she was named Employee of the Month. Leisha had left that job, however, and was currently working at an Italian restaurant.

Finally, English threw some money on the table and got up from his chair. He handed Young his business card. Young threw up his hands, palms toward Tal.

"No way. If Leisha finds that, I've had it. I can't imagine what she would do to me. One time, before the grand jury met, Rebecca Atchley gave me her card and Leisha found it. She was so mad, I thought she was going to explode. I don't want her to find out about this meeting—ever!"

Only a few days later, Young called English again, asking for another meeting at the same place they had met before. Young seemed a little less nervous than he had been at their first meeting. He told English he was leaving Leisha. He was moving to another home and he was in the process of getting a restraining order against her. Also, he was asking for temporary custody of their son.

Then Young pulled a folded piece paper, apparently torn from a legal pad. "Leisha drew this and it scared the shit out of me. I thought I should show it to you."

English studied the drawing and his heart began to pump. In the sketch, a figure, on which was printed the letter *S*, was restrained by a grid. Footprints led away from the grid toward an open door, through which could be seen clouds and a tree. Inside the door was a second figure, face down. In the lower right corner were five objects that sent a chill through English: a gun, a knife, a hypodermic syringe, a pair of handcuffs and a severed penis and scrotum.

Hurriedly, English thanked Young and left. Back at the office, English showed the drawing to George White. "What do you think?"

White shook his head. "Could mean anything. Or nothing. Could mean she knows more about Scott Dunn's death than she lets on."

English nodded. "Maybe Richard Walter can tell us what was going on in her mind when she drew this."

English sent the drawing to Walter. At the end of the week, Walter called Tal. He had examined the drawing and, in his opinion, Leisha had drawn a picture of the crime scene where Scott Dunn had been murdered. Walter promised to write out his interpretation of the drawing and get it to English right away. Within a few days Walter made good on his promise and his pictograph analysis arrived.

"In the lower left quadrant of the paper the drawing portrays the faceless victim, identified as S in a bondage-restrained position. The arms are stretched out and connected to a device similar to a wood pallet, grating or homemade device to accomplish the task. The victim appears to be wearing footgear such as socks, moccasins or slippers. The lower right quadrant shows five masculine symbols, including a hypodermic needle, gun, knife, handcuffs (could be a horse-related come-along device) and emasculated penis and scrotum.

"The left middle position shows barefoot footprints leading away from the bondage site to the doorway. They stop at the doorway with the fallen body beside them. The body has arms outstretched and is mirrored by a shadow figure opposite.

"The upper portion of the paper has a wide horizon line, which is broken by a doorway leading to the outside. At the end of the road are clouds and the sky.

"Interpretation: Inasmuch as the crime scene of the Scott Dunn murder occurred in a bedroom shared by the victim and author of the drawings, it is important to note the implicit/explicit inferences of information.

"In reference to the overall setting, it appears that the picture portrays only the bedroom setting. The horizon line represents the wall. The clouds outside represent everything outside of the bedroom.

"Referent to the lower left quadrant, the faceless body bound to the framework is labeled S, and representative of Scott. Consistent with that, with what is known by the murder investigation, the author portrays the victim held captive and vulnerable to acts of torture. Hence, we find the drawings of Scott Dunn being portrayed with the needle, knife, gun, handcuffs. The detached genitalia could infer sexual abuse with a dildo or, more than likely, it was representative of emasculation.

"The mid-point footprints represent an attempt to get away, which was stopped; in particular the fallen body with companion ghost and unattached handcuffs represent the fallen dead. Furthermore, the future, through the door, is clean and unused.

"In summary, it is believed that the pictographic drawings represent the murder and crime scene evidence of Scott Dunn. It is also believed that the author of the drawings was at the murder scene and drew these drawings for a personal pictorial diary."

English and White agreed with parts of the interpretation formed by Richard Walter. They believed that Leisha had participated in the killing of Scott Dunn. Beyond that, they left psychological impressions to the expert. The drawing may have reaffirmed their conviction of Leisha Hamilton's guilt, but it offered nothing in the way of proving it and would never be offered in court.

In March, Young met with English again. This time Young wanted to talk most about the perjury case against Leisha Hamilton. He said Leisha had talked with her daughter the night before her daughter was to testify before the grand jury. Leisha instructed her daughter what to say about the boat. Young said that he was aware at the time that Leisha had the boat. He said Leisha became paranoid during the time the grand jury was meeting; she thought the house and phones were bugged. She wouldn't talk to him unless they went for drives in the car.

Prior to the grand jury probe, Leisha had always spoken of Scott as having disappeared. Then when the grand jury began its investigation, she said Scott must be dead, because the investigators could prove it.

Young told English he believed Leisha had six children: two were around ten or eleven years old, living with their father in Georgia; a daughter, fifteen years old, lived with Leisha; another daughter, about fourteen years old, lived with Leisha's father; Leisha's oldest child, a son, lived with his adoptive father, possibly in Indiana. Young said Leisha didn't know who his real father was. Her youngest was their son.

Toward the end of May, Jim Dunn, who was pressing the police investigation on possible witnesses and alleged killers, returned to Lubbock. Jim refused to give up hope though he felt depressed following the grand jury hearing. He was eager to meet Lubbock County's new Criminal District Attorney, Bill Sowder. Most of the new CDA staff was complete and Sowder was already getting high marks from the police investigators who dealt with him and from the community at large.

The new district attorney cordially welcomed Jim and Barbara and told them he would look at the evidence in the case against Leisha Hamilton and Tim Smith. He had one problem, though. Prior to becoming district attorney, Sowder had been a defense attorney in partnership with Dan Hurley. When the LPD began its investigation into Scott's death, Tim Smith had hired Hurley as his attorney. To avoid conflict of interest now, Sowder could not participate in any cases in which Hurley had been involved. Already he had hired a special prosecutor for several cases and he would need to do so again in the Dunn case. He assured the Dunns he would get a prosecutor to look at the evidence and decide whether they had enough to present to a grand jury.

Jim Dunn thanked him. "We'll work with you and the special prosecutor any way we can."

The prosecutor Sowder had in mind was Larry "Rusty" Ladd, an assistant district attorney in Hale County, which joined Lubbock County on the north. He told Ladd that most of the investigatory work had been done in the Dunn case prior to the grand jury case in which Leisha had been indicted, although more might be necessary. He warned Ladd that there were some extraordinary evidentiary problems because the body had not been found and no weapon had been recovered. There were two suspects and not much else, as far as Sowder could tell. They had not found any witnesses or a weapon and neither suspect had confessed.

At Jim's request, Sowder arranged for the Dunns to meet Rusty Ladd with Tal English at their Lubbock hotel. Dressed casually, in jeans and a checkered shirt, Ladd impressed Jim as more than just a good ole Texas lawyer. Behind Ladd's lazy drawl and quick smile, Jim sensed there was a man who couldn't resist a challenge.

Ladd listened with palpable interest to Jim's story. Before leaving, Ladd promised to give Scott's case careful scrutiny. Jim assured him that Richard Walter would cooperate fully.

Ladd had been a police officer before going to law school, so taking a case that still needed some investigation done was not something of which he was afraid. To him it sounded like a challenge professionally, one he was eager to take on.

When Ladd started reading through English's synopsis and time line, he believed both Leisha and Tim had done the killing, but wasn't convinced there was enough evidence to get an indictment on Leisha Hamilton. Nevertheless, there were Tim's letters that established the relationship between the two, there was obvious evidence of her manipulation of Tim and it had to be put forth that Leisha wanted to kill Scott or to have him killed and would have needed some help with the disposition of Scott's body.

Leisha appeared to be a woman to whom sex was just one of several tools she used in order to accomplish what she wanted; she was crass about that. It also was evident that Scott Dunn, although he wasn't rich, had a father who, as far as Leisha was concerned, had a lot of money. Scott was good looking, he was charismatic, he had a line into a lot of money and a family history of money that Leisha may have seen as a potential source of security for her. Ladd could see easily that there might have come a point in their relationship when Scott said something to her, such as, "I will never marry you. You know that's never going to happen." And then there was his engagement, which seemed to occur close to his disappearance.

Ladd became convinced that Leisha felt scorned; when she realized she was never going to have a permanent relationship with Scott, she decided she would have him killed. Some of her motivation also might have been materialistic. She might have thought she could keep Yellow Thunder and the white Camaro, but there was no evidence to indicate that greed was her only motive. However, to Ladd, the main reason Leisha killed Scott or had him killed was that she was furious at him, because she thought he had used her and she wasn't going to put up with that. Of course, she would think that; she had always used people. That was her way of life.

Ladd contacted Richard Walter and asked him to come to Texas for a third time. Walter agreed. It would be difficult to say who was less impressed when Rusty Ladd and Richard Walter met at the airport in Amarillo. Walter took one look at the attorney, wearing his customary jeans, checked shirt and an old leather hunting hat with a floppy brim that almost touched his eyebrows, and his hopes for convicting Leisha Hamilton and Tim Smith plummeted.

Ladd, on the other hand, was neither impressed nor intimidated by the slim man in the elegantly cut suit and horn-rimmed glasses. He had no doubt, however, that Walter could be useful to him.

Walter explained his theory of the rationale of the crime. Ladd was impressed with him, because Walter brought to the investigative table pieces of the puzzle that only he could document and identify—the profiles of Leisha and Tim and the conversations with Tim, where Tim had let a bit of his guard down.

After the meeting with Ladd, Richard called Jim and expressed his misgivings. He was convinced Ladd didn't understand the psychology of the case and, consequently, he would not be able to get a conviction.

Jim begged Richard to give Ladd a chance to prove what he could do. "We need to help him all we can," Jim said. "He's our last hope."

Over the next few months, it took all the skills at negotiation and persuasion that Jim possessed to keep Richard on the case. Ladd made it clear to Jim that he would use Richard's expertise as he saw fit and if he thought some of the psychologist's theories and impressions wouldn't help him make his case, he would leave them out. Richard was appalled with Ladd's handling of the case, but Jim managed to keep him on board.

Making all of this even more difficult for Jim was the reappearance of his old nemesis, cancer, in the summer of 1995. Thirty years earlier, he had undergone radical surgery for a huge abdominal mass, which his surgeons didn't expect him to survive. Now, a new malignancy was in his prostate and he underwent radical surgery and radiation. He was determined he would fight the disease with every ounce of willpower he possessed. He had to. He would live to see Scott's killers convicted. If he didn't fight for justice for Scott, who would? Maybe that determination was what kept him alive; whatever it was, he survived the cancer and recovered his health.

By the time Ladd had finished his evaluation of the Dunn case and decided it was strong enough to take to a grand jury, it was early summer. In the intervening months, Sowder had added Ladd to his staff of prosecutors. That raised the issue of whether he could still be the special prosecutor. Ladd convinced Sowder that he could keep the case separate from all the other cases in the office and from anyone who might have been connected to the case earlier. But he assured Sowder he was going to take it to a grand jury at some point. Although he didn't discuss the specifics of the case with his colleagues, the entire staff knew what he was working on and gave him grief over it; to them it was a foregone conclusion that he would lose—big time.

Working with Tal English and George White as they prepared for the grand jury, Ladd took note of all the leads the detectives had followed that had led nowhere, but had entailed hundreds of hours of frustrating work on the part of the investigators.

While Jim was monitoring, impatiently, the progress Rusty Ladd was making with the grand jury preparations, Tal English told him about Lubbock County's Victim's Assistance Advocate, Pam Alexander. Tal said Pam would be following the case so she could be of service to Jim and Barbara. She would be calling Jim to tell him how she could help in the coming weeks and months. She would be able to get information to him if he was unable to reach either Tal or Ladd. She could keep him updated and offer moral support. Her role would continue throughout the grand jury hearing and the trial, if Leisha and Tim were indicted, and afterward.

Pam's knowledge of court proceedings, her optimism, her unwavering support were invaluable to Barbara and Jim over the long months that would intervene before the second grand jury was convened.

Finally, in October, the case was ready for the second grand jury. Rusty Ladd tried to be very cautious in his preparation for the hearing. He was going to pursue a single line of prosecution: that Leisha and Tim had killed Scott only because she was a woman scorned, one who was angry because Scott had told her he was going to marry another woman. Ladd believed that Scott Dunn's body was put in the Dumpster located only a few feet from the apartment where he was killed, that it was covered up with garbage, that it wound up in a garbage truck, was taken to the landfill and most likely would never be found.

Ladd felt Leisha Hamilton was a career crook, a woman who had been in trouble with the law all her life. On the other hand, Ladd did not see Tim Smith as that kind of crook. He saw Tim as a semi-tragic figure caught up in something that was much bigger than he. Tim might have been the one who actually beat Scott Dunn to death, but if he was, Ladd thought, Tim was still compelled, pushed, enticed and perhaps even induced by some drugs and his intoxication with Leisha to commit the murder.

Taking that into consideration, Ladd envisioned these two people in that bedroom where they had just killed a man. Scott was lying there, bleeding profusely. They had to get rid of the body and they didn't want it to be found—ever. Having the body discovered in his own bedroom would cast suspicion directly on Leisha. Ladd knew she was smart enough to realize that. Therefore, Ladd surmised, she would feel compelled to put the body where it would never be found. And she didn't have many options. She and Tim could put the body in the car and take it somewhere or put it in a place where someone else would dispose of it unwittingly. Either way posed a tremendous risk for the killer or killers. If they put the body in the back of the car, they could get stopped for a traffic violation and an officer might notice that the back end of the car was riding low. They could not take that chance. On the other hand, they could put the body in the Dumpster and hope that no one would find it before the garbage truck came by the apartment early Friday morning, many hours after the killing, depending on when the fatal blows were struck.

Ladd wanted the grand jury members to meet Jim Dunn and hear all he had done in the five year investigation and to see how committed Jim was to having the evidence presented to them so that his family could finally find peace and he would feel he'd done all he could to gain justice for his son.

Ladd also wanted the grand jurors to see the painstaking work Tal English had done over this long period. He would depend on English to provide the evidence that would establish a lovers' relationship between Tim and Leisha.

The prosecutor wanted the jury to see what Tim's mental character was at the time of the killing; he wanted to show that Tim was immature at best and at worst, a character living in fantasyland wanting to be Leisha's superman—her hero. Ladd believed wholeheartedly that Tim Smith would have done anything Leisha asked him to do. In his mind Ladd could see Leisha putting a crowbar in Tim's hands, telling him to go into the room where Scott Dunn was sleeping and kill the man who was keeping them apart. Ladd believed Tim would have been willing to do that.

Ladd decided not to call either of the defendants to testify at the grand jury hearing. He let them know that if they wanted to testify they could. Neither Tim Smith nor Leisha Hamilton chose to do so. Ladd presented the case as simply and concisely as possible: The grand jury deliberated less than fifteen minutes before returning indictments for both Leisha Hamilton and Tim Smith. It had been almost five and a half years since Scott Dunn had disappeared.

Tim and Leisha turned themselves in to authorities the following day and remained in jail in lieu of $50,000 and $75,000 bonds, respectively.

"Based on my experience as a police officer and a prosecutor, I doubt very seriously whether we'll find Scott's remains. I think his parents will carry that burden to their graves," Ladd told the media who already were picking up the part that Jim Dunn had played in making his son's killers accountable and were clamoring for interviews. However, he added that the lack of a body does not mean a case cannot be proven in court.

He went on. "I think there is ample evidence of Scott's death and of who the perpetrators are. That doesn't mean it's not a challenging case.

"This is a murder case," Ladd said. "Started out as a missing person, ended up as a homicide. It's one of those cases where trace evidence such as hair and fibers will play key roles. That means that good officers, doing their job, preserving evidence, did a great job in getting the case where it is today."

chapter fourteen

On Trial

His son constantly on his mind, Jim Dunn watched the days and weeks go by, never out of touch with all the investigators who might contribute to the coming case.

Rusty Ladd spent eight months preparing for the trials of Leisha Hamilton and Tim Smith. Since there was no body, no weapon and no witnesses, he knew a guilty verdict would hinge on two things: helping the jury understand how the forensic evidence tied Leisha to the killing and convincing the jury that Leisha was the type of person who could have committed such a crime.

He enlisted Roy Carper, a new prosecutor in the District Attorney's office, to act as his second. Carper had joined the staff the first of January that year. The Dunn case was his first major assignment.

Ladd gave Carper the file and highlighted the important aspects of the case for him. The biggest hurdle they faced was the challenge inherent in every case—to prove their theory "beyond a reasonable doubt." In this extraordinary case, however, they first had to prove beyond a reasonable doubt that a murder had been committed with no body, no weapon and no eyewitness.

To do this, their first challenge was to present the forensic evidence and argue it in such an organized way that the jury would be able to look at it and say, even without a body, a weapon or a witness, the prosecutors had built a case, one small, solid brick at a time, until it reached an inescapable conclusion—that this woman played a pivotal role in the death of Scott Dunn.

The second challenge the prosecutors faced was that, on the surface, Leisha had done a number of things to make it appear she was cooperating. Ladd wanted to be able to refer to those things and show either she knew nothing—and was an absolute idiot who didn't see her own house awash in blood, who didn't see carpet being cut out of her own floor—or she was the most cold, conniving, calculating person that one would ever have the misfortune to meet. He felt as did Jim Dunn that there was enough evidence in her relationship with Tim to show her as the latter type of person. Nevertheless, it was the formidable task of Ladd and Carper to convince a jury of this.

Ladd's philosophy was that if you approached a case and started thinking to yourself, this is a big, major case, then you started making mistakes. The O.J. Simpson trial was a prime example. He resolved that he wouldn't make those kinds of mistakes. This was a big case for a lot of different reasons: It was a high profile case because of the missing body aspect. James Dunn had proven that he wasn't going to give up until his son got justice. A tremendous amount of news coverage had already occurred and Dunn would get more. There also was the fact that it had gone to a handpicked special prosecutor. Ladd worked hard to focus on the case, not on its importance. He could not allow it to become one of those big cases that gets away from you.

Jim learned that Ladd and Roy Carper had different strengths as prosecutors and these strengths would prove to complement each other as the trial progressed. Ladd had a reputation for being what he called "a heart and soul kind of lawyer." Carper, on the other hand, was extremely skilled in taking the technical, forensic aspects of a case and presenting them in such a way that a jury could easily see the picture he was painting. So they divided the labors based on the different skills of the two men. Ladd chose to examine witnesses such as police officers who were close to the investigation, some of the expert witnesses with whom he felt rapport and the victim's family. Roy Carper would handle the more technical witnesses.

Two days before the trial of Leisha Hamilton, Jim and Barbara Dunn arrived in Lubbock. They checked into the same downtown hotel where they had stayed so many times throughout the past six years. One block from the hotel was the memorial statue of Lubbock's native son, rock 'n' roller Buddy Holly, who had died prematurely in a plane crash. That statue reminded Jim of his own end of innocence. Of the destruction of dreams. Lubbock itself had become a place to grieve. A place to reflect on what had been lost. All the nostalgic markers of his youth had turned into memories of his dead son.

The next morning, which was Mother's Day, Jim and Barbara drove to the cemetery where Jim's grandparents were buried and placed flowers on his grandmother's grave. He gazed with sorrow at the vacant space near her, the place he once thought of for himself and which now he had reserved in his mind for Scott. He had thought about putting a memorial marker there. Many times. But he couldn't bring himself to do it. Not now. Not yet. Maybe never.

Unless…unless, as a result of the trial that would start tomorrow, he might learn where his son's remains were. He still held out hope that some day he would have some tangible evidence of Scott's death and could give his son's remains a proper burial. The last thing he could do for Scott for whom he had so many dreams. Until then… the gravesite would remain barren.

The trial of Leisha Hamilton began on May 12, 1997, four days short of being six years since Scott Dunn's disappearance. Jim and Barbara Dunn, Richard Walter, Derry Harding, W. R. Collier, his wife, Mary Collier, and Pam Alexander, Lubbock County Victim's Assistance

Director, arrived early at the Lubbock County Courthouse and took their seats two rows behind the prosecutors' table. Leisha Hamilton, carefully coifed and made up, a slight smile on her face, walked with her attorney, Rick Wardroup, past the Dunns' group. Her tailored white blouse, black skirt and low heeled black pumps failed to hide the provocative swing of her long legs. Her dark brown hair swirled around her shoulders. She acted as if she had no cares in the world.

Jim felt himself grow tense. He wished he didn't have to look at her; on the other hand, he could hardly keep his eyes off her. How could she look so casual and so confident when she was facing a trial that could put her in prison for life?

The onlookers stood as Judge William R. Shaver made his entrance. Jim's attention turned to the square-jawed, silver-haired, distinguished-looking veteran who took his place behind the bench, sat down and then gazed down at them. Across the aisle from the Dunn group were seventy-two prospective jurors appearing for the *voir dire,* the process by which twelve members of the jury and alternates would be selected.

"Good morning, ladies and gentlemen. My name is Bill Shaver. I have been assigned to preside in the Ninety-ninth District Court during the absence of Judge Mackey Hancock, who is the duly elected judge of the Ninety-ninth District Court. Judge Hancock is with the Army Reserve in Bosnia. We are praying he will be back the first week in July to take over his court again.

"Members of the jury panel, this cause is the State of Texas versus Leisha Hamilton. Leisha Hamilton stands charged by indictment with the offense of murder. You are instructed by the court that an indictment is not evidence of guilt. It's merely a formal pleading to bring a case to trial and you shall not consider the fact the defendant has been indicted as any evidence of guilt.

"We refer to this as the *voir dire* examination. The attorneys are permitted by law to ask you questions in regard to your background and questions in regard to certain laws that may become applicable in this case, to determine in their minds whether or not you would be a fair and impartial juror in this particular case."

Judge Shaver then introduced the attorneys, Assistant Criminal District Attorney Rusty Ladd, seated at the prosecution's table, and next to him, assisting, Assistant District Attorney Roy Carper. "Representing the defendant in this proceeding is Mr. Richard Wardroup, seated at the head of the defense table. Mr. Richard Gore, seated in the jury box, will be helping him during the jury selection."

Judge Shaver gazed down upon the four attorneys. "Gentlemen, this jury panel was duly qualified in the central jury pool. They received their oath in the central jury pool, received the preliminary instructions required by law. You may question the panel for the State."

Keeping in mind the greatest hurdle he faced, proving beyond a reasonable doubt that Scott Dunn had been murdered in what he would refer to as "the killing room," Ladd began immediately to lay the foundation for proving that, not only had a murder been committed, but it had been committed by Leisha Hamilton.

Assuming his best "aw shucks, I'm just a good old West Texas boy" pose, the able prosecutor faced the jury. "Good morning, ladies and gentlemen. The process we are going through is called *voir dire*. If you remember, from high school or college or just your knowledge as a citizen, you're entitled to a fair trial whenever you're challenged by the State and accused by the State of doing something wrong.

"Let me ask you, who else is entitled to a fair trial whenever is jury is being convened to hear evidence? Who is entitled to a fair trial?

"The defendant is entitled to a fair trial before the State says we are going to punish you like a felon, in this case before we are going to call you a murderer, then we have to give you a fair trial.

"But who else is entitled to a fair trial?"

"Anyone." An unidentified panel member spoke up.

"Does *anyone* include the State of Texas?" Ladd asked.

"Yes," the man replied.

Ladd nodded. "Yeah, sure it does. This is the State of Texas versus Leisha Hamilton. Ms. Hamilton is entitled to a fair trial. So is the State of Texas.

"This involves the disappearance and murder of a fellow named Roger Scott Dunn. It started out as a missing person investigation. Mr. Dunn's body has never been located." Ladd went on to cite the prominence of the story in the media in the intervening years since Scott Dunn's disappearance.

Looking intently at the jurors, he said, "I'm not too worried about somebody having watched TV and read the newspapers. But the test on whether or not you can be a fair juror is, regardless of how much information you may have heard through the media about the case, whether or not you have already made up your mind about the case.

"And so that's the question I need to ask. Considering the extensive media coverage of Mr. Dunn's disappearance and some of the evidence that was in the newspapers regarding his murder, the subsequent indictment of Leisha Hamilton and a fellow named Tim Smith for Scott Dunn's murder, is there anybody here who, because of their exposure to the media, has already made up their mind one way or the other regarding Leisha Hamilton's guilt or innocence?"

A short discussion ensued between Ladd and several jurors who said they had already formed opinions about the defendant's guilt or innocence.

"The law says that a person is presumed innocent until they are found guilty. What's the standard that I have to find them guilty or the standard of evidence that I have to present to show that they are guilty?" Ladd asked.

The answer came back from several members of the panel. "Beyond a reasonable doubt."

"How about beyond any doubt whatsoever? Has anybody ever heard of that one? Is there a difference between beyond a reasonable doubt or beyond shadow of a doubt? How many say it's the same thing?"

Again, several hands went up.

"Let me see the hands that said it's the same thing. Nice and high. Be proud of your opinions." Again, hands went up. Ladd smiled at them. "I'm going to seek to change your opinion. Let's see if I can. If I cannot, be honest with me and tell me that I cannot. We are going to go on a twisty turn to get there, but hang with me on it.

"Y'all are hearing this is going to be a criminal case, that it's murder. You expect to see evidence, right? You expect to hear evidence. Is that right?

"What kind of evidence are you going to hear? There's basically two kinds. There's physical evidence, photographs, blood and things like that. And then there's testimony, people getting on the witness stand and saying, 'I saw this; I heard this; I did that.' Those are the two basic kinds of evidence. Testimony and physical.

Ladd moved slowly so that he could watch the faces of the jurors. "But even with physical evidence, if I'm waving around some photographs, I can't just hold the photograph up in front of the judge and say, 'Judge, this is evidence; I want the jury to have it.' I have to give it to somebody who's on the witness stand so they can say, 'Yeah, I remember when that photograph was made; and what you see there in that photograph, that's the way it looked that day; and here's what it means to the case; here's why it's important,' and they explain that.

"And then I can say, 'Judge, I want you to let the jury be allowed to consider this piece of evidence. Okay?'"

Ladd's voice rose. "That means that anything you see or hear in the courtroom is going to come through somebody sitting in that witness stand, in that witness chair. Is everybody with me? That means that everything you hear about this case, as far as evidence goes, is going to come from someone else.

"Don't you know there's always some little thought way back deep in the back of your head that says, 'Well, you know, they may have just arranged all of this. It could just be some kind of huge conspiracy against the defendant. The police and some witnesses out there, they may just not like her and somebody just might have got up here and spun together a whole big web of lies. It could happen, you know. All these people could be in cahoots together against the defendant.'"

Ladd paused. The room was quiet. The jury was paying attention. Then he went on.

"You might not be able to articulate any reason why you think that's true, except that everything you heard came from somebody else, every single piece of evidence. And the law says that I have to prove the case to you beyond a reasonable doubt.

"Now, here's my point. If everything you are hearing about the case comes from somebody else, how can you be absolutely, beyond any doubt whatsoever, beyond a shadow of a doubt, how can you be certain? Are you with me on this?

"How can you be certain, if it's coming from somebody else? How is the only way you could be certain about any piece of evidence or anything that I'm trying to prove? There's only one way, if it's certain beyond any doubt whatsoever. How would that be?

"You would have to see it yourself. If you saw it yourselves, what would you be? You would be a witness. You would be under subpoena sitting outside somewhere. That's why the law says we have got to have neutral people sitting in the jury box.

"And to have neutral people, we have to have people who don't know anything about the case or if they know something like we were talking about from the media or whatever, they have got to be able to set that aside and say, 'I am going to make a decision on this case, if I'm on this jury, based on the evidence I see and hear and that's it. That's all.' That's why the law says you only have to prove the case beyond a reasonable doubt, *not* beyond any shadow of a doubt. The law gives the definition.

"I would submit this to you. A reasonable doubt is a doubt you can look at and you can say, 'I have a reason for it. Here's my reason. This is my explanation.'

"I told you a while ago there's basically two kinds of evidence, testimony and then exhibits. There's another way to get that picture of what evidence is and that's circumstantial evidence and its opposite. What is the opposite?

"Eyewitness. There are two kinds of evidence when we are cutting it this way. One is circumstantial evidence. That means clues that indicate somebody was there or that something happened. And then there's eyewitness. I was there and I saw it happen.

"The reason I would like to be a defense lawyer one of these days, and I spent a while doing that, is because then I could stand up like defense lawyers can stand up and say, 'Ladies and gentlemen, you know this case is completely circumstantial.

"'Do you know what that means? It means they ain't got an eyewitness to this case and, you know, you can't trust that circumstantial scientific stuff.' That's what *I* would say.

"Then I come up with a case where I don't have a shred of scientific stuff. And do you know what a defense lawyer would stand up and say? 'Yeah. They have three eyewitnesses. Do you know what eyewitnesses do? They lie. They take an oath and they just lie. Where is the fingerprint? Where's the scientific stuff? Where's the—now what have we got since O. J.'s trial? Where's the DNA?'

"So I'm kind of caught in between. If I've got an all-circumstantial case, I should have the eyewitnesses. If I've got an eyewitness, I should have had circumstantial evidence.

"What does the law say about whether evidence is to be circumstantial or eyewitness? Here's what the law says: It doesn't matter. *It doesn't matter.* If the jury believes beyond a reasonable doubt that the evidence proves a person to be guilty, it doesn't matter if it was eyewitness, it doesn't matter if it's circumstantial. It doesn't matter if it's a blend of the two. The law says that if you have not a single shred of evidence, except the testimony of one witness—let me give you an example of how that comes up. How many people believe that crimes are committed out in broad daylight, most often, with twenty or thirty witnesses always readily available?"

He was rising to a crescendo.

"If you are a crook and you want to break the law—kill somebody, rape somebody, steal something from somebody, burglarize somebody—you try to do it somewhere nobody else sees you. So if you've got a convenience store robbery, that happens. The guy's been around before, he comes to the store, he uses a towel to open the door with, he walks up to the counter, he puts his towel down, reaches in and pulls out a gun and says, 'I want all your money.'

"She says, 'Okay,' and she gets all the money, she brings it out and puts it in a bag. The guy's got the towel still there. He turns right around walks off. He's never touched anything with his hands. The crime eye camera wasn't working. And three weeks later, because of another crime the guy may have committed, the lady is shown a picture of this guy and she says, 'That's the guy. I will never forget that face.'

"Any fingerprints? No. Any photographs? No. Any other witnesses? No. One witness who says she will never forget that face. The law says that if a jury believes that testimony beyond a reasonable doubt, they can find him guilty."

His voice was sonorous. "So it doesn't matter whether it's eyewitness, circumstantial, all of one, all of the other, any combination of the betweens. What matters is, whether or not you believe there's sufficient evidence to prove beyond a reasonable doubt."

Ladd could see by their facial expressions most of the panel members were engrossed in his discussion of the jury's responsibility and power. He paused a moment, took a deep breath and went to the heart of his case against Leisha Hamilton.

"Whenever I talk about evidence and I talk about murder, what's one of the things that you would expect to hear? If somebody gets murdered, what am I usually left with?

"A body. And many people believe you cannot prove somebody guilty if you do not have a body. If that's your opinion, you are entitled to that. But the law says you don't have to have a body to prove somebody guilty of murder. If I'm proving somebody is guilty of murder, I have got to prove somebody got killed. Right?

"My question to you is, do you believe that this could ever be done without producing a body? Do you believe that?"

"I have a problem with that," someone said.

"All right. What is the problem, besides the obvious one?"

"Simply because some people just hide and you can't find them."

"Does that mean that if I could not produce a body that you would say then there can't—"

Defense counsel Rick Wardroup stood up. "Excuse me, your honor. I am going to object to Mr. Ladd trying to get a commitment as to what purports to the facts of this case."

Ladd denied that such was his intention.

"You need to reword your question," Judge Shaver instructed.

"All right. Do you believe a person could be found guilty of murder if there was not a body?"

"I'd have a hard time," the man admitted.

"Here's the question," Ladd said. "If we made a law that says if you don't have a body, you cannot prove someone guilty of murder, then what's a murderer going to do every time?" Again, Ladd answered his own question. "If I can just get rid of the body, they can never find me guilty, ever. There would be more shallow graves than you could count, don't you think?

"The question is whether or not you can envision, I guess, any circumstances where a body had not been located that would still have enough evidence that the person had been killed.

"I have got to ask you this way, because Mr. Wardroup made an objection a while ago and it was one of those good objections. I cannot tell you what the evidence in this case is right now and then ask you to decide whether or not you could go along with that evidence or not, because then I would be asking you to commit to a certain piece of evidentiary point of view before you have even heard the evidence or taken an oath. So I have to ask you in broad terms about your opinions of the law to see if you can follow the law.

"The law does not say there must be a body to prove somebody guilty. The law says there must be sufficient evidence to prove beyond a reasonable doubt that the fellow got killed. If you heard sufficient evidence to prove beyond a reasonable doubt that the fellow got killed, could you decide the fellow had been killed without having to see the body?"

At that point, Judge Shaver interrupted, sharply reminding the attorneys and the jury panel that it was quarter past twelve and time for a lunch recess. When the court reconvened, Ladd resumed his *voir dire*, explaining his second line of offense.

"There's a concept in Texas law called the law of parties. It doesn't have anything to do with how many kids from Texas Tech can fit around a beer keg," Ladd said with a grin. "It has to do with the idea that if you help somebody do an evil deed, then you are just as guilty as the somebody. And that's essentially what the law of parties says. It says that a person who aids, assists, solicits, encourages or in any other way participates in helping someone else commit a deed, then that person is just as guilty.

"Texas law says, if you were just there and while you were there somebody else commits a crime then you are not necessarily guilty. But if you in any way participate in that, then you are just as guilty.

"Now use your common sense for a minute. There obviously is a difference between somebody who would kill somebody and then somebody who would help them do that. Where do we make some kind of decisions about that difference? Where do we make a difference in the way we apply the law?

"We have managed to prove a person killed somebody. And we have somebody else and we can show they didn't actually pull the trigger but they nevertheless participated in the act. Maybe they just weren't quite as bad as the first person who actually did the deed. Where do we make a difference in that? In the State of Texas, in a properly applied case, and this is one of those cases, a jury makes the decision. So at *voir dire* Mr. Wardroup and I have a double responsibility and that is to talk to you about the concepts of the law that have to do with guilt and innocence, like the law of parties, and to also talk to you about punishment, because the same jury that hears a case also decides punishment."

Finally, Ladd concluded his *voir dire*. "Ladies and gentlemen, you have been awfully patient with me. Let me encourage you—if I asked you a question that's just bugging you and you have not raised your hand and been put on the list to come up and visit with us privately a little later on, let me encourage you to do that when Mr. Wardroup is visiting with you.

"Thank you very much for your attention."

Attractive, smiling Rick Wardroup, Leisha's attorney, stood, faced the panel and introduced himself and his client. He talked about Leisha's having worked for several restaurants where members of the panel may have seen her. He called attention to the slightness of her frame. Then he went directly to his major argument and that of the prosecution—the question of whether a murder actually had occurred.

"There are two primary issues in this case. Number one is, has there been a murder? It's the State's burden of proof beyond a reasonable doubt to prove that there has been a murder. Now, back until 1974 the law of the State of Texas required that you provide the corpus delicti. You had to produce the body or part of a body to support a conviction for murder. When the new Penal Code came into effect in 1974, that part of the law was done away with.

"Mr. Ladd talked to you a little bit this morning about the possibility or the probability of being able to prove a murder without having a body. And many of you probably thought of the opportunity or thought of the situation if you saw somebody shoot somebody and drag a lifeless body off, well, you might be able to prove a murder without a body being there then.

"So you can see that maybe there are certain situations where that's possible. Now is there anybody who won't hold the State of Texas to their burden of proving beyond a reasonable doubt that there's been a death here? Anybody here who thinks the fact that a person hadn't called Mom and Dad in five years, that this alone would be enough?" He waited a moment, then continued. "I take it by your silence then that there's not."

After more discussion with the panel members about the State's burden of proof, Wardroup tackled the matter of punishment, reminding them that in any murder case, with the exception of capital cases, the range of punishment is from five years to ninety-nine years or life. He asked the jurors whether, if they found a person guilty of murder, if they could imagine a set of facts where they could assess only five years as punishment. Satisfied that the prospective jurors could envision such circumstances, Wardroup finished his statement.

By four o'clock that afternoon, the jurors had been selected. Solemnly, Judge Shaver called the names of those chosen, nine women and three men, along with two alternates, a man and a woman. He directed them to take seats in the jury box.

When they were seated, Judge Shaver announced that although it was getting late, the case would begin. "I will give you your instructions, we will then read the indictment, we will have the opening statements and then, if there's any time left, we will have one witness to testify."

When Judge Shaver completed his instructions to the jury, Rusty Ladd opened for the State.

"This is a murder case. In the State of Texas, things don't get more serious than the case you are hearing today. As you may have surmised from our discussion on *voir dire,* we don't have a body. And I can tell you right now, you are not going to hear any evidence of a particular weapon. So how, exactly, do I intend to prove this case?

"Leisha Hamilton is guilty, either herself or as a party, of the death of Roger Scott Dunn. Here is what I expect the evidence to show you." For the next few minutes, Ladd told the jurors about

Scott Dunn, his family, his relationship with Leisha Hamilton. Ladd pointed out that Scott and Leisha had been dating for a while, but that at the time of his murder, Scott had just become engaged to another woman.

"Ladies and gentlemen, you are going to hear from Mr. Dunn that he got a call from Leisha Hamilton, saying that Scott was missing, that his impetuous, possessive twenty-four-year-old son had suddenly dropped out of sight, gone, and no one knew where.

"You are going to hear that Mr. Dunn became more and more worried, because Scott used to call him at least every week or so. But after May 16, Jim Dunn never heard from Scott Dunn again.

"You are going to hear that, at some point, the police went to Leisha Hamilton's apartment, that they lifted a piece of carpet in the bedroom where she said Scott used to sleep and they found blood all over the concrete and carpet. They immediately suspected foul play."

Leisha's eyes were shooting daggers at his back. He wanted her to take his words personally.

"Scientific investigators came and processed the crime scene with a chemical that reveals the presence of human blood, and they found evidence of blood having been smeared, scattered, and splattered all over two walls inside that apartment. It had very obviously been cleaned up. The carpet that had to have taken most of the blood had been cut out and disposed of. But even after that extensive effort and cleanup, they found small particles and splotches of blood still there, a few on the wall, a few on the ceiling.

"You are going to hear evidence from a blood spatter expert who can look at the way drops of blood are shaped and tell how they got there." Ladd gazed with deliberation at each juror.

"You will hear him testify that the blood spots he saw from the photographs of the scene, taken from that apartment, indicate what he will call back-and-forth castoff, indicating that somebody rapidly and viciously lifted something, throwing blood one way and flung it back down, throwing blood another way. At least four blows." Now Ladd was ready to move in the direction he really wanted to go.

As he spoke, Ladd clasped his hands together, lifted them high above his head and brought them down with a resounding thud on the railing. Again, another thud, on the railing. A third time and a fourth. Jurors flinched at each blow. Ladd stepped back. "This expert will show you how he reached those results."

Ladd told of the relationship between Leisha Hamilton and Tim Smith, about the duct tape found in Smith's apartment and of Smith's attempt to hide it. Ladd summarized the scientific tests conducted on the tape. He looked at the jurors. Their expressions were intense.

"You are going to wonder—by the time you look at all the photographs we intend to introduce into evidence in this case, photographs that show how much blood was spilled in there, how big a piece of carpet was cut out of there and how big a piece of carpet was cut out of an adjoining room in Leisha's apartment—you are going to wonder how anybody, even if they were a little messy with their housekeeping, could have missed seeing that for two weeks, the time that elapsed between the time Scott Dunn was reported missing and the time the police came back to that location and found the blood in the carpet.

"You are going to wonder why the tape that was used to patch in that piece of carpet of Leisha Hamilton's room had Tim Smith's hair on it." Ladd closed his eyes as if in thought then opened them wide again.

"There are some questions that we're not going to be able to answer for you. You are going to wonder where Scott Dunn's body went and how it got there. In *voir dire,* Mr. Wardroup said there wouldn't be any evidence of a body. But there will be ample *evidence* of a body, there just won't be a body. By the time this trial is over, by the time you have heard the forensic evidence, the hair, the carpet, the blood, the blood stains, how they are shaped, what that means…"

Wardroup interrupted. "Excuse me, your honor. I am going to object to this not being opening statement. He is going into argument at this point."

"I will overrule it," Shaver said frostily.

Ladd exhaled in relief and continued. "By the time you have heard that, by the time you have heard about Scott's possessiveness with his stuff and then by the time you have heard the evidence we will present to you the record Leisha Hamilton's own web of deceit, the people she lied to about Scott's possessions, about her own memory of what happened that night, the next night after it and about the other lies that she told investigators and other people that she was involved with, there's not going to be a doubt in your mind that Scott Dunn was murdered in Leisha Hamilton's apartment. In the killing room.

"And by the time you have heard the rest of the evidence about Leisha's involvement in the case and the forensic evidence, there won't be a doubt in your mind that Leisha Hamilton is guilty of the murder of Roger Scott Dunn.

"Some of the evidence is tedious. Scientific evidence usually is. We will have to bring in people who will get on the stand and say, 'I took this piece of evidence from so-and-so and I gave it to so-and-so.' You are going to wonder why they are there. And it is because of what we call a chain of custody, to establish the validity of scientific testimony.

"Listen carefully to that. It gets hard to listen to, especially in the middle of a sleepy afternoon, but after you listen to that, you will have an opportunity to go back to the jury room and render a correct and true judgment. Thank you very much."

For a few moments Rick Wardroup, the well-credentialed, able defense attorney, glanced at the prosecution table as if in disbelief. Then he turned to face the jury and began his opening statement. "Ladies and gentlemen of the jury, please understand that what Mr. Ladd has just said is not evidence. What I'm about to tell you is not evidence. So, if you hear something different from us than what you hear from the witness stand, it will be your responsibility to go with what you hear from the witness stand.

"I want to tell you the story that I anticipate coming out in testimony…" Wardroup gave the jury a detailed account of Leisha's activities for the rest of the week, as she had indicated in her statement to the police. He told of Scott's illness, emphasizing that Leisha had taken care of him. Wardroup told of Leisha's coming home on the afternoon of May 16, finding Scott gone and of coming home the next day and finding the back door kicked in. Wardroup made sure the jury was aware that Leisha had called the police at that time, although he did not mention that she had done so at the instruction of the apartment manager; he pointed out that the police officer who had investigated had seen nothing unusual.

To rebut the impression the prosecutor had drawn, Wardroup repeatedly referred to Leisha's having volunteered information to the police. "There came a time that, for whatever reason, she thought, well, I better tell the police about this. Again, June 7, Leisha Hamilton calls the police, invites them to her apartment. They see the carpet gone from beneath the couch and asked her permission to look around, which she gives. She signs a voluntary consent to search her apartment. During this search, the police officers find the carpet that has been pieced in, pull up the carpet patch and find the things that Mr. Ladd has told you about." Wardroup looked over at the jury. Then he went on precisely, carefully.

"I think the bottom line is going to be that you will see pictures, you will hear the testimony from the experts. We anticipate the evidence is going to be that they could account for approximately one and a half units of blood. That's all.

"Ultimately, I think the evidence is going to leave questions in your mind: first of all, is Scott Dunn still alive today? Secondly, if he isn't alive today, why is she the one on trial and not Tim Smith? Thank you."

Judge Shaver glanced at Ladd. "All those you know to be witnesses who are present, would you have them stand and be sworn at this time?" After the witnesses were sworn, Judge Shaver, in a sonorous tone, reminded them that the rule had been invoked, meaning that all witnesses must wait outside the courtroom until they were summoned to testify.

"You are instructed not to discuss this case among yourselves or in the presence of other witnesses, nor read written reports of testimony of other witnesses," Judge Shaver warned them. "You may discuss it with the attorneys separately and apart from other witnesses."

Jim Dunn, along with Richard Walter, W. R. Collier and Derry Harding, were escorted to a small witness room nearby. Jim, who had been the driving force behind the investigation from the first day he knew his son was missing and who had been so personally involved in the investigation for six years, went very reluctantly. He dreaded the hours in the small, windowless room, not knowing what was happening in the courtroom, waiting, unable to do anything, while others decided the fate of the woman he was convinced had murdered his son.

Jim Dunn could tell that his wife Barbara was glad about the presence of Pam Alexander beside her in the courtroom, especially since, as a witness, he was sequestered. Pam had contacted them several months earlier, telling them it was her job to work with them as they prepared for trial and during the trial as well. Her knowledge of the judicial system, her contacts with police and CDA investigators and her knowledge of the case already had been and would continue to be of tremendous value to the Dunns. The two women waited tensely as Judge Shaver gave his instructions to the jury. Barbara Dunn stared fiercely at Leisha Hamilton as she sat at the defense table, her head held high, a glimmer of a smile touching her lips.

Then, the prosecution called Scott Dunn's mother as its first witness.

In response to Ladd's questions, she identified herself as the former wife of Jim Dunn and the mother of Roger Scott Dunn. She testified that, under the direction of a police officer, she had given a blood sample to be used in the reversed DNA testing to determine if the blood found in Leisha's apartment belonged to her son Scott.

Wardroup said he had no questions for the witness and she was excused. That ended the proceedings for the first day. Judge Shaver called a recess until 9:00 AM Tuesday.

Pam accompanied Barbara to the small room where Jim waited. "I think we got off to a good start," she told Jim. "I don't think Rick Wardroup made anyone mad on *voir dire,* but I believe the jurors liked Rusty better."

It was around dark when Jim, Barbara and Richard Walter went back to their hotel to have dinner. Throughout the meal, they discussed the day's happenings, but Jim found it hard to think about anything but the trial he had waited for so long, in which his son's killers had to be held accountable. He had to make the jury understand why this was so important, but could he? He would be the first witness called the next morning. He felt anxious and tense. Jim spent a sleepless night. Over and over in his mind he reviewed all he'd done to bring this case—the people he'd interviewed, his meetings with nationally known criminologists, including the Vidocq Society, the forensic consultant for Scotland Yard who determined that someone had been bludgeoned to death in the killing room, the United States' foremost DNA expert, who proved the blood found in Scott's bedroom was his, and the well known blood spatter specialist who determined the minimum number of blows that were struck and the type of weapon that was used. He had tried to do all that he could to bring the truth to light, to gain justice for his son. But had it been enough? That question haunted him. What he would say to the jury when he faced them the next morning? Watching as the first light of day filtered through the window, he wearily got up to face the second saddest day of his life.

chapter fifteen

A Father's Vow

On day two, Jim Dunn and Richard Walter went directly to the tiny, claustrophobic witness room where they were supposed to wait until they were called to testify. Frustrated, Jim watched the parade of attorneys with their clients pass the door. Later there was a lull in the traffic. Then he heard footsteps approaching and recognized Leisha Hamilton's voice. In a moment, she and her parents passed the open door without a glance inside, continuing on toward the courtroom. Jim forcefully restrained himself from confronting her.

Barbara Dunn and Pam Alexander were already seated in the courtroom when Leisha walked in. Barbara compressed her lips and reached for Pam's hand, squeezing it hard. Pam's eyes were on the defendant. She shook her head in disbelief. Leisha, again dressed modestly in a beige shirtwaist blouse, a brown skirt that reached below her knees and low-heeled pumps, walked almost jauntily. She had a smile on her lips; her long brown hair glistened in the light as it swung around her shoulders. Greeting her attorney vivaciously, she sat down beside him.

"She's flouncing around like she's at a party," Pam whispered to Barbara. "What is she thinking?" Barbara shook her head and watched Leisha in grim silence.

All stood as Judge Shaver entered the courtroom. When he was seated, he called for the jurors to come in. Jim Dunn was the prosecution's first witness.

Jim made his way through the crowded courtroom. He paused for a nanosecond at the row in which his wife sat and gave her a slight smile. Quickly, he moved on to the witness box and was sworn in. He closed his eyes for a moment, letting his mind drift back to the day he learned his son Scott had disappeared.

Rusty Ladd wanted Jim to tell all of his story, from his first conversation with Leisha Hamilton to his total involvement in furthering the investigation of his son's death. Ladd wanted the jury to empathize with Jim, to see him as a grieving father, but one determined to see justice done in his son's name. He wanted the jury to see Scott through his father's eyes.

First, taking a step back, assuming his more relaxed, friendly position, Ladd led Jim through a series of questions about himself, including his formative years in Lubbock County. Jim's voice broke as he told the jury he was the father of Roger Scott Dunn, who would have been thirty-one if he had lived. Feeling like a fist had wrapped its way around his heart, Jim paused to regain his composure, then went on.

"Scott was about five years old when his mother and I divorced," Jim said. Then he told of their lives as divorced parents, trying to rear Scott as normally as possible. "He came and lived with me parts of the summer, holidays and other times. When Scott was in about the seventh grade, he seemed to be a very bright kid, but he was having some problems in school, so I had him tested and it turns out that he was dyslexic or had a learning disability. Even though he had a photographic memory, he had problems with reading and math, skills like that, so I took him out of school in Texas and brought him to Pennsylvania and put him in a private school that focused on learning disabilities."Visions of his buoyant, high-spirited son flashed through Jim's mind.

After eliciting more information about Scott's adolescence and early adulthood, Ladd paused in his questioning to show Jim photographs that would be introduced as evidence. "Jim, I want to ask you to look at all of these photographs, then I will ask you some questions about all of them together."

With no objection from the defense table, Ladd asked Jim to explain each photo to the jury: One was the picture of Scott and Jim taken when Scott was finishing a semester at Phelps School in Millvale, Pennsylvania; one was a picture of Scott in his uniform, taken after he finished his basic training. With him in this photo was Jim's grandfather.

Ladd indicated another photo. "Was that Scott's car?"

Jim said sadly, "That's Scott's car."

"It looks like the car was well taken care of."

Jim half smiled. "Yes. You could eat off the motor in that car."

The pictures were handed to the jury members and Jim watched intently as they examined them closely. It seemed to him that they took a longer look at the pictures of Scott and himself.

Having established Scott's background and his relationship with his father, Ladd moved toward the events in what he termed the killing room. The courtroom was deathly silent.

"Jim, when did you first learn of Scott's disappearance?"

Jim recounted his first telephone conversation with Leisha Hamilton, when she told him Scott had disappeared. He noticed several jurors had leaned forward to hear better.

Ladd gazed sympathetically at Jim. "Sometimes my profession calls upon me to ask a question that I know is stupid and may hurt you, but I need to ask it anyway. Since that time, have you ever seen, heard from or talked to your son Roger Scott Dunn?"

Jim shook his head. "Absolutely not."

"When you were talking to Leisha Hamilton that night on the phone, did you ask her any questions about Scott's disappearance?"

Jim said he had asked Leisha if she had any idea what could possibly have happened to Scott. "She denied any knowledge about Scott's disappearance." Jim said he also asked Leisha if she knew of any problems that Scott was having with anyone—problems severe enough that someone might have harmed him. At that time, she said she did not know of anyone.

Ladd asked Jim if he knew whether or not Scott was involved with any girl other than Leisha Hamilton at the time and Jim told the jury about Scott's Mother's Day phone call, telling of his engagement to Jessica Tate.

"Jim, let me ask you a few questions about your and Scott's relationship. Did Scott typically stay in touch with you while he was away?"

Vivid memories flashed through Jim's mind. "Scott was in touch with me every few weeks."

"And you said the last time you had talked to him was on the phone, Mother's Day, May 12; is that correct?"

"Yes."

"Was it characteristic of Scott to just disappear for months and months at a time?"

Jim quickly replied, his voice firm. "No. Scott always called. I never, ever lost contact with Scott."

"When was the next time that you talked to anybody in Lubbock about Scott's disappearance?"

Anger flashed across his face when Jim told of calling Leisha at the restaurant where she worked the following Tuesday morning.

Then, getting no satisfaction from that conversation, he said he had called Max Gianoli at ProSound Electronics. Gianoli said he furious because Scott just ran off and left him.

"Were the Crank It Up contests very important to Scott?"

"Apparently they were. I never talked directly to him about them, but this was apparently a big one. Gianoli said this was a very important one and they were building a system they were sure was going to win."

Ladd made an almost imperceptible nod of the head and asked Jim about any other Lubbock contacts he had made regarding Scott's disappearance. Jim said that he had waited a few days, hoping Scott would call him. But no call came. The next Friday night, he had talked to Leisha, who had not heard anything from Scott. She had told Jim she had picked up Scott's car from ProSound Electronics. He told the jury, "I was shocked, because when I talked to her on Sunday night, she had not told me she was going to get the car."

"Jim, did Leisha tell you, in that Friday, the twenty-fourth, conversation with you, anything about somebody coming back into the apartment?"

"She said Scott had left his keys in the apartment the day he disappeared and that the following day, someone had come and kicked the back door in and had taken some more clothes."

"Did she ever tell you anything about Scott's wallet or any money he had?"

"She mentioned that when he was sick on the night of the fourteenth or fifteenth, she got seven or eight dollars out of his billfold, which was in his pants, to buy food and some kind of medication, because he had a sinus infection. She said that she picked him up at Max Gianoli's house on that Tuesday afternoon and apparently he had some kind of a sinus infection or some kind of a condition that made him almost delirious. That night she went to the store. She bought a thermometer. And he had a temperature of 102 degrees on that Tuesday night."

"She told you the exact temperature he had?"

"Yes."

Ladd moved on to the day when Scott finally was reported missing. "Jim, at some point did you decide it was necessary to file a missing persons report with the police?"

"I filed that report on May 31, late in the afternoon."

"Had you ever talked to Leisha about what was necessary before the police would accept a missing person report?"

"We talked about it that day. She told me she didn't think a missing persons report could be filed because there had to be some evidence that some harm had come to him and that she didn't think I could file a missing persons report."

"She certainly didn't tell you anything about having any kind of evidence like that, did she?"

"No." Jim told the jury that when he finally talked to Detective Tal English, the investigator said these missing persons things happen all the time and within a few days, the people usually show up. It was not a high priority for the police department at that time, he grimaced.

"Was there a point at which it became a high priority?"

Jim took a moment to think, then said, "Yes. I called Tal the next Friday afternoon, June 7, between four and five o'clock. It had been one week since I first reported Scott missing."

"After visiting with Tal over the phone, were you aware that Tal and other detectives possibly were going to conduct an investigation that evening at Leisha's apartment?"

"Yes."

"When's the next time that you visited with Tal?"

"The next morning, Saturday, June 8, at about eleven. A day that I will never forget."

"Is that the point at which the missing person investigation turned into a murder investigation?"

"Yes."

"Was there a time when you came to Lubbock yourself?"

Jim explained that he and Barbara came to Lubbock on June 17 and stayed a week, leaving the following Friday.

At that point, Ladd questioned Jim about giving blood for the reversed DNA test. Jim steeled himself, trying not to think about his feelings that terrible day, and gave Ladd the full details of how the blood was taken. He then identified the voluntary consent form he had signed, which had been entered into evidence.

Abruptly, Ladd switched the questioning back to the trip Jim and Barbara had made to Lubbock in June and asked if Jim had an opportunity to talk to Leisha while he was in Lubbock. Jim said he had called Leisha to see if she would have dinner with him and Barbara that night, so they could talk about Scott's situation in more depth.

"Jim, did she mention to you that night, or any time prior to that, that she was involved with a fellow named Tim Smith?"

"After the blood was discovered…" Jim bit his lip pensively, then went on, "She said she was involved with a man named Tim Smith. She said she started seeing Tim Smith when she found out about Jessica Tate, basically to try to make Scott jealous and that Tim Smith had come to her apartment the afternoon of the day Scott disappeared and that Tim had spent the night in her apartment."

"Did she tell you that was on the night of the sixteenth?"

"Yes," Jim said quietly. He kept his emotion under check with difficulty.

"After she originally told you she had spent the night with Tim Smith at her apartment on the sixteenth of May, did you talk to her after that about Tim's spending the night with her on the sixteenth?"

"Yes," he said definitely. He wanted to get it all in, tell it right so the jury would see the truth as he had. He went on, "And she said, 'I didn't tell you he spent the night at the apartment that night. I told you that he spent the night with me the next night, that I don't remember anything that happened the night of the sixteenth.' She didn't remember where she was, she didn't remember anything that had happened that night."

"Now, this is the same Leisha Hamilton who had given you a graphic description of Scott's fever and a blow-by-blow description of everything they had done when she brought him home sick that night?"

"That's correct."

"She didn't remember what happened the night of the sixteenth?"

Jim thought for a moment of facts, seeming random but linked together, and began. "She said she remembered exactly what happened the night before; what they had to eat, what they saw on television. She went to work the next morning at 5:30; she took Scott a glass of water and gave him a sinus tablet. She came home at 2:30. Tim Smith came down and met her and after that she's a total blank."

Abruptly, Ladd switched the subject back to Scott's yellow Camaro. "Did you and she talk about Scott's car when you went out to dinner together?"

"Oh, definitely." Jim nodded. "At that point I wasn't sure what the situation—like I said, she was very interested in Scott's car."

Wardroup challenged the statement. "Excuse me, your honor, I am going to object to this as not being responsive to the question."

"Your honor, I asked him about the car," Ladd said firmly stepping in. "He is going into that conversation, Judge."

"Overruled."

A bit exasperated, Ladd turned back to Jim and tried again. "You said she was real interested in the car?"

"Yes. She said she went to ProSound and picked the car up. She wanted to have that car and asked if I would let her have the car. I said it was Scott's car, but when we found Scott, she could have the car."

"What did she say in response to that?"

Sitting up, Jim remembered how he'd found her answer almost a body blow. "At that point she looked straight at me, and said, 'What if Scott's not found for four or five years?' I said, 'I guess we will have a long wait.'" He paused, his voice broke with pain, but he was able to continue. "And she was right. It's been six years."

"When is the next time you talked to Leisha?"

"I talked to Leisha on the phone the next night, June nineteenth."

"And what did you talk about then?"

"We talked about the car, because the police had gone out that afternoon and picked it up and she was very upset, wanted to know why."

"Do you know why the police picked up the car?"

Jim tried to answer as matter-of-factly as his strong feelings permitted. "Not precisely, but we had met with the police—Detective Randy McGuire and Detective English—that morning and I had told them of her extreme interest in the car."

"This was before the car got picked up?"

"Yes."

"And the police picked up that car, as far as you know, in response to the conversation you had with them about what Leisha had said the night before?"

"Yes," Jim said grimly.

"When you and Leisha talked about the car on the nineteenth, what did she tell you?"

"She said, 'Why are they taking that car? The car should be right here. You told me I could have the car.'

"I told her the police had the car and they would keep it until they were through with it. And besides that, it was Scott's car."

"Did you talk to Leisha again before you went back to Pennsylvania?"

"Yes, we did. I don't remember the exact date, but I think it was the following day, we had another conversation. I was talking to Leisha about her involvement with this other man, Tim Smith. And she told me that she was pretty sure that Tim Smith had something to do with Scott's disappearance."

"Did she tell you why she believed that?"

"Because he was acting strange, following her around. She said she just felt suspicious that he had something to do with it."

"Is that the first time she had ever told you that?"

Jim could not suppress the slight tremor in his voice. "As far as him having something to do with it, with Scott's disappearance, that he had done something to Scott, that was the first time she had ever said that. I asked her if she had told the police what she thought. She said she hadn't. I told her we should go down and talk to the police about this. And she agreed to do that."

"Have you tried to stay in touch with the main people involved in this investigation ever since Scott's disappearance?"

The pulse in Jim's forehead clenched. "Absolutely," he said, showing signs of stress and pain. "Because—I just wanted to know—I wanted to find Scott's body so we could give him a decent burial. And that's been my intent since day one, to try to find out what happened to my son so we could have his remains and have him buried," Jim bared his soul.

"You have never been able to do that, have you?"

"No," he said almost mournfully.

On this somber note, Ladd concluded his questioning of Jim Dunn.

Wardroup announced that he would reserve cross-examination of the witness.

Judge Shaver, an unabashed look of sympathy on his face, called for a short recess.

Although Jim's testimony was over, he had been told there was a chance he could be recalled, so he was relegated to the tiny, windowless, airless room once again. Richard Walter, also under the rule, sat with him. Pam, who had left the courtroom and come to see him for a few moments, squeezed Jim's arm encouragingly. He gave her a half smile through his pain.

"You were great," Pam said smiling back. "You made a good impression on the jury. I can tell you right now, Leisha is not making a good impression on anyone. Except, maybe that one man in the jury box who keeps making eye contact with her. It's almost like she's flirting with him. Once, I saw her wink at him!"

"What? You've got to be kidding!" Jim exclaimed in distaste. For a second he froze in disbelief. Then angry feelings rose to the surface.

"Don't worry. The judge sees what's happening. I saw him glaring at her a few minutes ago."

chapter sixteen

The Trial Moves On

Ladd's next witness was Pat Taylor, who had worked with Scott at ProSound Electronics and now was general manager of the store.

Taylor testified that Scott had been very good at his job, that he could not recall ever getting any complaints about Scott's work. He also confirmed that Scott was extremely possessive about his belongings and he rarely ever saw Scott lending a tool to anyone else. "I can't imagine that Scott would simply drop out of sight, leaving everything he owned behind him."

Having covered the subject, Ladd changed the course of questioning, directing Taylor's attention to Scott's cars. Taylor remembered the Camaro that he called Yellow Thunder. "Would you tell the jury how well Scott took care of his car?"

Taylor ran his hand through his hair then said, "He took very good care of his car, especially the stereo system that he had in it."

"Can you imagine Scott, with the attitude he had about his car, just dropping out of sight and leaving that car behind?"

"No."

"Was Scott staying with anybody else? Did he have sleeping privileges at anybody else's apartment besides Leisha's?"

Taylor hesitated a moment as if thinking. Then he said, "At Max Gianoli's."

"Have you heard from Scott since he disappeared that May?"

"No," Taylor said definitively.

"Have you heard any word, letter, phone call or heard of anybody else getting any letters, phone calls or word from Scott?"

"No."

Ladd glanced up at Judge Shaver. "I pass the witness, your honor."

On cross-examination, Wardroup asked Taylor about Mike Roberts. "When Mr. Roberts started working at ProSound, did your relationship with Scott change?"

"Yes, it did. We didn't go out together as much. They worked together in the bay all the time and they would go out together."

"Do you remember telling Detective English that Mike Roberts's personality changed drastically, that he became more violent and irritable, after Scott Dunn disappeared?"

"He did at one point. I remember Mike and I started arguing a bunch about installs."

"And did Mr. Roberts continue to work at ProSound?"

"No, he did not."

Taylor was excused and Ladd recalled Jim Dunn to the stand.

"I think you already testified that Leisha was upset when the police picked up the car. And I asked you how the conversation with her that night ended. You said it just ended with that. She was upset and you told her the police weren't finished with the car. Did you and she talk about that car any time after that?"

Jim couldn't help the sigh which escaped his lips. "Many times."

"What was the gist of those conversations?"

"Leisha called me on several different occasions and asked when was she going to get the car back, that the police were through with the car and it had nothing to do with the investigation. She wanted the car back as soon as possible. She said she had talked to Detective English, who told her they were through with the car and that she could have it back. It could be released to her if I gave her a letter signed that she could have the car back."

"Were you willing to give her that letter?"

Jim shook his head. "I wasn't willing. I told her that I would give her the car when Scott was found."

Again, Wardoup, who was well aware of the sympathy Scott's father evoked, had no questions for Jim Dunn.

The morning's testimony was over. Judge Shaver agreed to call the noon recess a few minutes early and asked the jury to return early. Following the lunch break, Ladd called the former ProSound employee Mike Roberts to the stand. A slender, athletic-looking man, Roberts walked quickly and stepped into to the witness box.

Under direct examination, Roberts said that he now lived in Tacoma, Washington and worked in automotive electronics, installing car stereos, alarm systems, power windows and other electronic apparatus. He said he was married and had a son. He said that he and Scott had been good friends. He also knew Leisha Hamilton and pointed her out at the defense table.

Pam Alexander, sitting next to Barbara Dunn, whispered, "Look at Leisha. She just winked at him! Can you imagine anyone flirting at a time like this?" She stared at the defendant, who was smiling at Roberts, leaning forward, as if she couldn't wait to hear what he was going to say.

"Do you know anything about any other girlfriends he had at the time besides Leisha?" Ladd asked.

"Not any actual girlfriends, no. He had a lot of acquaintances who were girls."

"When was the last time you saw Scott?"

"It was about five days after he went home sick." Ladd did not challenge his account of the time. Scott more than likely had been dead within three days after he became ill that fateful Monday.

"Scott called the shop, talked to Max. Max told me that he wanted me to see Scott after work, so I did. We talked for about forty-five minutes," Roberts said. He said Scott was very concerned about their being able to get the van ready in time for the upcoming contest.

"About what time of the night, day, were you talking?"

"It was somewhere between, say, midnight and one o'clock in the morning."

"Do you recall seeing anybody when you went into the apartment to talk to him that night, seeing anybody else standing around outside?"

"No, I didn't."

"Did you see anybody outside when you left the apartment?"

"No."

"Have you ever seen or heard from Scott since that time?" Ladd gave a glance in the direction of the jurors.

"No."

Ladd was almost finished with his direct examination of Roberts. He asked if Roberts and Scott had discussed Scott's coming back the next morning to take him to work.

Roberts told of the plan to pick Scott up at about quarter of nine, and of receiving no response to his knocking. He tried the door to see if it was unlocked.

"Did you look around any of the rest of the apartment, around the outside, to see if there was anybody inside?"

Roberts didn't hesitate. He said he went around to the bedroom window and it was shut and the shade drawn.

"The parking lot where you parked was in the same area that the window was?"

"Right next to the window."

"Every time you had walked from the parking lot to the front door of the apartment you could see through the window into that bedroom?"

"Yes. Except that morning."

"When Scott failed to show up at work on May 16, where were his cars?"

"They were at the shop. Then, I believe Leisha came to pick the yellow one up."

After a few more questions, Ladd let the witness go.

On cross-examination, Wardroup asked if Leisha's car was at the apartment that morning. Roberts said it was not.

"Did you ever hear Scott mention Jessica Tate?"

"Yeah, I believe so."

"Did you have any knowledge that Scott might be engaged to Jessica at the same time he was living with Leisha?"

"No, I didn't."

"Were you there when some of Scott's girlfriends would drop by the shop?"

"I had never seen anybody other than Leisha stop by the shop to visit him."

Wardroup told the witness he could step down.

Ladd's next witness was the father of Tim Smith, Leisha's co-defendant. The older Smith, his foot bandaged, used crutches to maneuver awkwardly to the witness stand. He was a stocky man, his graying hair in a stiff brush cut. Ladd gave him a few extra minutes to get settled in the witness box. Then he began his questioning.

Smith said he had talked to Tim a little bit about the case. He knew a romantic relationship existed between Tim and Leisha and had learned after the fact that they were living together, but he didn't know when they began living together.

When asked if Tim had ever talked to him about any of the evidence in the case, Smith said his son had mentioned that he had found a roll of duct tape on a Dumpster near his apartment about the time Scott Dunn disappeared.

Next, Ladd asked Smith to describe where they had lived when Tim was at home. He described the small enclave. Smith said that eventually, his son wanted to live in Lubbock, so Tim moved. Tim was about thirty years old when this occurred.

"Was he married?"

"No. He's married now. For two years. And he has one son."

"How did you feel about Leisha and Tim being together?"

The older Smith stroked his chin for a moment, then said, "I didn't like it. I didn't think it was right. They weren't married. I expressed that concern to him."

"Has Tim ever written to you?"

"Yes."

Ladd showed Smith the packet of cards and notes Tim had written Leisha and asked Smith to look at them just long enough to see if he recognized the handwriting. Smith thumbed through the exhibits and said the writing on each was that of his son Tim.

Ladd stepped back. "The documents that I just showed you are Tim's handwriting?"

"Yes."

"And he signs this one Tim, doesn't he?"

"Yes, sir." The older man's face showed the wear and tear of worry over his own son's predicament.

"Also signs it as the Flash and Superman, doesn't he?"

Smith gave a faint smile. "Yes, sir."

"Did you ever know him to use those nicknames in regard to himself?"

"No, sir."

"Mr. Smith, thank you very much. I pass the witness."

The witness was excused, subject to recall by Wardroup for the defense.

Next, Ladd called his first police witness, the man who had worked so devotedly with Jim Dunn and had done such a diligent investigative job. The long hours and the strain showed on the young, attractive face of Detective Tal English of the Lubbock Police Department. Ladd led English through his early investigation, when Scott was presumably missing. The attorney asked English about his first telephone contact with Leisha, when she told him of the items that were missing from the apartment, then the break-in and items that disappeared that day.

"Did she say anything about his wallet?"

"I believe she said the wallet was missing."

"Did she say anything about his car keys?"

"His car keys were left there, I believe she said."

"Did she show you those car keys herself?"

"I later got those car keys."

"Who did you get those from?"

"From Leisha Hamilton."

"So you don't know whether there were any other keys originally on the ring or not?"

"I do not."

Next Ladd asked English about his first visit to the apartment with George White. "When she told you a piece of carpet was missing from underneath the couch, what did you think?"

"I believed there was something wrong, definitely. I immediately wondered what was on that carpet—why it was missing."

Ladd showed English several photographs, which he identified as pictures of the interior of the apartment, taken on his first visit. He pointed out to the jury the couch and the area under it that showed beige padding.

"Tal, did you ask Leisha about the piece that was cut and whether she had ever noticed that before?"

"Yes, sir."

"What did she tell you?"

Tal leaned forward, his voice earnest. "She said that up until—I believe it was the twenty-eighth of May, she had not noticed it, because she had been sleeping on the couch and had sheets that hung down where she couldn't see under the couch."

The remainder of the pictures were of the bedroom carpet as it appeared when the detectives first saw it, the stained padding that was revealed when the patch of carpet was removed, bloodstained concrete underneath the padding and tack strips and the specks of blood on the walls. Ladd asked English to explain the chain of custody used to preserve the integrity of the evidence. Then he asked Judge Shaver for permission to let English read to the jury the statement Leisha had made to the police on the day following the discovery of the crime scene. Shaver granted the request, but, since it was almost four o'clock, he called a fifteen-minute recess.

When court reconvened, Tal English began to read Leisha's statement, emphasizing first that when the statement was taken, she was a witness, not a suspect.

Ladd did not go through the statement point by point; instead he asked the detective if Leisha had made any comments while they were examining her apartment.

"Did she seem agitated or upset over the blood being found, over Scott's being a victim of some kind of foul play?"

"Her emotional state didn't really change at all that I could tell."

"Just matter-of-fact?"

"Yes, sir."

"Was that the same emotional state that she had when she pointed out a hair or what she thought was a hair sticking out of the blood on that wall?"

"Yes, sir." English's calm demeanor impressed the jury.

Ladd moved on to more photographs, some showing the exterior of the apartment building and its proximity to the parking lot and to the Dumpster in the alley just a few feet away from Apartment 4. Then he showed Tal aerial photos, showing the entire apartment complex, including adjoining buildings, the alley and the Dumpster. English explained to the jury the proximity of the buildings and the parking lot.

"You visited the apartment several times yourself; is that right?"

"Yes, sir."

Ladd spoke quietly. "What's the easiest place to park when you want to drive a car next to that apartment?"

"It would be that north parking lot."

"If you wanted to park your car as close as you could to Leisha Hamilton's front door, how far away would you be?"

"Actually, you could park about a yard away, I guess."

"Is there a Dumpster in that parking lot?"

"Yes, sir. It sits next to the alley."

When English had answered all of Ladd's questions about the crime scene, the prosecutor moved on to other aspects of Leisha's statement. Now that the picture had been drawn of the crime scene, it was important to sketch out the two people who had ended Scott Dunn's life and just how this was done. Ladd asked English to explain to the jury how Tim Smith had become involved in the case. English told of Leisha's saying Smith had been acting strangely and that she thought he might have hurt Scott. Then he told of the visit he and George White had made to Smith's new apartment, where they found the roll of duct tape.

It was even more important that the jury visualize what had taken place, because there were no witnesses, no weapon, no body. The evidence was all circumstantial, but in this case it conveyed, Jim and Ladd believed, a powerful and telling motive.

At this point, Judge Shaver interrupted, noting that it was five o'clock, time to call the evening recess.

chapter seventeen

The Temptress
and Cirsumstance

When court reconvened at 9:00 AM on Wednesday, May 14, Leisha, in a clingy, teal blue and white polyester dress, belted at the waist, made her way to the defendant's table. Pam and Barbara glanced at each other. Leisha had dressed demurely the first two days of the trial. Had she tired of that look and decided to flaunt herself? Possibly. Leisha's coquettish smile and spiritedness in the presence of the jury now seemed pronounced.

Detective Tal English returned to the witness stand. Rusty Ladd asked him what he had done with the duct tape he and George White had found in Tim Smith's apartment. English explained that he had found green carpet fibers and several hairs adhering to the sticky edges of the roll. He said that Leisha Hamilton had voluntarily given him a sample of her hair and Scott's hairbrush, which contained some hairs she said probably belonged to Scott. Tim Smith had been subpoenaed to give hair samples. Those pieces of evidence were presented and identified for the jury.

English also prepared the way for the forensic experts who would be testifying later on in the trial, by telling how he maintained the chain of custody of all the blood taken from the apartment and sent it to the various agencies for testing.

Wardroup conducted only a brief cross examination of the detective, emphasizing the voluntary cooperation Leisha Hamilton had given the police—i.e., voluntarily giving a statement, willingly giving her blood and hair samples for DNA testing and volunteering information about what she saw as Tim Smith's erratic behavior.

Ladd had a few more questions on redirect examination, hammering on Leisha's formal statement. "You had taken a statement from her asking her what had happened and she explained to you what had happened on the fourteenth and fifteenth; is that correct?"

"That's correct."

"You asked her to account for her activities on the sixteenth as well, did you not?"

"That's correct."

"Was she able to tell you what happened on the fourteenth and fifteenth of May?"

"Yes, sir."

"Part of that detail is what the jury has heard in that statement she gave you?"

"That's correct."

"Does that strike you as being vague or very detailed?"

"It was very detailed."

"When you asked her what happened on Thursday night, the sixteenth, what did she tell you?"

"She couldn't remember."

"She could not remember a thing that happened Thursday night?"

"She said that she either went to her favorite club, as she usually did, or Tim Smith might have come down to her apartment, then left. She couldn't remember."

"Did she ever tell you that she slept with Tim Smith in order to make Scott Dunn jealous?"

"Yes, sir."

"Did she tell you where that act took place?"

"On one occasion it was at her apartment and maybe another time at his."

"Did she tell you what room she and Tim slept in?"

"The living room."

Ladd had no further questions for English at that time and called as his next witness Jim Thomas, the supervising criminologist at the Lubbock Department of Public Service laboratory. Thomas explained the process he had used for performing the Luminol testing of the bloodstains in Leisha Hamilton's apartment.

Thomas identified photographs of the interior of the apartment as the crime scene where he had done the Luminol test. He said that he found some fluorescent patterns on the wall in the bedroom, which appeared to be fingerprints. This could not be confirmed, since there was no detail, but the size and shape were indicative of fingerprints. He described the area on the wall that indicated a wiping type of action had been performed.

"Suppose the blood had been spattered against that wall in kind of an arbitrary fashion and somebody had wanted to clean it up and they used water and soap or other cleaning agent to wipe across the wall. Would traces of the blood show up all the way across that wiping pattern?" Ladd asked.

"I think it would be consistent with that, because as you're trying to clean the blood it becomes diluted with the water or the cleaning material and so it would tend to just spread the blood throughout that area. Luminol is very sensitive to blood. So it would be difficult to dilute it to such an extent that it would not respond."

Ladd showed Thomas a dozen photographs, which Thomas identified as pictures that had been taken during the Luminol test in the apartment. Ladd directed Thomas to leave the witness stand and use the pointer to show the jurors what they were seeing in the photographs, which had been mounted on poster board. Almost as one, the jurors stared at the photos with indrawn breath. The stark contrast between the dark walls outside the area containing Luminol and the bright, wiping pattern illuminated by the Luminol was shocking.

Thomas pointed out that in some of the photos, the wiped area reached as high as five feet from the floor. When they had finished examining each photo, Ladd referred Thomas to a scale model of the bedroom that had been previously introduced.

"Using your notes and photographs, would you be able to indicate for the jury the general range of where those blood smears were? I don't mean the exact location of where they were, but the general range and shape of where those occurred on those walls."

Nodding, Thomas said he could. With a pen he marked an area beginning to the right of the window on the east wall and all around the area where the carpet had been cut out next to the south wall and around the light switch, a distance of several feet along each wall.

Wardroup conducted a long, thorough cross-examination of Thomas. Finally, he excused the witness.

Roy Carper stood and called the State's next witness, Jessica Tate. A hush settled over the courtroom as she entered. Jessica, a slim young woman, was attractive in a pink jacket, trimmed in black, worn over a just-above-the-knee-length black skirt. Her long, dark hair was swept back and away from a smooth brow. She walked slowly but with quiet dignity to the witness box and sat down.

"Ms. Tate, my name is Roy Carper. I'm the Assistant Criminal District Attorney here in Lubbock. I believe we spoke on the phone yesterday and again this morning."

"Yes, sir."

"We are here on a case involving the murder of Roger Scott Dunn. Do you know or have you known in the past Roger Scott Dunn?"

"Yes, sir, I have."

Carper showed Jessica a photograph and she said it was a picture of Scott Dunn.

"Would you explain to the jury, please, how you met Scott Dunn and what your relationship was?"

"In Abilene, Texas, I went to a store called ProSound Electronics to have a stereo installed in my car." She smiled but her eyes glistened with tears. "I tried to talk him down on the price of the stereo."

"Did it work?"

"Yes, it did."

Carper moved slowly and carefully, his face tense. His questions led her through her first dates with Scott when she was a senior in high school. She said they had become very close and that although they had been separated for a while when she left for college, the relationship had resumed in March, just a few weeks before he disappeared. Under Carper's skillful questioning, Jessica testified to the facts surrounding her relationship with Scott Dunn, up to and including her telephone call to Scott when Leisha Hamilton answered and told Jessica she was Scott's wife. She looked for a moment like a deer caught in the headlights, frightened and apprehensive. It was as if having to say it made Leisha's conversation and Scott's disappearance happen all over again.

"Were there any other conversations that took place between you and Hamilton?"

"Honestly, I don't recall. I do remember that we were both upset, because obviously neither one of us knew about the other. I believe I hung up on her." Jessica's face was pale. Her hand shook as she stroked her brow.

"After you returned to Texas, did Scott tell you that he was going to be coming through Dallas at some point in time and wanted to meet with you?"

"Yes. He said he was going to be coming to the DFW airport and wanted me to come to the airport and see him."

"When would that have been?"

"I don't have an exact date. It was very shortly after I had returned from school. It was right at the time when he had come up missing, because I spoke with him one day and he said he was going to call me the following day with his flight information so that I would know where to meet him at the airport. And he never called me back."

"In any of the conversations you had with him in the late spring, did he ever mention a ring?"

"Yes, he did. He had told me several times he was so excited about the ring that he was having made for me and that he was making payments on it. That was one of the reasons he wanted me to meet him at the airport. He said he had one payment left on the ring and that he was going to make that payment, pick up the ring and bring it with him to the airport."

Carper gave her a long, somber look. "Is that the last time you ever talked to Scott Dunn?"

Time froze. The courtroom seemed to have sucked in its breath.

"Yes, it is," she said. The words seemed wrenched from her heart.

Carper took a step back to let them linger. Then he went on.

"Has he ever contacted you in any manner since that time?"

"No, sir."

After a few more questions, Carper relinquished Jessica Tate to Rick Wardroup's cross-examination.

Though Wardroup asked only a few brief questions, one created a slight buzz among the spectators.

"Did Scott ever mention the name Leisha Hamilton to you?"

The spectators all seemed to lean forward as if poised for the reply.

"No, sir."

When Jessica left the witness stand, Pam Alexander slipped from her seat and followed her out of the courtroom. She introduced herself to the younger woman and asked if she would like to meet Scott's dad. Jessica said she really would like that, so Pam escorted her to the witness room where Jim waited.

Jim had talked to Jessica several times by telephone, but he had not met her. His first thought was how beautiful she was! Her bright, vivacious smile captivated him instantly and he sensed that she was both loving and giving. Jim felt she was the kind of girl you told your dad about, the kind of girl you brought home to meet your parents. How wonderful it all would have been, had Scott and she gotten engaged.

Jessica told him she had finished college and her field was banking and finance. She spoke of a future that Jim imagined would have been shared with Scott—Scott's future if he had lived. He would have married Jessica and been truly happy. But he hadn't lived to see that life.

Now Jim felt a new sense of loss. Not only had he lost his son, but he had also lost the prospect of having this charming, intelligent woman for a daughter-in-law and the grandchildren he might have had. All gone.

When the trial resumed, Roy Carper called three police officers in quick succession to establish chain of custody of various bits of evidence. The first was Detective Gaylon Lewis, the LPD Identification Officer who had collected the blood, hair and fiber evidence from the crime scene on June 7, 1991. Following Lewis, the police officers who had overseen the collection of blood from Scott's parents testified to their actions. Then, the prosecution called Tal English back for a short redirect for the purpose of introducing into evidence Tim Smith's notes to Leisha.

English said Leisha had given him the notes, saying that Tim had left them on her car and in her apartment. Most were not dated, but from Leisha's statement and certain references in the notes themselves, they were written around the time Scott disappeared. English was instructed to read all of the notes into evidence. When he had finished, Ladd asked him to re-read one of them.

"I want to direct your attention to one of these cards. I think you may have missed a line there. I want you to tell the jury what it says after the end of that sentence, 'You are even prettier when you smile.' Why don't you read through the whole card again?"

"Good morning, green eyes," English read. "You look very pretty. I hope you are feeling much better today. I know you are going through a lot right now and I just want to help you get through it all. Please let me help you. You are even prettier when you smile. Love you, Superman."

"And after 'you are prettier when you smile,' he has some kind of drawing of a face with a smile; is that correct?"

"That's correct."

"Do you recall one of the cards, which the jury is looking at right now, making a reference to Mother's Day?"

"Yes, sir," he said firmly.

"Happy Mother's Day?"

"Yes, sir."

Mother's Day had fallen on May 12, just three days before Scott disappeared. Other letters introduced had been dated April 28, so it was clear that Tim Smith's love obsession with Leisha Hamilton had begun at least a few weeks before Scott's murder.

English's testimony carried over into the lunch hour, so Judge Shaver recessed the court until 1:15 PM. Barbara Dunn joined Jim and Richard Walter in the tiny witness room, where they decided to go to the courthouse cafeteria for lunch. As they started through the line, Jim turned to pick up some silverware and almost bumped into Leisha, standing not eight inches from his elbow. Behind her stood her mother, who had been glaring at Jim when she saw him outside the courtroom. Jim ignored the two women and moved on, but his heart pounded with rage. Leisha was out on bail, moving about freely, while his son was dead and he had no idea where Scott's body was. The injustice was almost more than Jim could bear.

Returning from the lunch break, Jim and Richard resumed their vigil in the tiny witness room. Barbara returned to the courtroom, where Pam Alexander joined her. A few moments later, Rebecca Atchley, the former assistant district attorney who had presented the case to the first grand jury, came in and sat down next to Pam. Atchley had gone into private practice after the election of the new district attorney, but she still felt strongly about the case and had come to see how it was going. Pam nudged Rebecca when she saw

Leisha come in. "Look at her prance!" she whispered. "Did you ever see anything so blatant?"

At that moment, Leisha caught sight of Rebecca and froze in her tracks. For a long moment, the two women locked gazes and it was apparent to Rebecca and Pam that Leisha remembered how her relationship with Atchley had been. Leisha finally turned, moved slowly and sedately to her place at the defense table. Apparently Rebecca's presence had put a damper on Leisha's cavorting, for she sat very quietly and demurely for the rest of the afternoon. Gone were the flirty tosses of her long dark hair; gone were her seductive glances toward the male juror who had captured her interest.

During that afternoon session, a procession of technical experts testified regarding tests on hair and fiber samples submitted to them. Richard Fram, an agent in the FBI's trace evidence unit in Washington, D. C., discussed how he compared the hairs removed from the duct tape underneath the carpet to the head hair samples of Timothy Smith and Leisha Hamilton. He said that he found a head hair that exhibited the same microscopic characteristics as hairs in the known head hair sample from Timothy Smith. That hair was consistent with coming from Smith. Fram also said there were numerous head hairs that exhibited the same microscopic characteristics as hairs in the known head hair sample from Leisha Hamilton and those hairs were consistent with coming from her.

Rick Wardroup declined to cross-examine the witness.

Carper next called Scott Williams of the DPS laboratory in Lubbock, who had compared the duct tape that had been found in Tim Smith's apartment with the carpet fibers clinging to it to the tape found under the carpet in Leisha's bedroom, and with fibers of the carpet from that room. Williams said he found the two samples of duct tape to be indistinguishable.

He also told Carper that the green carpet fibers from Scott's bedroom were consistent with the fibers found on the duct tape from Tim Smith's apartment, but the brown fibers from Smith's carpet were not consistent with the samples from the duct tape.

As the morning passed Cathy McCord, the serologist at the Lubbock DPS laboratory, was called to testify. McCord said that when she received the evidence from the Dunn crime scene, she analyzed it to determine the presence, the origin and the type of the different blood samples that were submitted. She said she had a blood sample from Leisha Hamilton, a hair sample off the south wall of the bedroom, one sample of Sheetrock scrapings from near the light switch of the same apartment and blood scrapings from the floor of the room.

Wardroup objected to the introduction of these samples into evidence, citing problems with chain of custody. Shaver sustained the objection. This meant Detective English would have to be called back to the stand. Before that, however, Carper asked McCord to explain the two different types of DNA testing. "One," she said, "is called RFLP, restriction fragment link polymorphism. The other is called PCR, or polymerase chain reaction. In our laboratory," McCord said, "we do PCR testing, in which a smaller amount of blood is needed for the test, but which does not give as much information as RFLP."

Ladd set out his case piece by piece. He knew each part had to fit for the jury to make the final connection.

Detectives Tal English and George White both testified as to the chain of custody of the items in question and Carper then called David Young, a forensic serologist, DNA analyst and hair analyst with the Texas Department of Public Safety, working in the Lubbock office. A relationship between the hairs on the duct tape under the bloodstained carpet had been established. Now it was time to turn the jury's attention to the hairs on the roll of duct tape found in Tim Smith's apartment, for these were important pieces of the circumstantial evidence that the jury would have to consider.

Young said he compared nine hairs off the roll of duct tape to the hair from Scott Dunn's hairbrush. He also compared the nine hairs to previously mounted slides from the FBI that contained hairs from Leisha Hamilton and Timothy Smith. Two hairs from the duct tape roll exhibited microscopic characteristics that were consistent with hair from Scott's hairbrush.

"None of the hairs that I pulled off of the roll of duct tape were microscopically consistent with Leisha Hamilton or Timothy Smith's head hair," Young said, his voice quiet but firm as he held the attorney's eyes.

On cross-examination, Wardroup pounced on one paragraph in Young's report. "The next to last paragraph of the report that you sent to Tal English says that some hairs don't possess sufficient individuality to be used as a basis for positive personal identification; is that right?"

"That's correct."

"With regard to the two hairs that you compared and found similar to Scott Dunn's, did you have full hairs?"

"Yes, they were full hairs."

"But none of the nine hairs that you found on the roll of duct tape compared favorably to Tim Smith or Leisha Hamilton?"

"That's correct."

When Rusty Ladd called Dave Hayden to the stand, Hayden told of how he had met Leisha. Ladd asked him if the relationship had ever become sexual, Hayden replied that they had sex probably three times. He said the first incident occurred about a month or so after Scott Dunn's disappearance.

In response to Ladd's questions, Hayden said he knew Tim Smith, that he had seen him at the restaurant where Leisha worked. Later, Hayden said, he had seen Smith at Leisha's apartment. Hayden told the jury that he had been working at the restaurant at the time and he also gave his impression that Smith came in not to eat, but to watch Leisha.

Ladd wanted to be sure this registered with the jury. He reemphasized Smith's preoccupation with the defendant. "Just to watch Leisha? Kind of sat there, like a big old puppy dog watching her, didn't he?"

"Pretty much."

"Did he stay there one hour, two hours, the whole shift?"

"Sometimes the whole shift."

"Did Leisha talk to him?"

"They were mostly arguing."

"When Tim was at the restaurant sitting there watching Leisha, did you ever see him order any food?"

"No, sir."

Then Ladd carefully led Hayden through the scene in Leisha's bedroom, when Tim walked into the apartment while Hayden and Leisha were in bed together.

"Were you and she engaged in the act of having sex when you saw Tim in her apartment?"

Hayden nodded. The courtroom was pin-drop quiet. "We were having sex and he came in. He barged in on us and wanted to talk to Leisha. And Leisha got upset, because he came in and he wasn't supposed to be there. She asked him how he got in there. And he said he had a key."

"Did he knock before he came in?"

"No."

"You said Leisha got upset?"

"Yes, sir. She got up and was telling him to leave. She slapped him and he wouldn't leave. He just kept saying that he wanted to talk to her. And she said no."

"Did he do anything violent toward Leisha Hamilton that night—after she slapped him?"

"No."

"Did she push him around?"

"Not really push. She was trying to get him out of the apartment."

"She was in his face, wasn't she?"

"Yes, she was." He pursed his lips.

"Was she screaming at him?"

"Yes."

"Was she dressed?"

"No, sir." A little gasp arose from the spectators. All eyes were craned on Leisha for a few moments. Ladd waited for quiet then he went on.

"She didn't have anything on at all?"

"No, sir."

On that note, Ladd dismissed Dave Hayden and called Burt Todd. Todd told about his romantic relationship with Leisha, which began shortly after Scott disappeared and which lasted three or four months. He said his and Leisha's break-up had been messy, because he was moving away without her and she had told him she was pregnant with his child. He said he had no way of knowing if this was true. Todd said he told her if she was pregnant and he was the father, he would accept his responsibility. He never learned if she actually had a child.

Ladd then directed the questioning toward Tim Smith. Todd confirmed the information Dave Hayden had given the court. Ladd asked about Leisha's reaction to Scott's disappearance. "Did she seem upset about his leaving?"

"More mad than upset, because they had moved there together and had signed a lease."

"Are you aware of whether or not Tim was dating her while you were dating her?"

"Through hearsay only."

A picture of Leisha, the temptress, was emerging. Ladd kept drawing it.

"You never saw Tim at her apartment while you were there or saw him come into the apartment afterwards or anything like that?"

"He was there, but according to her, they weren't dating at that time."

"Okay. Did she ever tell you that she was scared of Tim?"

"One time she said she was scared of him."

"Based on what Leisha told you about her relationship with Tim, would it surprise you to find out that she and Tim began to live with each other?"

"It did when I heard it, yeah."

Ladd had no further questions and Wardroup indicated that he did not want to cross-examine.

Ladd called to the stand Karl Young, who testified that he and Leisha Hamilton, the mother of his youngest son, had started dating when Leisha was in jail for perjury. He said he received thirteen or fourteen letters from Leisha and talked on the telephone to her many times.

"During any of those conversations you had with her, or in any letter that she ever wrote to you, did she ever talk about the absence of Roger Scott Dunn's body?"

"Yes. There were a few times that she'd respond that with the absence of the body they couldn't prove the case."

"Did she ever say anything about the absence of a weapon in the case?"

"Yes. She always stated that without a weapon and without a body they had no case."

"She said, 'If they don't have a body they can't convict me,' didn't she?"

"That is true."

"And she told you that if we didn't have a weapon we couldn't convict her?"

"That is true."

On brief cross-examination, defense attorney Wardroup got Young to admit that Leisha had never acknowledged knowing anything about Scott's death.

The stage was set for the third day of testimony, Thursday, May 14, when Richard Walter and the experts in DNA and blood spatter analysis would take the stand.

chapter eighteen

The Profiler

Calling Dr. Richard Walter was a calculated risk for the prosecution, but Ladd knew that Jim Dunn had absolute faith in the profiler from the Vidocq Society. Ladd recognized Walter as a consummate professional, without whose suggestions to Tal English and other detectives working the case; without whose contacts with forensics experts such as Dr. Shepherd in England; without whose assessment and profiles of principals in the case, which fueled the investigation when it sputtered—without all those qualities Walter brought to the investigation, Ladd would more than likely have had no case to bring to trial. This assessment in no way belittled Jim Dunn's complete involvement. It was Jim's time and energy, devoted first to finding his son and then, when it was learned Scott wasn't coming home, to finding his son's killers and ensuring justice was done, that had prodded the investigator to bring the case to its day in court. It would have been easy for some harried investigator to give up because everything seemed to lead to the inevitable dead end: no body, no weapon, no witness. If an investigator had made the decision not to continue, no one would have faulted him for it. But, inspired by Jim Dunn's devotion, they could not, did not give up and Dunn was resolute in his insistence of Walter's testimony being crucial.

What bothered Ladd about putting the profiler on the stand, though, was Richard Walter's belief that there was a conspiracy surrounding Scott's death—a conspiracy that included not only Leisha and Tim, but at least one other person, perhaps several others. Walter believed that someone at Scott's place of work was engaged in illegal drug activities, Scott found out and said he was going to go to the police. Therefore, the person involved either coerced or encouraged Leisha into killing Scott, helped her with the murder or paid her to do it. Walter's investigation of how sick Scott had suddenly become led him to believe that an attempt was made to poison Scott at the party he attended on Monday, May 13. When the poison attempt only made Scott extremely ill, it then became necessary to eliminate him immediately and forcefully. Consequently, Scott was bludgeoned as he slept either Wednesday night, May 15 or in the early morning hours of May 16.

In spite of Walter's strong belief in his conspiracy theory, Ladd had no tangible evidence to support it. He did, however, have strong circumstantial and scientific evidence to link Leisha Hamilton and Tim Smith to the murder, so he wanted to confine his case to that evidence. Ladd did not want to risk letting the defense get time to counter Walter's theory. He was anticipating that if Wardroup found out about the conspiracy idea, and if he saw that the prosecution could prove a murder had occurred, he would try to direct the jury's attention to another suspect. Walter's theory would fit perfectly into the defense attorney's plans.

For these reasons, Ladd was reluctant to call Walter as a witness, even though his assessment of Leisha and Tim added valuable facts. Ladd's only hope was that, since crime profiling was considered, at best, an inexact science by those in the judicial system and, as far as he could determine, there was no precedent for utilizing crime profiles as testimony in Texas jurisprudence, the judge would not allow this part of Walter's testimony. Finally, Ladd decided to go with Jim's gut feeling about Walter and call him, but it was with some trepidation. Nevertheless, Richard Walter was called to the stand.

After Walter was sworn in, Ladd asked him to explain crime assessment and profiling.

Walter described the investigative technique and said that it was a recognized tool used by various police agencies across the United States and around the world. He said he had testified many times as an expert in this area of investigation.

Explaining that a profiler could use recognized patterns of behavior to see in terms of all the evidence if a pattern was present, he commented, "It's a systematic way to evaluate that. That also includes looking at the pre-crime behaviors, at the crime behavior and post-crime behavior. Just because the body dies doesn't necessarily mean the evidence ceases. And so one then continues past that point. What are the issues? What should one expect in terms of post-crime behavior? That's the assessment—"

Ladd tried to lead Walter down the path he had laid out. "Let me interrupt you for just a second. When you talk about making an assessment of pre-crime, crime episode and post-crime behavior, does that include an assessment of a *victim's* pre-crime behavior as well as an assessment of any *suspects* or *defendants* in the case as to pre-crime behavior?"

"Exactly."

Ladd pressed on. "Does it include a post-crime assessment of the defendants or suspects in an investigation?"

Walter nodded. "Yes. And it's designed basically to rule out, in terms of what you can exclude. The pre-crime behavior may be consistent with a particular suspect or the crime behavior may be consistent with that suspect, but the post-crime behavior may be inconsistent with that individual. It's one way to create doubt so that one can try to exclude a point of fact. A false positive."

Ladd looked over at the jurors to see whether they were watching—they were. "Try to exclude what?"

Walter pursed his lips. "Try to exclude a wrongful pursuit down a line of investigation. And that assessment is going to feed the investigator, because crime assessment talks about a type. It doesn't talk about a specific individual. Therefore, the fancy word is the probability, the likelihood of it."

"Did you make any kind of study in the field of crime assessment and profiling in regard to the investigation of Scott Dunn's murder?"

Walter said that he had done so.

"Did you make any opinions or reach any kind of conclusions regarding crime assessment and profiling in the Leisha Hamilton/Scott Dunn murder investigation?"

"Yes." Walter replied firmly.

Rick Wardroup interrupted. "Your honor," he said politely, as was his style, "excuse me. May we approach the bench?"

Judge Shaver motioned for the attorneys to approach.

Wardroup began, "I believe the opinion this witness intends to give is based on evidence that's hearsay, that the person who provided that evidence is not going to be called as a witness by the State."

Wardroup was referring to Dr. Richard Shepherd, the British forensic expert who had made the first determination that a murder had been committed. "And if that's the case, then I think going on with Walter's testimony is improper. And I would ask the opportunity to question the witness outside the presence of the jury."

Nodding, Judge Shaver said quietly, "I think you are entitled to that."

Turning to the jury box, he instructed the jurors to retire to the jury room. Wardroup then began to question the witness.

"First of all, have you ever testified as an expert in the State of Texas?"

Walter said he had not.

"As I understand the reports regarding your work in this case, they were dependent on some information that was developed by Dr. Shepherd; is that correct?"

Walter hesitated a minute as if weighing the idea. "That's only part of it," he said.

Wardroup frowned. "Tell me what part was dependent on what Dr. Shepherd did, please."

"What Dr. Shepherd did was involved with the evaluation of the material sent by the Lubbock Police Department to him for an opinion as to whether the crime scene was consistent or inconsistent with life."

"So any opinion you would have on that issue would be based on information that Dr. Shepherd developed and provided to you and the LPD; is that correct?"

"In part, yes," Walter conceded.

"What other information do you have or what other opinions do you have about this case that are based on your own direct observations?" Wardroup asked dryly.

Walter stared at the defense attorney disdainfully. "I interviewed Leisha Hamilton, your client. I have also interviewed Tim Smith and Mike Roberts. I have also interviewed Max Gianoli. My information has been predicated upon working with the LPD, so I have been privy to the evidence. I have also been privy to all the police reports and the accumulated evidence in written form."

Ladd looked at the judge to see how he was taking this. His expression was inscrutable.

"During the interview with Leisha Hamilton, was her lawyer present?"

"No, he was not." He shook his head.

"Was she warned of her rights before the interview was conducted?"

"Yes, she was."

"Do you have on your person any written waiver of rights that she executed?"

"No."

With that, Wardroup turned toward the judge. "Your honor, I am going to object to this witness's testimony, first of all, as to the situation surrounding the crime scene. It is based on evidence that's hearsay to this witness and from a witness who is not going to be called by the State, as I understand it. Secondly, as to any impression he has regarding an interview with Ms. Hamilton, unless and until there is a written waiver of rights, I think that's inappropriate for the jury."

Ladd leapt up. "Your honor, it's well recognized as a matter of law that experts can review police reports, written statements, statements by other people who are involved in an investigation, in order to make expert opinions in their field of expertise. By what Mr. Wardroup is saying, no experts could testify regarding their expert opinions unless they had been actually present at the crime scene and done all that work themselves. Experts are able and entitled to testify regarding their expertise based on police investigative reports, statements and evidence they have had access to."

Judge Shaver's face was thoughtful. "You understand that the Texas Supreme Court and the Court of Criminal Appeals are very restrictive on what constitutes an expert who can go before a jury. And in fact, sufficient predication has to be established to the judge to determine whether or not this so-called expert has expertise sufficient to go before the jury—their background, publications and so forth."

"Yes, sir."

"Go into that. I'm not about to go ahead and rule on that at this time."

"Yes, sir. We are prepared to go into that."

"Well, you go into it outside the presence of the jury."

"Very well, your Honor." For the next fifteen minutes, Ladd led Walter through a detailed recitation of his qualifications as a psychiatric profiler. He asked Walter about the dozens of crime investigations, nationally and internationally, in which he had assisted. He asked Walter about the papers he had published and courses he had taught on the subject to various law enforcement agencies.

Judge Shaver interrupted. "Do you have a single case in the State of Texas where crime assessment and profile was accepted as a scientific, reliable study in this state? A single case?"

"Not offhand, Judge." Ladd responded.

"I'm not talking about with law enforcement agencies. It may be accepted by law enforcement agencies, but we are talking about a much higher burden for a field to be accepted in a courtroom. Do you understand that?" Shaver asked.

"I understand what you are asking about, sir. And the answer to that is, I do not. I'm not sure if research would turn any up, but I do not know of any right this minute."

The questions ricocheted back and forth.

"Do you have *any* authority on it?"

Wardroup spoke up. "I sure don't, your honor."

Judge Shaver looked up. "Anything else?"

"Your honor, I see where the court's headed regarding its ruling in terms of expert evidence, but I want to be able to go into conversations that the witness had with Leisha Hamilton. Mr. Wardroup's already made reference to an objection he would have based on Miranda rights. I wanted to flesh that out. We probably need to do that outside the presence of the jury as well," Ladd conceded.

Judge Shaver waved his hand. "Go ahead."

With the jury still absent, the State continued its examination of Walter, eliciting from him the fact that the conversation he and Detective Tal English had with Leisha Hamilton had taken place in the car outside of the restaurant where Hamilton worked. Walter admitted he was not a police officer, but had been invited to become a part of the investigation by the Lubbock Police Department.

In response to Ladd's questions, Walter said that Leisha was advised of her Miranda rights, although she did not sign a waiver form. Walter observed that Leisha did not appear to be drunk or intoxicated and her state of mind was such that she appeared to understand the questions he asked her. "Furthermore," he said, "she was coherent in her responses to those questions."

"Did you talk to her about Roger Scott Dunn's disappearance?"

"Yes. I referenced it as a murder. She had, by previous police reports and understanding, inferred a number of times that Tim Smith might be the guilty party. So I wanted to find out from her whether she had any evidence of that or whether it was supposition. She made the comment that she had an alibi for the time of the murder and I asked her how she could have an alibi when she didn't know when the murder occurred or we don't know when the murder occurred. The only person who knew that was the killer. She said, 'Oh, yes, well, I guess I don't have an alibi.'"

"Did you ask her anything about her romantic involvement with

Tim Smith, the co-defendant in this case?"

He frowned. "Yes. I had asked her why, if she believed that Tim Smith might be the guilty party, why she moved in with him afterward. And she said that they did not have a sexual relationship, that it was a roommate relationship."

"Did you ask her about whether she had ever been sexually involved with Tim Smith, in particular at or about the time of Roger Scott Dunn's murder?"

"Yes, I did ask that. And the answer was no."

"She said she had not been sexually involved with Tim Smith at any time; is that correct?

"That's correct."

"Did you talk to Tim Smith in regard to his role in Scott Dunn's disappearance and murder?"

"Yes."

"Were you with Tal English when you talked to him?"

"Part of the time."

"Was Tim advised of his Miranda rights before he spoke to you?"

"Yes."

"Richard, do you recall when you talked to him?"

Walter's voice hardened. "It was the day that he was taken to the Sheriff's Department for hair samples."

"Do you remember whether or not the conversation you had with Tim Smith was on the same trip to Lubbock as when you had the conversation with Leisha?"

"Oh, yes. It was the same day."

"When you talked to Tim, where did that conversation take place?"

"It took place in the hallway of the Sheriff's department or the Sheriff's building. We started chatting and he spoke about the issues."

"Did you ask him about his romantic involvement with Leisha Hamilton?"

"Yes. He claimed it had been consummated many times."

"Did he ever admit to you directly being involved in the homicide of Roger Scott Dunn?"

"No."

"Did Leisha Hamilton ever admit to being involved in the homicide of Scott Dunn?"

"No."

Ladd turned to the judge. "Those are the questions I would ask in the presence of the jury."

Judge Shaver was ready with his ruling. "The court, after having heard the evidence submitted, is of the opinion that crime assessment and profile has not been established to be a scientific, acceptable expertise to go before a jury. The information I have received here shows that he may have the expertise to assist for crime enforcement officers, but there's not a showing that it's been accepted in the scientific community as reliable information to go before a jury or to be acceptable. The court will, therefore, sustain the defense objection.

"Insofar as the matter of the statements made, he was acting as an agent of law enforcement at that time. The statute was not complied with, was not reduced to writing. I will sustain any objection to that line of testimony. And I'm sure that the State has many, many objections to the ruling of the court."

An angry Richard Walter left the courtroom. He was incensed by the judge's ruling. His work was internationally known and respected and now a small-town judge in Texas was telling him it was not acceptable. When Richard told Jim, still consigned to waiting outside the courtroom, what had happened, Jim was bitterly disappointed. To him, Walter's assessment was nothing short of miraculous and proved beyond doubt that not only was Leisha Hamilton capable of killing Scott, but that she had actually committed the murder. But Jim knew they had to accept the judge's words and press on. They could not give an inch now. Not if Leisha was to be punished for what, Jim was very sure, she'd done to Scott.

The prosecution called as its next witness Dr. Charles Harvey, a deputy medical examiner for Lubbock County. Harvey explained the responsibilities of his position, which included the primary function of determining the cause and manner of death in all unnatural deaths and all unattended deaths within its jurisdiction.

Ladd pushed ahead. He was on surer ground now. And he was determined to leave nothing to chance. "I want to talk to you about blood, blood loss and how a person dies from blood loss. What kind of tissue is blood?"

Dr. Harvey answered, "Blood is a fluid tissue that flows within a confined space called the vascular system. It provides oxygen to all of the living cells in the body. It helps to transport nourishment to all of the cells of the body."

"Consider the case of a twenty-four-year-old male, average size, a little more than average height, average weight—about how much blood would that person have in his body?"

"Between four and five liters. A liter is roughly equivalent to a quart."

"Are you familiar with the terminology a hospital would recognize as a unit of blood?"

"A unit is half a liter."

Slowly, carefully, precisely, Ladd examined the expert. "So how many units of blood would a person, a twenty-four-year-old male in good health, average height and weight, normally have in his body?"

Harvey spoke in a quiet, effective way, which was firm but not argumentative. "He would have between eight and ten units of blood."

"How much blood could a person lose without being at risk of losing his life?"

"It's usually safe to withdraw one unit of blood without too much untoward effect. People may experience some lightheadedness. Loss of two units of blood usually brings about symptomology. And one's life becomes endangered after the loss of three to four units of blood. There is a distinct risk of loss of life."

Ladd held each aspect unearthed up to the light. "At what point, in your opinion, would loss of life be certain, based on a loss of blood?"

"I'd say loss of half of the blood volume, four or five units. If that were not replenished within twenty or thirty minutes, then the vascular system would go into a situation that's called hypovolemic shock. And it can't recover from that."

"Doctor, you said that when a person lost two units of blood there would be a certain symptomology. What do you mean by that?"

"They would be lightheaded. They'd be possibly on the verge of losing consciousness. Standing up, they would run the risk of passing out and losing consciousness, because they don't have the volume of blood in the vascular system needed to maintain the circulation to the head. And by standing up, the blood is dropped lower and they can become dizzy and black out."

"You said that if a person lost between three and four units of blood, their life would be in danger. Why is that?"

"Once you get below a certain level of blood volume, the blood is unable to provide oxygen to the vascular system itself."

Ladd kept on, though he knew from casting glances their way that the jury members were getting antsy. Still he had to prove this part of the case for the record.

"If a person has lost two units of blood, is he normally capable of responding on his own to his circumstances?"

"He might be."

"You said a while ago that a person might be lightheaded if he lost that much blood?"

"Yes."

"Would a person's ability to respond to his circumstances—to defend himself, fight for himself, drive a car, manipulate locks and doors, get himself dressed and go to a medical treatment center—would that begin to be impaired after the loss of two or three units of blood?"

"Yes, it would."

"When the cause of death has been as a result of bludgeoning or beating to death, is that normally associated with head or facial injuries?"

"Not always, but I would say that the vast majority of times that I'm dealing with blunt force trauma deaths, there is a head injury."

Now Ladd wanted to circumvent any posturing by the defense.

"I want to direct your attention to your involvement in the Roger Scott Dunn/Leisha Hamilton murder investigation. Did you do an autopsy in connection with this investigation?"

"No, I did not."

"No body was ever produced to you, nor was any request for an autopsy made; is that correct?"

"That is correct."

At that point the prosecution passed the witness, reserving further interrogation until other expert testimony was heard. Defense counsel reserved his cross-examination of Dr. Harvey until that time.

Ladd and Carper had decided that Carper would direct the examination of the next, crucial witness, who would testify to the infallibility of DNA testing for reversed paternity.

It took the better part of an hour for Dr. Arthur Eisenberg to detail for the jury all his qualifications to be an expert witness in the field of DNA testing. It was crucial to the State's case that the prosecution prove that Scott Dunn had died in the killing room and Dr. Eisenberg's testimony was needed to demonstrate that, beyond reasonable doubt, it was Scott's blood that had been spilled on the carpet and splattered on the walls. When the court had accepted Dr. Eisenberg as an expert witness, Carper asked him to explain reversed paternity.

"The term 'reversed paternity' is used in cases where we have an unknown biological sample and we are trying to establish the identity of the person who contributed that biological sample. We can do that by comparing the potential parents of the person whose sample is unknown to determine if that sample originated from the offspring of the individuals being tested. We perform many of those tests."

Carper then asked about the tests Dr. Eisenberg had performed to determine the origin of the blood in Scott Dunn's bedroom.

"We were sent three pieces of evidentiary material. These were blood scrapings from a tack strip that's used to hold down carpeting, a sample from carpeting and a sample from the padding underneath the carpeting. And we received two vials of blood: one from the mother of the missing individual and one from the father of the missing individual."

Knowing that Wardroup was going to try to use the exceptionally long, six-year investigation to cast doubt on the authenticity of the evidence, Carper led the witness through all the laborious details of establishing and maintaining chain of custody.

Nevertheless, Wardroup renewed his ongoing objections to the authenticity of the samples.

"It is understood. As restated, the court will overrule your objection. Seventy-nine, 80, 81 and 82 are received in evidence," Judge Shaver ruled.

Carper looked at the jury, who despite the complexity of the evidence seemed to be following every word. He asked, "Did you compare DNA from these samples with those two known samples from Scott's mother and father?"

"Yes, we did. Only two of the samples on the first pass actually yielded DNA. The best sample was obtained from the scrapings from the tack strip. The carpeting, when we first isolated it, did not yield sufficient high molecular DNA to do the type of procedure necessary. We also got a small amount of DNA from the padding, which also yielded results."

For a few minutes, Dr. Eisenberg detailed how DNA can be used for identification purposes.

"At conception, that first cell, all the DNA that a person will have in his lifetime, is brought together. Half of the DNA comes from the mother in the egg; half of the DNA comes from the biological father in the sperm. So every cell in the body originates from the doubling of that first cell. Therefore, any cell in the human body can be used to identify the origin of where it came from, who contributed that cell.

"And, in fact, the DNA from one individual to another is unique, with the exception of identical twins. By looking at enough regions of DNA, we can distinguish any two people in the world, with the exception of identical twins. We look at regions of DNA that have many different variations. By comparing the variations between a mother or child and the alleged father, we can determine parentage. And we could also do, as I described, reversed paternity to try and determine the origin of an unknown sample of evidence.

"In DNA testing we look at several different regions, one after another, and we get a pattern from each of those regions. When we look at the pattern of DNA from a child, we compare it to his or her mother. One of the pieces of DNA must match the mother; the other piece must match the true biological father of that child."

"Is it ever possible to get a false positive reading in one of these DNA tests?" Carper asked.

Eisenberg's jaw jutted out like a knight's shield, "When we talk about potential errors or potential mistakes, any type of error or mistake would result in an exclusion. So in terms of error, any error tends to result in a false exclusion, not a false match."

"Doctor, if a sample had been contaminated, would that tend to give a positive reading or just how would that affect the sample?"

"I'm not sure what you are referring to, but in my mind there are two types of contamination: one contaminated with another sample of human DNA or human cells, or bacterial contamination. The only effect that bacteria potentially could have is causing the DNA to degrade to a point where we will not get a pattern. We will *never* get a false pattern," Dr. Eisenberg said firmly.

"We will either get a pattern that is truly representative of the DNA from the individual it originated from or we will get no result."

"Doctor, if you had a blood sample that had been mixed with, say, a cleaning solution, would that deteriorate it or degrade it to a point that possibly you could not get a reading?"

"Sure. There are certainly chemicals that potentially could be added to DNA that can destroy it. Many chemicals can destroy the DNA or degrade it to where one methodology may not be useful and perhaps it could be destroyed to a point where no analysis can be done. You will *not* get a false result. You will destroy it to a point where you will get no result."

"Doctor, did you make a comparison of the samples you obtained from Scott Dunn's parents to the unknown sample you obtained from the tack strip, carpet and carpet pad?"

"Compared to the tack strip and the carpet padding, yes, we did."

"And do you have those results with you?"

"Yes, I do."

"May I see those, please?"

Wardroup tried gamely to rebut the testimony. He objected to the seven posters that had been displayed, reflecting results of the DNA testing on the Dunns' blood samples and blood from the tack strip, carpet and carpet pad. To the untrained eye, the photos looked like a series of bar codes on a white background. His objection was noted by Judge Shaver, but the jury was looking grim.

Indicating the pictures, Eisenberg said, "The end result is that in all seven regions of DNA that were examined, there was one band in common with the blood stain with the mother, there was one band in common with the father, James Dunn.

"Given the results of the DNA probe analysis, it is greater than *10 billion times* more likely that these two people are the biological parents of the individual whose dried blood was recovered from the tack strip, as opposed to them being unrelated to the contributor of the bloodstain.

"So what that translates into probability is ninety-nine with seven nines after that. Simply based upon the way the statistics are done, it can never be 100 percent. But certainly based upon this analysis, there's absolutely no doubt in my mind or *scientific fact* that the bloodstain originated from the offspring of those two individuals."

Carper nodded. "I'll pass the witness."

Dr. Eisenberg had been impressive. The jurors seemed to follow his words closely. His photos of the DNA bands made a compelling picture of the matching of strands between the blood samples from

the crime scene and those of Scott Dunn's mother and father. There
were no doubts. Blood from the crime scene belonged to Scott.

"You may cross-examine, Mr. Wardroup," said Judge Shaver, who
had been listening intently to Dr. Eisenberg.

"Doctor, let me show you exhibits that have previously been
marked State's 34, 36, 38, 33, 37 and 35, and represent to you that
there have been blood spatter pointed out in each one of these
exhibits. The amount of spatter that you see in these exhibits, is that
potentially enough for you to run your DNA testing on?"

"My expertise is not in blood spatter analysis. I *can* tell you that
on a drop of blood about the size of a pin head, DNA is intact and
sufficient for us to do an analysis."

"I take it by your testimony, then, that there were no wall scrapings, Sheetrock scrapings or any of that sort of thing presented to
you for testing?"

"No, sir, there were not."

"Was there any scraping from a door knob in the bedroom?"

"No, sir."

Though there was little redirect, Carper did elicit from Dr.
Eisenberg the fact that, based upon his experience and knowledge,
not every sample submitted to a laboratory is sufficient for DNA
analysis.

Dr. Eisenberg was excused and Judge Shaver adjourned for the
noon recess.

During the next break, Barbara described the photos and Dr.
Eisenberg's testimony to Jim. He was glad the evidence had been so
overwhelming, yet, for a long, painful moment, he could not help
wishing Dr. Eisenberg had been wrong, that the DNA had not
matched his, but Jim knew his wish was not reality. The moment
passed. With agonizing reluctance but growing certainty, Jim had
accepted during the long course of the investigation and amassing
evidence that his son was gone, forever.

chapter nineteen

Blood Tells...

When court reconvened at 1:30 PM, the prosecutor called Dr. Tom Bevel, the blood spatter expert from Oklahoma City, to the stand. After the court had accepted Bevel as a qualified expert, Ladd asked the witness to explain what he did and why it was so important to this case. It was hard to read the jury and Ladd knew they would have to all pay close attention if they were to glean what was crucial from the scientific evidence.

The courtroom was quiet. Bevel spoke in a deep voice that attracted and held attention.

"In an analysis of the blood as it appears on the walls or the floors or the victim or sometimes the suspect's clothing, we try to determine what occurrences are possible that could have produced those stains as they are found. For example, if we had some blood, let's say, on a white screen, one of the first things that I would try and do is to break that down into one of three general categories. That would be a low, a medium or a high velocity type of an occurrence.

"For example, if I have a cut finger and blood is adhering to the end of my finger due to the surface tension of the blood droplet, of course, gravity is trying to pull it down. Once enough weight in that blood droplet is able to overcome the surface tension, then it will break away and simply fall straight downward. That would qualify it in the area of a low velocity blood droplet."

Some in the courtroom seemed to audibly intake their breaths.

"If I start moving my arm around, the gravity isn't the only thing overcoming it. It is actually the movement of the arm and the centrifugal force breaking away. That would make it fall into the range of a medium velocity. We are not talking about how fast the blood travels in air, but rather what it was that broke it away from the blood source. One of the most common areas where you find medium velocity is in beatings. If I hold my hand up high and then if I grab it with the other hand, that force will break the blood up from the blood source and that will then create what is referred to as blood spatter. It will fall either to the ground or to the podium or to the wall, depending upon where you are." Ladd saw that Leisha's face was pale, as if she knew where Bevel was going.

"The last general category would be a high velocity. If I had my hand up in front of a white screen and if it were shot with a bullet and the bullet exited the opposing side of the hand, blood would travel in the same direction as the bullet. If we are up in front of the screen, the blood is considerably smaller, because there's a higher energy or a higher force that is impacted on the blood than either the medium velocity or the low velocity. So looking at the general pattern type, we are able to identify it as being consistent with a high velocity, which could be a gunshot, high speed machinery, expectorant blood, something along that line. Or a medium velocity generally associated with a beating. Or low velocity, simply gravitational pull."

The jurors' heads were moving as Bevel gestured. It was a good sign—for the prosecution. Ladd pressed him.

"Are you saying that by looking at blood in some kind of pattern, you can make some determinations about the kind of incident that put that blood there?"

Bevel nodded. "Yes, sir, you can. You are looking at not just simply the bloodstain itself but, for example, the size of the bloodstains, the numbers of them, the placement, the distribution, the angularity or the direction they are traveling. All of that will help shed light on what might have caused it."

"Are there any other descriptions of bloodstain or pattern you need to explain to the jury in order to describe to them any conclusions you reached in regard to Roger Scott Dunn's murder?"

"I would say at least two other areas. One of the things that's important is the direction the blood is going. You are able to determine that by the long axis of the individual blood droplet. One of the other things that certainly is important in this case is castoff stains. If I am swinging my arm or an object in my hand back over my shoulder, the bloodstains will go out in the direction of the swing and ultimately the long axis will be consistent with the direction the arm is swinging.

"Now, if we have not lost all of the blood as we come back in the other direction, they are going to point just in the opposing direction. So one of the things that is important when we find castoff stains is to determine whether or not it's a back or a forward swing, or if the long axis from one stain is lining up with another stain, which would help us to identify those two stains as being in the same swing."

"Why would it be important to look at blood castoff and find whether or not they were lined up on a particular axis?"

Bevel took a deep breath and said, "One of the things that we try and identify is the minimum number of blows that might have been struck in a beating, which is where you typically get castoff. If you have five bloodstains and you run a straight line through them and they are all basically on the same angle, then likely those all came from that one particular swing."

One jury member gasped. His reaction rippled through the spectators.

Bevel waited for quiet and then went on. "If, however, you have a bloodstain over here that is going in one direction and then beside it you have another one that's going in this direction, those obviously did not come from the same swing. So we would consider that as representing two separate swings.

"We also have to have a blood flow in order to create the castoff. You have to have the weapon striking into an area where there's already sufficient blood flow in order to have enough blood get onto the instrument to either cause spatter or to cause castoff."

To clarify, Ladd asked, "If I were striking you in the head with some object that was heavy enough to do some kind of damage to you, would my first blow have blood on it?"

"No, sir, it would not."

"Why is that?"

"It may have blood on it, but not in sufficient quantity for the centrifugal force to pull a blood droplet off."

"So if I understand your testimony correctly, I'd have to deliver at least a second blow into the same area that I delivered that first blow to have enough blood to cause castoff?"

Bevel nodded. "Either castoff or spatter."

"I want to show you some photographs that have already been introduced into evidence and ask you to take a look at those. Do they appear to be from the same area of a room?"

"They do."

"And what area would that be?"

"That would be the ceiling."

"If it pleases the court, let's step down in front of that microphone so we can show the jury a little bit better what we are talking about."

Moving purposefully, Bevel took his place near the exhibits.

Ladd asked, "Would you describe for the jury what they are going to be looking at in terms of your science in these photos?"

Bevel pointed to the first photo. "This is the ceiling of the northeast bedroom. There are three bloodstains in one area and two in another area that my fingers are pointing to.

"What you are going to be looking at is the long axis of the bloodstain, showing the direction. It is running along the bottom edge of the photograph. I will keep the photograph the same direction, but I am going to show another bloodstain that is beside it. And it is running a different direction. So the long axis is not following the same line as the first bloodstain that we looked at.

"These are consistent with castoff. So there is an object that has some blood on it that is swinging below the ceiling. The blood is coming off with that swing, going up to the ceiling.

"We have at least three different long axes on the bloodstains that are not following the same line. So that would be consistent with three separate swings as opposed to just one swing."

"From the drops that you've discussed on the ceiling, Tom, can you make any conclusions or opinions about whether or not those are low, high or medium velocity?"

"Those would certainly be consistent with a medium velocity, which is having come from a castoff or an item that is swinging, projecting the blood off of it, and the blood traveling upward until it strikes the ceiling."

"Is there any way those drops could have been put on the ceiling by somebody being shot?"

Bevel shook his head. His face was intense and purposeful. "No, sir. We are dealing with an entirely different size of bloodstain. A pretty good rule of thumb basically states this: As the energy or the velocity of whatever it is that is breaking the blood away from the blood source increases, there's a decrease in the size of the blood droplet. When we start talking about a high velocity such as a gunshot, it is not going to produce the size of bloodstain we are seeing on the ceiling and is also not going to get to that distance. It is not consistent with what I expect to find from a gunshot."

Ladd paused to scan the jury. They looked weary. Now Ladd raised his voice emphasizing his next words. "Have you ever seen blood spatter castoff that was made as the result of somebody being killed or hurt with a knife?"

"I have seen castoff from knife wounds, yes, sir."

"Is this consistent with a knife wound?"

The jurors were alert now, leaning forward.

"On a knife, because of the way that it is typically swung, the majority of the blood comes off of the tip end. That's a very small surface area; therefore, you get a very small blood droplet. It will not produce something like this and certainly not going to the ceiling."

"Is there anything else that you can think of besides a beating, a bludgeoning, that would account for that kind of castoff on the ceiling of that room?"

"Not that I can think of, no."

"Have you ever seen castoff as a result of somebody swinging an ax, hatchet, some sharp-bladed instrument that is also used with a lot of weight and force?"

"Certainly. If you are able to get blood on the blunt end as opposed to the sharp end, you can get something like this. If you are talking about the blade edge, because of it coming to such a narrow point, the blood size usually ends up being pretty small."

"It would have to be a blunt ax?"

"Certainly."

Ladd turned the questioning toward a second set of photographs. "Would you explain to the jury what we have there?"

"It's the south wall of the northeast bedroom. The one that is going to be on your right shows the long axis, both going up and also going down, so opposing directions."

"In reference to the kind of velocity that's needed to make that kind of blood spatter and that kind of blood castoff, you describe that as medium velocity?"

"That is correct, sir."

"Put in some kind of measurement that a layperson can relate to, what kind of measurement of force are we talking about?"

"Medium velocity by definition is from five to twenty-five feet per second. Either one of them can produce what is referred to as medium velocity."

"All right. Why don't you go ahead and have a seat?"

Ladd had found his stride. It was time to focus in on the real evidence that Scott Dunn had been violently killed.

When the witness had returned to the box, Ladd asked, "Tom, considering the blood on the ceiling and the blood on the wall, are you able to make any kind of conclusions about how many times the person would have been struck?"

"I can, if I can explain. We have got a little bit of a problem, in that I didn't get to see the crime scene itself and context was very important. From the photographs and from questions that I've asked, I am not able to align the bloodstains on the wall with those on the ceiling.

"If they are in different places and they do not align, then that increases the number of blows that would be required. But it's certainly possible that they actually do align. And if they do, then I don't have as many blows. If they are in separate areas, then the blows increase."

"Well," Ladd said, "to be safe, let's assume that the bloodstains that you were seeing on the wall align perfectly with bloodstains you are seeing on the ceiling. Then how many blows would have been delivered, including that first blow that wouldn't have had any blood on it?"

"It would have been a minimum of four blows." One of the jurors winced.

Ladd didn't miss the reaction; he pressed on. "You said in order to deliver the kind of drops we were seeing in the blood spatter and castoff, it would have had to have been delivered at five to twenty-five feet per second?"

"Yes, sir."

"How fast would the weapon that is delivering those droplets have to be moving in order to create that blood spatter and castoff?"

"In my opinion, it is going to be in the upper end, certainly for the spatter. But I cannot conclusively give you an exact speed based upon what we have here."

"Would fifteen to twenty-five feet per second be—"

"It would be easily within that range, yes, sir."

"Keeping within that range, is a blow that's being delivered with some kind of hard object capable of doing any kind of injury to a human being?"

"Most certainly."

"What can it do?"

Wardroup interrupted. "I'm going to object to this witness not being qualified as any kind of physician at this point, your honor."

"I will overrule your objection," Judge Shaver said firmly.

Ladd began again. "I had asked you what type of injury it could cause."

"If you are being struck with a blunt object in the torso, the limbs, you certainly can have internal bleeding, for example, and you get a lot of bruising." Bevel was unshakable in his certainty. "That alters considerably if you change the target to the head. The head will produce considerably greater volume of blood that will be found external of the body as opposed to being struck in the chest with a blunt object. So, it depends what and where."

"You stated earlier that you worked twenty-seven years as an Oklahoma City police officer. Have you ever been to a crime scene in which a bludgeoning death occurred?"

"Yes, sir."

"Most of them are to the head, are they not?"

"The majority of the time, yes, sir."

"If someone were being struck at the speed that we have talked about with a hard object in the head, could that break the skin?"

"Yes, sir."

"Could it break the bone?"

"Yes, sir."

From time to time Ladd glanced over to Leisha, who was studiously ignoring him. He knew it was just an act. She heard everything. He went on.

"Could it break the skull?"

"Yes, sir."

"Is it possible that whoever was being hit as a result of that blood spatter and castoff could have been hit more than four times?"

"It is certainly possible. Generally, when we talk about blows, we refer to it as the minimum number. It certainly could have been more."

Ladd showed Bevel a piece of bloodstained carpet and a similar section of carpet pad, which had been marked for identification. "Do you recognize these?"

Bevel replied that Tal English had mailed them to him only a few weeks earlier, toward the end of April of the current year.

"Tom, what kind of tests did you perform on these?"

"A saturation test to try and identify how much blood it takes to give a like area of coverage, reference the carpet and the pad, using carpet that was from the same residence."

"Would you explain to the jury exactly how you did the saturation tests, the processes you went through?"

Bevel explained that he had used carpet and padding that approximated the thickness of the sample carpet and pad from the crime scene. "We were trying to determine how much blood it takes to absorb naturally and to wick into this particular pad."

"And when you actually did the saturation test, you were pouring blood?"

"We were using whole human blood that was Hebronated and it was poured not actually onto the pad, but through the carpet. Hebronated means that it had been treated with an anticoagulant so that it wouldn't coagulate too quickly and become unusable. In actuality that made the test more conservative, because the Hebronated blood is thinned and will spread faster and it's an anticoagulant, as opposed to blood that is freshly out of the body, which will not spread quite as fast."

Ladd saw the jury growing fidgety but he had to lay it all out once and for all for them and the record.

"How does it make the results of your test more conservative?"

"Simply because the area of saturation would be reached faster with a smaller volume of Hebronated blood, as opposed to blood directly from the human body," Bevel clarified.

"If you are using Hebronated blood to make the saturation test and the person who is the source of the blood that made that stain did not have blood thinner in his bloodstream, then your test would show less blood than what he actually lost?"

"That is very likely, yes, sir."

"All right. Would you go ahead with your explanation of how you did this test?"

"This was done on a cement floor. A piece of plastic was placed over the cement floor, taped down, which would represent the plastic covering from the pad. The reason that we did not use the pad from the crime scene is that it had insufficient areas that were not already bloodstained. And the danger of having my test blood travel over to an area that we were using for a control area was too great, so we chose not to do that. The carpet was placed over the plastic on the floor and then we started adding 200 milliliters of the whole human blood at a time, pouring it on the carpeted area. We were waiting about forty-five minutes to an hour to allow the natural absorption and then noting the size."

"When you added all the blood you needed to approximate the same size of the stain that you outlined on the carpet pad, how much blood did it take to make a stain of that size? Is that a precise amount or is that described in terms of a range of volumes?"

"We described it in terms of a range. And that came to 875 milliliters on the lower end to 933 milliliters on the upper end. To approximate what that actually is in other terms, if you give blood at a blood bank, what they refer to as a unit is 500 milliliters. So when we are talking about 933, we are talking about 67 milliliters less than what you would have in a two-unit volume of blood. And 875 milliliters is 375 milliliters more than one unit of blood."

Ladd kept his voice up to hold the jurors' attention. He wanted them with him when he cut to the chase. "You attempted, at my instructions and because of the way you are, to make every estimate of blood saturation and loss conservative; is that correct?"

"That is a correct statement."

"Did your test account for the blood that would have been lost from an individual in a beating death that would have been soaked up by his hair?"

"No, sir."

"Did your test account for the blood loss that would have been associated from a beating death with blood lost in sheets, blankets, mattress or mattress pad?"

"No, sir."

"If there were towels, dish towels or other things of that nature used to clean up the blood left over after a beating death, did your saturation test take into account that amount of blood?"

"No."

"Tom, let me ask you to step down to this model of the northeast bedroom of Leisha Hamilton's apartment." Bevel stepped out of the witness stand again and stood beside the model apartment.

"If you would, let's assume that the blood lost in this crime scene was identified as human blood and the clean-up you see in this area on the walls represent the range of the wiping motions. Do you have any opinion about what kind of crime was committed in that room?"

Bevel looked Ladd straight in the eye. "Yes, sir. A bludgeoning."

"Would that have occurred to the head area?"

"It is more likely to have occurred to a head area than any other area, yes, sir."

"If the person who was the subject of that bludgeoning normally slept with his head placed toward that end of the room, does that increase or decrease any of your opinion?"

"I would say it actually increases."

"And how many times, at a minimum, would that person have had to be struck in the head to cause that kind of blood spatter, castoff, clean-up action?"

"Based upon the castoff stains, it would have been a minimum of four blows."

"Is there any way that blood could have been placed there on the ceiling, on the wall, by a high-powered nose bleed or somebody's leg being bashed with a hammer or some other hard object?"

Once again, the courtroom was pin drop quiet.

"No, sir," Bevel said firmly.

Bevel had been an excellent witness—extremely well prepared with his answers, but not above the jury's heads. Ladd returned to the prosecution table. "I pass this witness."

On cross-examination, Wardroup introduced another element into the case: Okay, he theorized, someone may have been killed, but not Scott Dunn.

"With regard to your opinions as to the castoff on the wall and on the ceiling, if that's from a different blood source than the person who was injured, then you can't draw an opinion as to how many times that person may have been hit, could you?" His question pointed to a new line of defense

Bevel hesitated for a moment then said, "If it is a different person, then I could draw some conclusions as to how many times that person was hit. But it will not correlate to this one, if it is a different person," Bevel replied.

"So if the blood beneath the carpet was type O and we don't know what the blood on the ceiling and the wall is, then you can't draw all of the conclusions, without question, that you did for Mr. Ladd, can you?"

"Without knowing that it is a consistent blood source, I cannot," he admitted.

Wardroup had no further questions.

At the prosecution table Ladd's face was flushed. He knew he needed to refocus the jury's attention on Tom Bevel's direct testimony, so Ladd asked the witness to repeat his estimation of blood loss. Bevel was adamant: at a bare minimum, just under two units of blood.

The witness was excused. Roy Carper, again taking over for the prosecution, called DPS serologist Cathy McCord. Carper showed McCord the Sheetrock scrapings from the bedroom ceiling. McCord said she had examined the scrapings at two different time periods, having received the samples from Detective Tal English on both occasions.

The first time she examined the samples, McCord said, she determined only that human blood was present in the sample. On the second submission, she attempted to determine the DQ Alpha, the blood type.

Carper offered the samples for the State. Then he directed her attention to the carpet and padding, which already were in evidence. She said she had conducted some tests on both, which had been submitted to her by Detective George White.

"First, you determined whether or not human blood was present. Then I believe you attempted to determine the ABO blood type and then you attempted to determine the DQ Alpha type. If you would, please, tell the jury what your findings and conclusions were."

In easy to understand language, McCord told the court that the human blood she had found on the carpet padding, the tack strip and the carpet itself was type O.

She said she also examined a sample of Sheetrock scraping from the wall near the light switch and found human blood, but in a quantity insufficient for further testing. She found human blood on scrapings from the concrete floor under the padding, but not in sufficient quantity for typing purposes. McCord said human blood was present on the scrapings from the ceiling, but she did not attempt to type it.

Then McCord told of examining the pubic hair from Tim Smith and the blood submitted by Leisha Hamilton. Neither was consistent with the blood on the carpet, padding or tack strip.

When Carper questioned McCord about her examination of the hairs from Scott Dunn's hairbrush, she said those hairs had not had roots; therefore, she could not get a DNA result.

"So you cannot say for certainty that the DQ Alpha type of the blood on the carpet nailing strip and carpet pad came from Scott Dunn from your DQ Alpha analysis?"

"No," she admitted. There was a moment of silence.

"However, what Dr. Eisenberg did is a completely different test. And based upon the reversed paternity situation, he could make that determination, couldn't he?"

"Yes," she said, her face open and honest.

During a brief recross-examination, Wardroup asked McCord about her testing of a doorknob that had been taken from Leisha's bedroom door. McCord said she had found a spot of blood on the knob and had determined it to be type A.

Wardroup moved on to another area of questioning, asking McCord if she had checked the carpet sample for bone fragments.

She nodded and said she had conducted such tests, but found none. Prodded by Wardroup, McCord said she had found no evidence of skin, brain matter or human tissue other than blood.

Returning to the blood on the scrapings taken from the ceiling, Wardroup asked McCord again if she had determined a blood type.

"There was not sufficient quantity to try it."

"So any of the droplets or castoff or whatever that are marked by little Xs here on the ceiling or here on the wall, you can't tell what ABO type they are?"

"No."

"And you can't tell the jury that they are the same or different as Scott Dunn's blood?"

"No."

"There's not any way for you to know how long that blood spatter had been in place on the wall or the ceiling, is there?"

"No," she said quietly.

The defense had scored a few points. Leisha had a glint in her eyes.

The witness was excused.

Determined not to let the jury be swayed, Rusty Ladd recalled Dr. Charles Harvey, the deputy medical examiner from Lubbock County.

"Doctor, this morning we were talking about blood loss and how much blood a person could lose. Do you recall that testimony?"

"Yes, sir, I do."

"If you would, assume that somebody is lying on the floor, on top of a bunch of blankets, in the approximate center of the area marked by the semicircle against the wall. Assume with me that this person has been struck in the head area at least four times with enough velocity to cause blood to cast off with a velocity five to twenty-five feet per second, probably fifteen to twenty-five feet per second.

"Now assume with me that the blood loss in just the carpet itself is anywhere from approximately 1.3 units of blood to 2 units of blood. Assume that the person lost that blood through an injury to his head, caused by those blows. Would you expect that person to be able to function on his own without immediate medical help?"

"No, sir, I don't think so."

"In your medical opinion, if a person had suffered those kinds of injuries, would those injuries be fatal?"

"I would expect they could be fatal. I think that, in the hypothetical that you presented to me, we are talking about serious injury to the head."

"Would those kinds of injuries render a person unconscious?"

"I would expect that, yes."

"Would those kinds of injuries cause actual damage to the brain itself?"

"More than likely."

"Would you expect to see brain matter in the same quantity and the same places as you would expect to see blood in a bludgeoning death about the head?"

"No, I wouldn't."

"Doctor, I am asking you to look at the size of the outline stain roughly in the center of the carpet. And then, if you would, let's look at the back and the size of that stain. If you would assume with me that a person whose head is lying about where those stains were made was also lying on any kind of blankets, mattress, sheets, pillows, that sort of thing, would you expect those kinds of things to affect the amount of blood that might be lost?"

"Yes, I think they would."

"And you testified earlier that after a person had lost two units of blood you would expect that he would begin to get shocky? And after a loss of three to four units of blood, he begins to approach a fatal condition?"

"Yes, sir, that's correct."

In the total silence that followed, Ladd looked over to Leisha, who had assumed a defensive posture. He couldn't entirely suppress his smile as he turned the witness over to Rick Wardroup for cross-examination.

"If the assumption Mr. Ladd asked you to make regarding being hit four times with a blunt object isn't proved, if the blood spatter up here on the ceiling and on the wall is not shown to be from the same person Mr. Ladd says was lying on this carpet and you don't know where this blood came from, if it just came from a leg or something like that, would that affect your impression or your opinion as to whether or not that person might have been *in extremis?*"

"I'm not quite sure what you are asking here."

"If we throw out the so-called spatter on the ceiling, because it's not shown to be type O, or the wall, because it is not shown to be type O, and all we have is type O on the carpet, we are not assuming anymore that anybody's been hit in the head; all we can assume now is that we have X amount of blood loss. Okay?"

"Yes, sir."

"Now, would that affect your opinion as to whether or not the person would be *in extremis* or would potentially die?"

"Our estimate of the blood loss that's in the carpet is between one and a third and two units of blood. With the possible hypothesis that there is additional absorbing material that exists in between the carpet and the floor, so that we are looking at probably more than two units."

Wardroup raised his eyebrows. "You say probably. You may be saying maybe more than two units, isn't that right?"

"No, I am saying that we're with the assumption that there's other absorbing material in between the body of the deceased and the carpet."

"That was Mr. Ladd's assumption. I am not asking you to assume that."

"Then the only assumption that I can make is that we have what's measured in the carpet."

"Exactly."

"Two units of blood is not necessarily lethal," Dr. Harvey admitted.

Wardroup announced that he would reserve further cross-examination.

On redirect, Ladd asked Harvey, "If I lose even a unit of blood, because I have had some kind of accident—I have been cut, stabbed, hurt—isn't there usually some other kind of tissue damage that, along with the blood loss, would make me seek some kind of medical treatment?"

"That's frequently the case."

"And as the loss of blood increases to one and a half, two units of blood or more, the likelihood that someone would need immediate medical attention also increases, does it not?"

He looked over; the jury was with him now.

"Yes, it does," Harvey said grimly.

Silent for a few moments, Ladd let the information settle in. He wanted the jury to know just how important this evidence was. He glanced at the jury. They were intently watching the witness. Then he indicated that, subject to recall, the witness could step down.

chapter twenty

Wherein Lies the Truth

The tension was building inside Jim Dunn as he waited in the room reserved for witnesses. The prosecutor called his next witness, Patrick Lane, the mechanic who had been helping Scott Dunn reconstruct his white Camaro. The compact, pugnacious Lane strode to the stand, looked for a moment at Leisha, then looked away. Ladd didn't miss the visual exchange.

In response to Ladd's questioning, Lane said Scott had never mentioned Leisha Hamilton to him. He was surprised when he got a call from her after Scott turned up missing and she told him she was Scott Dunn's girlfriend.

When Ladd began speaking his voice was low. The witness leaned forward. "What did she ask you?" Ladd questioned.

"She asked me if I had seen Scott."

"Did you ask her anything?"

Lane spat out the next words. "I asked her how she got my phone number."

"What did she tell you?"

The witness didn't miss a beat. "She told me she was looking through Scott's billfold and found it."

"Was that the end of the conversation you had with her?"

"Pretty much."

On cross-examination, Wardroup asked Lane the date of Leisha Hamilton's call. Lane said he couldn't recall the exact date, but it was the day after he and Scott had discussed changing the motor from Scott's white car to the yellow one.

Wardroup pounced. "So you talked to Scott the very day before this phone call came?"

"Yeah. He was sick."

"But the lady didn't tell you when she had looked in the wallet. It may have been a week before, it might have been the day after, whatever?"

"Well, the week before I wouldn't think he would have had my phone number."

"When did he get your phone number?"

"That day I was talking to him."

Wardroup indicated he was through with the witness.

Ladd had nothing on re-direct. He asked Judge Shaver for two minutes so that he could check to see if Tal English was in the building. He wanted to recall the detective for one important question.

When English returned to the witness stand, Ladd pinpointed one of his meetings with Leisha.

"Did you talk to her at that point about the whereabouts of Scott Dunn's wallet?"

"Yes, sir. She told us that his pants had been lying on the couch, his wallet was gone, but his keys were still in his pocket."

"She said his wallet was gone?"

"Yes, sir."

Wardroup indicated that he had no further questions of the witness.

Judge Shaver addressed Rusty Ladd. "All right. What says the State?"

Ladd replied, "Your honor, the State of Texas rests its case."

Judge Shaver nodded solemnly. "All right. Members of the jury, it's now three-thirty. We will recess for twenty minutes and then commence further testimony."

After the short recess, before the jury returned to the courtroom, in a move that was no surprise to Ladd or to Jim Dunn when he heard about it, Wardroup moved for an instructed verdict of acquittal. "In support of that motion, we would respectfully show that the State has wholly failed to show the *corpus delicti,* that there has been a killing in this matter. The court, I am sure, is aware of the three opinions in the Fisher case, which say that while there's not a requirement of a *corpus delicti,* all the cases referred to in that case have either a confession or some evidence of a death. We don't have any of that in this case.

"Furthermore, the second ground for this motion is that there's been no showing that even if Scott Dunn is no longer living, Leisha Hamilton in any fashion caused the death, either as a party or as the direct actor. For those reasons we would request the court to instruct a verdict."

Judge Shaver's voice was decisive. "Motion denied," he said.

And so, six years after anyone had claimed to see Scott Dunn alive, Rick Wardroup began to present his case in Leisha Hamilton's defense. He called Detective Tal English as his first witness.

After a few preliminary questions, Wardroup went straight to the heart of his defense: Scott's not dead, but if he is, someone else killed him.

He asked English about all the places detectives had searched for Scott's body. English told him about searching the section of land close to where Tim Smith grew up, at the area around an aircraft training facility where Tim Smith went to school at one time and south of Shallowater.

"Did there come a time you interviewed a man who lived in Shallowater by the name of Alan Parks?"

English's reply was short, clipped and to the point. "Yes, sir."

"And was he a suspect in the disappearance of Scott Dunn?"

"Yes, sir."

"Did you believe he told you the truth?"

English didn't hesitate. "No, sir."

"Did you ask him or did you request a subpoena or a search warrant for a sample of his blood or hair?"

"No, sir."

"Regarding Tim Smith, did you ever request a search warrant for his blood?"

"No, sir."

"Did there come a time that a man named Doug Holden was a suspect in Scott Dunn's disappearance?"

"His name was given to me as possible, yes, sir."

"Did you interview Mr. Holden?"

"Yes, sir, I did."

In mind-numbing detail, Wardroup went over the same ground as Ladd's direct, trying to find holes or inconsistencies in English's testimony.

"And was there ever a request made for hair samples or blood samples from Mr. Holden?"

"No, sir."

Then on cross-examination, Ladd meticulously addressed every aspect of Wardroup's direct.

The jury was growing weary. Even the judge had closed his eyes.

"You have been assigned to this case from the time it happened all the way up to appearing in court; is that right?"

"That's correct."

"Over that course of time, isn't it true that every two-bit amateur in Lubbock County and from a lot of other places has some kind of opinion on what happened there?"

English nodded. "Yes, sir."

"That often results in some kind of 'lead' being passed on to the police department; is that right?"

"Yes, sir."

"From all sorts of other people?"

"That is correct."

"Did you follow down all those leads as best as you could?"

"Yes, I did."

"Did you have any evidence to present to anybody that Alan Parks might be involved in this murder?"

"No, sir."

"Did you have any evidence that you believed to be credible to present to anybody regarding Doug Holden?"

"No, sir."

"Did you have any evidence to present regarding anybody else's involvement in this crime except Leisha Hamilton and Tim Smith?"

"No, sir."

"If you had, you would have presented it, wouldn't you?"

"Yes, sir, I would."

"In regard to the burglary that was reported at Leisha and Scott's apartment, did you get any information about the whereabouts of those items from anybody except Leisha Hamilton?"

"No, sir."

"She gave you those nuggets of information bit by bit as the investigation progressed, didn't she?"

"Yes, sir."

Ladd dismissed the detective.

Nothing so far had surprised Ladd and Carper. They had expected that Rick Wardroup's first line of defense would be that the State could not prove that Scott Dunn had been murdered. That second defense posture would be that, if Scott had been killed, someone other than Leisha Hamilton had committed the murder. And, the prosecutors had expected that Wardroup would do his best to shift the focus to Alan Parks. However, when Wardroup next called Beth Parks, now Beth Bartin, the two prosecutors glanced at each other, eyebrows raised.

Beth Bartin, small and blonde, wore a navy blue dress, which rustled as she walked forward.

With a few well-chosen questions, Wardroup led Beth through her background and her first knowledge of Scott Dunn. She said she had known Scott when he lived across the street from her in Shallowater, but they had lost touch when he moved to Abilene. Then, right before he disappeared, she saw Scott at a fast food restaurant one night, the first time she had seen him since he left Shallowater. At that time, she was living with Alan Parks in what she described as an abusive relationship.

In a soft voice she recalled that Scott had promised to help her get away from Alan. In fact, the day he disappeared, he was supposed, according to Bartin, to pick her up at her mother's and take her to the home of a friend who lived east of Lubbock, at Buffalo Lake.

Wardroup interrupted the flow of her narrative. "The plans you made, were they even longer range than all of that?" Then he asked her if they were romantically involved.

"No, we were good friends."

"All right. So he was going to come get you."

"Right."

"And did he come get you?"

"No."

"Did you call his work?"

"Yes. He had gone home sick."

"And what happened after that?"

"I waited and I waited and I waited and he never showed up."

Wardroup asked her about her conversations with Alan Parks regarding her relationship with Scott. She said he had threatened her and Scott.

Beth squirmed in her seat; she looked ready to cry. "They were deadly threats. When Alan found out I had Scott's work phone number, he grabbed my hair and told me that if he ever caught me and my little boyfriend, that he would kill both of us. That he was going to have words with Scott."

"Was Alan Parks an only child?"

"No."

"What kind of siblings does he have?"

"He has two brothers."

"When Scott didn't show up, what did you do?"

Beth folded her hands across her breast and said almost in a whisper, "I waited until it was nighttime and then I figured he was not going to show. I stayed with my mom that evening, then I went home to get some clothes and I came back to my mom's house. I was really, really, really upset, though."

"Did Alan come home that night?"

She shook her head. "No."

"How do you know?"

"Because I know Alan. If I wasn't there, he was going to go look for me."

"Beth, what happened the next day?"

"Let's see, Alan came home about—Fred, Alan's brother, came there first. It was about three or four o'clock in the morning. I asked him where Alan was. 'Well, he went to Mom's house to change.' I was like, why, we have a shower here, you know. He didn't answer why. He said, 'Well, I guess he fell in the mud.'"

"Did it strike you as unusual that Alan didn't come home to clean up?" Wardroup asked.

"Well, yeah, because that was our home. We had a perfectly good shower there."

"When was the next time you saw Alan?"

"He came in, I guess, shortly after that."

"Now, did you have any conversation about Scott Dunn's disappearance?"

"Once, my mom handed me the newspaper to read about Scott's disappearance. And I just read the first couple of lines and Alan took the paper, tore it up and said not to ever look at that stuff again."

"When you said 'stuff,' I had the idea that wasn't the language used," the defense attorney remarked.

"No, it wasn't the language."

"What did he do after that?"

She looked around, her blue eyes widening with apprehension. "He just told me not to ever look at it again because he would kill me."

Wardroup next directed his questions toward Alan Parks's reputation for violence. "Had Alan been in the service?"

"Yes. He was in the Marines."

"And did he have any special training that you were aware of?"

"Special training? I don't know. I mean he told me, basically what they do is train to—"

Carper objected to the question on the grounds of hearsay and Judge Shaver sustained his objection.

Wardroup resumed. "Beth, did there come a time that Alan admitted he knew where the body of Scott Dunn was?"

"Yes."

"Was he intoxicated when he told you? Was he high?"

"He was high."

"What happened?"

"He had told me, 'Well, guess what, I know where your little boyfriend is. And he's dead and he's buried ten miles south of Shallowater.' And he told me 'I took care of the problem; you will never see it again.'"

Beth said she had not given the police this information then, because she was "scared for her life." She said that, finally, she became so upset, she called a hotline counselor.

"After that, did there come a time that Detectives English and White came to visit with you?"

"Yeah."

"And did you tell them what you've told us?"

"Yeah."

Wardroup looked at the jury. They seemed caught up in Beth Bartin's story. He pressed on.

"Did they ask you about Alan's propensity for weapons or whether he had weapons—"

"They came in and checked for weapons. They just asked if we had any kind of weapons around the house. And I said that the only weapons we had were what Alan had from the Marines, a couple of machetes."

"Did Alan indicate to you how he would get rid of a body when he had committed a murder?"

"Yes."

Again, Carper objected to the question as hearsay.

"Sustained."

"What kind of work did Alan do?"

"Construction, concrete, tearing up concrete, pouring concrete, stuff like that."

"Did Alan ever do any carpet laying work to the best of your knowledge?"

"Yes."

"Where did he do that?"

"He did it for little odd jobs. Alan Parks has never held a job for very long. He's always had little side jobs with his family, friends, whatever he could get."

"Did you ever see him patch carpet?"

"With his cousin, I guess."

"So he had that capacity?"

"Yes, yes."

"Beth, are you scared of Alan Parks as you sit there right now?"

"Yeah, I am scared," she said with a slight tremor in her voice.

With that, Wardroup relinquished the witness to the prosecution.

Ladd leaned toward Carper. "Do you want to take this one?" Carper nodded, then rose to his feet to begin cross-examination. Beth Bartin's testimony was potentially damaging to the State's case unless he could find some way to cast doubt on her credibility.

Under a barrage of rapid-fire questioning, Beth Bartin admitted that when she was in high school, she got pregnant and now, at the age of twenty-three, she had three children, all of whom had different fathers.

"Then, I got mixed up with Alan. I went to high school with him. We were friends. He went to the Marines and when he came out, I got with him—Alan was a real sweet talker. He could sweet-talk any woman into doing anything he wanted. He was very manipulative.

"But he beat me up a lot of times—broke my arm. He beat me while I was pregnant with our daughter and the doctors told me she had an 80 percent chance of dying at birth."

Backing away from her, Carper asked a few more preliminary questions and then, moving up close, he got down to the major ones.

"You said that the night that Scott Dunn came up missing, you had packed some things and you were waiting on him to come get you?"

"Yes, at my mom's."

Carper picked up the pace. "Why were you waiting at your mom's?"

"Because I couldn't be picked up at my house, you know."

"Why not?"

"My neighbor was kind of Alan's friend."

Carper wasn't about to be put off. He said aggressively. "Listen to my question. Why couldn't you get picked up at your house?"

"Because I was living with Alan."

"Did Scott Dunn pick you up?"

"No."

"What did you do when he didn't pick you up?"

"I waited. I didn't do anything."

"Where did you wait?"

"At my mom's."

"At what time did you go back to your house?"

"It was later that evening. I went home once about eight o'clock, I guess."

"Why did you go home at eight o'clock?"

"To get my clothes. I had a little girl at the time. I had to get all her diapers and her clothes."

Carper was intent on making his point. "Now, you went back to your house at eight o'clock and got your diapers and your clothes and then you went to your mom's?"

"Right."

"And what time was it you left your mom's and went back to your house?"

"I stayed with my mom that evening."

Carper looked at the jury to see if they were taking in this line of questioning. "Ma'am, I believe your testimony was that later that night, first Alan's brother came in and you said, 'Where's Alan?' and the brother said—"

"That was the morning," Beth said, her voice quavering.

"The next morning?"

"Correct."

"Okay." Carper felt sorry for the girl, but he felt even worse for the parents of Scott Dunn. Despite her discomfort, Carper knew he had to get the full story. "My question is, when did you go back to your house?"

She shook her head and tears began trickling down her cheeks. "I don't remember. It was late that evening. I don't remember."

Carper wasn't about to get distracted. "You said morning. Now, is it morning or evening?"

"It was morning."

"What time that morning did you go back to your house?"

"That morning? It was before four, because that's the time they showed up, because I remember looking at the clock and saying, 'It's four o'clock in the morning. What are you doing out—'"

Next Carper turned to her credibility. "Do you have a conviction for theft?"

The tears were flowing faster and Beth swallowed before she spoke. "This was when I was in college."

Sympathetic or not, Carper needed the truth out in the open.

"Yes or no, ma'am?" Carper said quietly.

She nodded reluctantly. "Yes. This happened—"

He repeated. "Ma'am, it can be answered yes or no."

"Somebody else did this to me."

"Ma'am," Carper's insisted. "It can be answered yes or no."

"Yes."

"Do you have a conviction for theft?"

"Yes," she said with a shudder.

Carper had what he needed; he wasn't going to hammer the young woman.

Carper passed the witness, who sat motionless, eyes downcast, letting the tears course down her cheeks. Wardroup rushed to shore up his witness's shaky testimony.

Looking at his witness Wardroup asked, "Beth, are you okay?"

She sighed, "I'm tired."

"Is there anything that you have said today that you hadn't already told the police?"

"No."

"Would you like to help find Scott Dunn?"

"Yes."

Wardroup said grimly, "I will pass the witness."

On re-cross, Carper asked, "Did Alan often brag about killing lots of folks?"

"Yes."

Carper sat down. "Pass the witness."

When Beth Bartin had been excused, Wardroup said, "Your honor, the defense rests."

The courtroom buzzed.

Shaver held up his hand for quiet. "What says the State?" Shaver looked at the prosecution's table.

"Your honor, the State closes." Rusty Ladd announced.

Judge Shaver turned his attention to the jury and made a brief statement. "Members of the jury, both sides have closed the evidence. This means the court must submit its charge to the attorneys and give them an opportunity to examine it, state their objections thereto.

"I will try to be ready to read you the charge at nine in the morning."

That night, Jim and Barbara and Richard Walter went to a Mexican restaurant for dinner. They allowed themselves, for the first time, to feel optimistic. Jim was really glad he would no longer be confined to the suffocating waiting room for witnesses. It had gotten increasingly hard for him to sit still when Leisha's mother or Leisha walked by the open door and glared at him or made rude remarks. Jim didn't want to match stares with Leisha, but her green eyes were mesmerizing, drawing his gaze, and for a moment the two would glare at each other. Her face tightened and Jim could see hatred there. He felt sure his face reflected his own determination to gain justice for Scott. Unyielding. Unflinching. Each day he waited in the tiny space had inched by. At night he tossed, sleepless. Despite his weariness now, he looked forward to tomorrow morning. He would be allowed back in the courtroom to hear the attorneys' final arguments.

chapter twenty-one

Leisha's Verdict

Friday morning, May 16, the courtroom buzzed expectantly. Jim, Barbara, Richard and Pam arrived early, eager to hear attorneys for both sides present their final arguments. The three of them watched grimly as Leisha Hamilton walked briskly to the defense table, laughing and talking with her mother and father, appearing to be totally at ease. She smiled at the jurors as they filed into their customary places. Most of them avoided eye contact with anyone. One, the man on whom Leisha had focused her attention throughout the trial, looked at her but did not acknowledge her smile.

The prosecution would speak first, then the defense, then the prosecution would conclude. Although the prosecution would have two opportunities to speak, each side would have an equal amount of time for its argument. When Judge Shaver had been seated and the session officially called, Roy Carper rose and began summing up the case for the State of Texas.

Carper reminded the jury that this was the sixth anniversary of Scott Dunn's death. "And here we are. Still nothing heard from Scott Dunn; no word to anybody."

Next, Carper explained the charge, saying that it set out what the offense of murder entails: "That a person intentionally or knowingly causes the death of an individual or, intending to cause serious bodily injury, does an act clearly dangerous to human life, which causes the death of an individual. That constitutes the offense of murder."

The charge also set out two ways that murder can be committed, Carper told the jury. "One is by direct act by the defendant, Leisha Hamilton. Another is by acting as a party in concert with some other person in causing the death of Roger Scott Dunn."

Carper explained again that this was the law of parties. "If she did anything at the time leading up to, during the commission of or in the time following the death of Roger Scott Dunn, which aided, abetted, assisted, encouraged or solicited, then she is as guilty as if she were the one who had done the bludgeoning herself."

Carper moved on to the subject of alibi. "An alibi says, 'Well I wasn't there when it was done.' But when you have the law of parties, you have to look not just at the time the killing was done, but during the time leading up to, during the time of the commission of and during the time immediately after the commission of the offense. So she can't have an alibi, if she did an act during the time leading up to, during the commission of and during the time immediately after the commission of the offense, that aided, solicited, encouraged, abetted the person who actually did the killing. She is as guilty as the person who swung the weapon that killed Scott Dunn."

Addressing the portion of the charge dealing with reasonable doubt, Carper said, "It is inconceivable how a person could live in an apartment that small, could have slept in a room for such a long time and still not know that a carpet sample was missing from under the couch, that a carpet patch was made in the bedroom. It's impossible that she did not know what happened. It's impossible that she did not help clean that up."

Then, briefly but graphically, Carper reviewed all the evidence. He pointed out that the odds were 10 billion to 1 that the blood that was recovered from the killing room was Scott Dunn's. "There are not 10 billion people on the planet Earth," Carper said, "so the blood came from Scott Dunn."

Pointing to the testimony of Tom Bevel, the blood spatter expert, Carper said, "There's no doubt that he lost a lot more than 1.7 units of blood. And although losing 1.7 units of blood does not necessarily create a medical emergency in and of itself, if you have someone who's been hit four times with medium velocity blows that create the type of blood spatter you saw in those pictures, there is a medical emergency and that person, if he's not dead already, better seek immediate medical help. That didn't happen in this case.

"You heard the most damning testimony of all: in conversations with Leisha's former lover, she said, 'There's no way I can be convicted, because there's not a body and there's not a weapon.'

"Ladies and gentlemen, I submit to you that we may not have skin and bone, but we have blood, and its components make up a body. We have a body; we just haven't been able to find it. And that body is the body of Roger Scott Dunn. He was killed in that apartment and it was done, either directly or as a party, by the defendant, Leisha Hamilton."

In his closing statement, Rick Wardroup also reviewed the testimony and the evidence, as well as his theory of what had happened. Wardroup talked about Karl Young's testimony, to which Carper had referred as perhaps the most important part of this case. "He may be right," Wardroup said, "because he told you two things. He told you that Leisha Hamilton never changed what she said, never ever, even years after. What Karl Young told you about Leisha saying 'They can't convict me because they don't have a body and they don't have a weapon,' is nothing more and nothing less than her resolution to the fact that she can't prove her innocence. And thank goodness, the law won't allow the State to prove her guilt, because it's not there."

Wardroup derided Carper's statement that there was none of Scott Dunn's hair beneath the carpet. "That is not the case! There was no testimony that any of Scott Dunn's hair was removed from that tape, but they told you they removed a limited number of hairs from the tape. And so the fact that they didn't testify about it doesn't mean it wasn't there. It means they didn't look for it or didn't find it or they did find it and it wasn't enough of a sample for them to tell. That's what it means."

Wardroup next reminded the jurors that type A blood was found on the knob of the bedroom door and its source was never discovered. "Who brought you the evidence of the type A blood? Was it the State? No. They have somebody's blood that's neither Leisha Hamilton's nor Scott Dunn's in the room and they didn't tell you about it."

Here, Wardroup abandoned his theme that there was no proof a murder had been committed and used a different tactic. "Throughout the trial, there came times when I would question closely certain doctors or certain experts the State brought to testify. And obviously the issue there was whether there was evidence enough to persuade anybody beyond a reasonable doubt that Scott Dunn was dead. Although proving murder was an important part of the State's case," Wardroup said, "it's not that important a part of our case, because the bottom line in the defense of this case is, it doesn't matter whether Scott Dunn is still living today or whether he lost his life back in 1991: there is not any evidence that points a finger at this young lady."

From here, Wardroup began to talk about his next theory: Someone else did it. "When you first saw this slight lady on Monday morning, your common sense told you this lady couldn't do that alone. The State knew that, too. And so they have tried desperately to tie Leisha Hamilton with Tim Smith. What do we know about Tim Smith? We know he was infatuated with Leisha, that he would sit around the restaurant where she worked, like a lost puppy dog, watching her. Does that make him a murderer? I don't think so.

"We know there was hair similar to Tim Smith's on the under-side of the carpet that patched the bedroom carpet in the northeast bedroom in Leisha's apartment. Do you know absolutely that this was Tim Smith's hair?

"We don't have the exclusion of Alan Parks. Don't you wish you knew right now what color Tim Smith's hair is, what color Alan Parks's hair is? Maybe we could exclude them that way."

Wardroup ridiculed the notion that, because Tim Smith had a roll of duct tape in his apartment and tried to hide it from the police, he was guilty of any crime. He reminded the jury of Tal English's testimony that Tim had just moved into a new apartment when the detectives discovered the duct tape. There were boxes with duct tape on them in Tim's new apartment. Wardroup put forth the theory that Tim picked up the duct tape in Leisha's apartment some time after Scott disappeared and used it to seal his boxes for moving. And just because he hid it from the detectives didn't prove his guilt, accord-ing to Wardroup. Maybe he was just embarrassed for having taken something from a girlfriend's house.

Wardroup recapped Leisha's actions following Scott's disappear-ance. He spoke of how she had not used a carpet cleaner to elimi-nate evidence. "If you are guilty in any fashion of commission of murder in a bedroom in your apartment and you've got two weeks before the detectives come out and look in that bedroom, what do you do? You steam clean your carpet."

"Every single witness who knew Leisha and Scott testified that she called them when Scott disappeared. What did she say? She said, 'Have you seen Scott Dunn?'

"Well, how did she seem? She seemed mad. She seemed hurt. But she did not say to a single person and Tim's notes to her don't say, 'Hey, we are getting away with this.' Because it didn't happen that way.

"In a few minutes, Mr. Ladd will have an opportunity to visit with you. Mr. Ladd is very talented and very persuasive. Listen carefully to what he has to say to you, to see if he answers the question about Alan Parks's hair. Was it similar to what we found on the tape under the carpet?

"If he answers, we still don't know if Tim Smith's blood is type A. Wouldn't that be helpful?

"I submit to you that your job will not be completed until you enforce the law that Judge Shaver has read to you and that you will have the opportunity to take back into the jury room with you. And when you do that, you will find Leisha Hamilton not guilty. Thank you."

Rusty Ladd was prepared for the third and final argument. He walked slowly back and forth in front of the jury box, looking into the eyes of individual jurors. His tone was emphatic. "Ladies and gentlemen, I ask only that you use a little bit of common sense and apply that to what you have heard in this case—not just the physical evidence, but also to the testimony you have heard.

"Apply your common sense to the argument you just heard from Mr. Wardroup: *Alan Parks and the Parks boys killed Roger Scott Dunn.* It is good to hear Mr. Wardroup acknowledge at last that Roger Scott Dunn is dead and that he died in that killing room six years ago today. It is not a happy memory for his family or for anyone else.

"Let's talk about Alan Parks for a minute. The only evidence you have about him was from Beth Bartin. We don't intend, when we start out cross-examining someone, to reduce them to tears, but we do have the right to test what they have to say and to test that by asking questions about themselves, about their own credibility. She made poor life choices in the past; is she making one now, by telling a lie?

"She got convicted of a theft in the past. That lets you know she has been unreliable in the past. So we're entitled to ask those questions. If someone cries because we ask that and we insist on getting a straight answer, I'm sorry. She is just going to have to cry, because we are entitled to a straight answer.

"And when you got a straight answer out of Beth, this is what you got: Her ex-Marine ex-husband drinks a lot; he gets high a lot; he brags a lot. When he said those things about his killing Scott, he was high and he bragged about killing lots of people. That's the kind of evidence we are supposed to have to convict someone like Alan Parks?

"Tal English is a police investigator; he talked to Alan because Beth told him her husband had made some incriminating statements. You heard Tal say he didn't think Alan Parks was telling the truth, but he ruled him out as a suspect.

"What was he not telling the truth about? Alan Parks denied making the statements to Beth and to others. He lied to Tal about that. Does that mean there is evidence there to present against Alan? Surely not the fairytale story you just heard, especially when you consider this: Alan Parks, ex-Marine, can kill with his hands, lays carpet and can patch it in, takes exquisite care to clean up every single drop of blood.

"But this same man, who takes such exquisite care to clean up that mess, blurts out the fact that he killed the guy to two or three different people. Does that make any sense?

"Alan Parks did not kill Roger Scott Dunn. The Parks boys didn't ride into town and kill him. Leisha Hamilton and Tim Smith killed Roger Scott Dunn."

He paused, took a deep breath and, looking at the jury, his voice took on a razor edge. "Your job is to examine the physical evidence you heard about—and there is plenty of physical evidence that ties Leisha Hamilton to that crime scene.

"The simple fact is that she lived there, but she said she didn't see this huge piece of carpet had been patched. Didn't notice all the blood that was beginning to seep out around the sides. And she didn't see that a big scrap of carpet had been cut out from under her sofa. She lived there for a long time after Scott Dunn disappeared. And for at least two weeks, she just didn't notice that those two pieces of carpet were messed up.

"Liars do well when they are answering questions they expect. She had been asked what she was doing on the night of May 15. She had known she would be asked that question and she was prepared. She gave a long statement in exquisite detail. You can look at it. It has been entered into evidence.

"Then Tal English asked her a question she did not expect. 'What were you doing on the night of May 16, *after* you discovered that Scott was missing?' *Uh-oh*. She didn't expect to have to answer that question, so she didn't know how to answer it. She hadn't manufactured any answer for that question. And so her answer is, 'I don't remember.'

"*Excuse me?* She remembers all the details of everything that happened the day before. She remembers every single thing that happened up to the point she said he disappeared. And then she doesn't have a clue about *anything* that happened in her life that next night? Just couldn't recall a thing?

"That's what a liar does. A liar prepares a story. She tells Jim Dunn some carpet is missing, but she doesn't expect Jim Dunn to ask her if she had checked through the rest of the apartment to see if she could discover what happened to it. So when he asked her that question during their phone conversation, her answer was 'yeah.'

"What? She had checked through the rest of the house and she missed seeing that big, huge semicircle of carpet, crudely matched to the surrounding carpet with the blood staining it?"

Ladd moved on to Tim Smith, "the guy who comes in and sits at the restaurant, stares at her, writes notes, got the notes that say 'I love you, I love you, I had my first taste of sex with you and I just like what I'm feeling with you,' and then signs it 'Superman; Flash.'

"One other thing you know in this case is that Tim Smith is a wimp. He lets her push him around. Remember what happened the night that she was in the arms of another man—Dave Hayden? Remember Dave's testimony?

"Remember when Tim Smith came into the room in the middle of the night, without knocking, into an apartment that was not his? Tim comes in—big, bad, bold Tim, who committed a murder all by himself, a Tim with that kind of driving force and personality? He comes in, sees his baby in the arms of another man and they are in the act of having sex.

"What does he do? Get mad? Blow up? Start to hit? No. He says, 'I want to talk to you, Leisha.'

"And Leisha jumps out of bed, without anything on, slaps him up against the wall, gets in his face and runs him off.

"Let's not kid ourselves about some things. Leisha Hamilton uses men like you and I would use Kleenex. Blow your nose on it and then throw it away. She used Tim.

"We don't have to prove to you she was the one who actually hit Scott or whether she invited Tim over that night to hit him or whether she just held him down or got him to sleep or stroked his hair and then let Tim hit him. All we have to prove to you is that, beyond a reasonable doubt, she was involved in Scott Dunn's murder.

"Remember, she lied about the carpet; she lied about Thursday night; she lied about the wallet. If someone is telling the truth, she doesn't have to worry about keeping things straight. But even if you are a good liar, a smart liar, an intelligent liar, you get your stories mixed up. You get things wrong. Like when she told Patrick Lane that Scott was missing and Lane wanted to know where she got his phone number. She said she got it out of Scott's wallet.

"But she had told everyone else that Scott's wallet disappeared when he did. If you are lying, you can't cover all your bases, no matter how smart you are.

"Do not take your common sense off like a jacket and hang it up before you go back into that room. When you obey the challenge of your oath, look at the evidence, look at her lies. There is no verdict possible, except 'guilty beyond a reasonable doubt,' of murder."

Judge Shaver charged the jury and sent them out to begin their deliberations. Jim, Barbara, Richard and Pam were directed to a nearby room to await the verdict. Jim was thankful that this new room was somewhat larger than the witness room where he had spent the last four days. At least this room was large enough that he could pace while he waited. And he did.

Just over five hours later, at 4:20 in the afternoon, Tal English, standing in the hall outside the door to the jury room, was shocked to hear a chorus of cheers come from inside the room. He knew the jurors must have reached a verdict, although he had no way of telling what the verdict was. He would learn later that, for hours, the jury was deadlocked eleven to one. When the deadlock was broken, the jurors were so relieved they let out a roar of relief.

A few minutes later, Judge Shaver called the interested parties back into the courtroom and admonished them. "I don't want any of the spectators to forget that this is a court of law," he said sternly. "I want absolute silence in the courtroom."

Of all the spectators Jim, the most anxious and anguished, watched as the jurors filed in. All of them kept their eyes averted, even after they had taken their seats. Jim's heart throbbed as the judge read the verdict:

"We, the jury, find from the evidence, beyond a reasonable doubt, the defendant is guilty of the offense of murder as charged in the indictment."

Leisha Hamilton, who had appeared unworried and sure of herself throughout the trial, looked absolutely stupefied. Her mouth fell open and she sat, immobile, for an instant. A moment later, she threw her head back and closed her eyes. Then her head fell forward and she began to cry.

Jim and Barbara Dunn looked at each other for an instant, as if disbelieving that this momentous moment of closure had come. Then Jim threw his arms around his wife and held her as if he would never let her go. His ordeal was over! It was over at last.

The judge then announced that, after a ten-minute recess, they would proceed immediately to the punishment phase of the trial.

When they reconvened to consider Leisha's punishment, Rusty Ladd called no witnesses. He did, however, read into evidence portions of an official document from Bernallilo County, New Mexico, stating that Leisha Hamilton "was convicted of embezzlement, a felony offense, occurring in the State of New Mexico, and was sentenced to the corrections department in the State of New Mexico for a term of three years." The document went on to say that the sentence was suspended and Leisha Hamilton was placed on probation for five years.

Following this, Ladd made a motion introducing all of the State's evidence from the guilt phase of the trial. Then the State rested.

Rick Wardroup called only two witnesses. The first was a young woman who had been a babysitter for Leisha's youngest child. The former sitter said she thought Leisha was a wonderful mother who should not have to go to prison. After being told that this was not an option, she said Leisha should receive the minimum sentence.

His second witness was the manager of the restaurant where Leisha was employed. He testified that she had worked for him for two years and was a good employee. He did not socialize with her outside of work, so he knew nothing of her lifestyle.

Judge Shaver gave the jurors the choice of deciding on Leisha's punishment that night or waiting until the following morning. It had been a tedious, demanding week and they wanted the case to end, so they decided to finish that night, even if it took them until after midnight.

That decided, Roy Carper again closed first. "The range of punishment in this case is a maximum of life or for a term of not less than five nor more than ninety-nine years and/or a fine of up to ten thousand dollars. Your sentence can be no less than five years and no more than life. You must set a proper punishment and I know you will do that."

Then Rick Wardroup made his closing argument, saying that the punishment should fit the crime. He asked that they consider the minimum, five years in prison. He reminded the jurors that no amount of punishment would make restitution for the pain Jim Dunn had suffered.

Ladd, whose words would be ringing in the jurors' ears when they retired to deliberate the punishment, also asked for punishment that fit the crime "and the criminal." Then he reviewed Leisha Hamilton's history.

Concluding, he said, "When she wants to, when it is necessary for her to do right—at work, in front of you—she can do whatever is necessary. She can cry, she can be on time, she can be pleasant with her customers.

"She needs to be punished for what she did. And when you are thinking of that, thinking of the value that we place on human life, what are you going to tell the rest of this county? When you kill another person in such a brutal fashion, when you do your dead level best to hide that until you are ready to orchestrate its being uncovered, when you hide behind lies and prolong the process this long—what kind of punishment do you deserve?"

When the jury had retired, Jim and Barbara Dunn, Richard Walter and Pam Alexander retired once more to the room where they had waited for the guilty verdict. They could have waited in the courtroom, but Leisha's family had chosen to await the sentencing there. Jim couldn't bear to sit in the same room with Leisha and her parents.

Almost two hours passed before the jury signaled it had reached a decision. Everyone trudged wearily back into the courtroom. Because of all they'd been through, and with Leisha still withholding the truth about what had happened to Scott, Jim wanted Leisha to get the maximum sentence, but no one else in his group gave him encouragement. Nevertheless, they all prayed she would get a significant punishment. There was a visible intake of breath as Judge Shaver read the jury's verdict aloud. "We, the jury, having found the defendant, Leisha Hamilton, guilty of the offense of murder, assess her punishment at confinement in the Institutional Division of the Texas Department of Criminal Justice for a period of twenty years."

Leisha looked altogether astonished. Rick Wardroup asked that the jury be polled and each juror answered, without looking at the defendant, that this was indeed his or her vote.

Jim stared at the woman who had brought such pain. If she served twenty years, Leisha would be in her fifties when she was released. Realistically, though, with parole rules in Texas so lax, he knew it was unlikely that she would serve her full time. But he determined in that moment to commit all in his power, the resources of time, health, energy and money to keeping her in prison as long as possible—at least until she was ready to tell authorities what she had done with Scott's body.

At the press conference he and Rusty Ladd held that evening, Jim told reporters that the jury had made their decision and he would go with that. Later, however, lying sleepless, he knew he could not rest completely until he found out for sure what had happened to Scott.

The next morning, Jim and Barbara decided to buy a headstone to mark the place where Scott's remains would be interred when they were found. Jim directed that an engraved likeness of Yellow Thunder, which in his mind he now called Silent Thunder, be carved on the marker. Then Jim and Barbara drove out to City of Lubbock Cemetery, where the bare gravesite waited, alongside the headstone of Jim's grandmother. They stood in the warm May sun, a gentle breeze drying the tears on Jim's cheeks. Jim looked toward the azure sky and prayerfully said, "It isn't over yet, son. It won't be over until I find you and give you a proper burial."

chapter twenty-two

In Search of Justice

Leisha Hamilton's trial had ended on the sixth anniversary of Scott's death. Rusty Ladd assured Jim Dunn that Tim Smith's trial would be set for later that summer, probably August. Tim's original attorney had withdrawn and Tim had retained a local legend, Floyd Holder, to represent him. Whether they liked him or not, people in West Texas generally agreed that if they ever needed a criminal attorney, Holder, a powerful presence, was the one they would want.

Holder filed a series of motions and it was more than a year before Smith actually faced trial. Rusty Ladd and Roy Carper again were the prosecutors.

In one of his pre-trial motions, Holder asked to exclude the testimony of Dr. Tom Bevel, the blood spatter expert from Oklahoma City who had conducted the saturation test in an attempt to determine how much blood had been spilled in the murder room. Judge Mackey Hancock, who had returned from Army Reserve duty in Bosnia, now was presiding. Hancock granted Holder's motion to exclude the saturation test on the basis that it was not scientific, had never been performed before and had no guiding parameters. He would, however, allow Bevel to testify about the blood spatter evidence, which indicated how many blows, at a minimum, had been struck and at what velocity those had been delivered in order to create the pattern of blood found at the crime scene.

When the trial actually began, on June 1, 1998, Ladd and Carper chose to present their case against Timothy Smith in a manner almost identical to the one used in Leisha Hamilton's trial. They focused on the grieving but determined father, Jim Dunn; they hammered on the law of parties to convince the jury that regardless of who had actually struck the blows that had killed Scott Dunn, both Leisha and Tim were equally guilty; that Leisha was the instigator and motivator and Tim Smith had been so smitten, he did anything she asked.

The make-up of the jury was of some concern to the Dunns. There were eleven women and one man, all comparatively young, possibly none more than forty years old. It might be easy for them to identify with Tim Smith and his wife, who were in the same age range now.

From the outset, it was apparent that Holder had two goals in mind: to paint Scott Dunn in the worst light imaginable and to portray his client as a clean-cut, well-dressed, born-again Christian, who, prior to meeting Leisha, had never been in trouble with the law and who now led an exemplary life with his wife and three-year-old child.

Beginning his depiction of Tim Smith as a victim of his passion during the jury selection, Holder made reference to his own wife, who sat in the courtroom. She was in the last stages of a terminal illness that appeared to have drained the life and vitality out of her, leaving her frail and white-haired, looking much older than her actual years. Holder, with tears in his eyes, talked about how strong can be the love of a man for a woman.

"I remember a long time ago, sitting in a bus station, and the prettiest girl I'd ever seen sat down next to me. And all these years later—here we are," he said, glancing at his wife.

It was apparent to Jim that several of the woman jurors were visibly moved.

In Leisha's trial, Rick Wardroup had not even cross-examined Jim. Holder, however, pounced on Scott's character and Jim's lack of presence during Scott's childhood. No matter how hard Holder tried to make Jim angry, Jim kept his composure. It was evident that despite his anguish, he was a man of values and conscience.

Again, Tim's father was a witness for the prosecution. He was no longer on crutches and this time he strode to the witness stand, seemingly more self-assured. Tim's mother and father had separated by then and although his mother was in the courtroom, she sat farther back, head down, paying absolutely no attention to her ex-husband.

Holder led Smith through a series of questions that left the impression that Tim had grown up in a strict, authoritarian home, where love was equated with punishment. It seemed evident from Smith's responses that his father had controlled every aspect of the son's life until Tim was almost thirty years old.

Smith's demeanor on the stand was different from that in Leisha's trial. Holder portrayed him as an abusive father who had never given his son any recognition; until this trial, he had never given any sign of caring for his son. If Holder's implications could be accepted, Tim had been a victim all his life and it was not surprising that he fell victim to Leisha, a vicious, scheming, self-centered female who held absolute power over him.

While Smith was on the stand, Rusty Ladd read a letter in which Tim asked Leisha to choose between him and Scott. In the letter, Tim wrote that he loved Leisha even though he knew about her relationship with Scott. He referred to Scott as an asshole and a snake. "If Scott wasn't here anymore," the letter said, "we could be happy together."

Ladd then asked Tim's father if his son was capable of killing someone and Smith said no. Nor would his son be capable of helping plan a killing, the older Smith said.

Again, Jim Dunn and Richard Walter were relegated to waiting outside the courtroom.

When the prosecution showed the jury the piece of blood-stained carpet from the bedroom, some of the jurors sucked in their breath. These dried, crusted, fading bloodstains were all that was left of Scott. It suddenly seemed impossible that this young man who had been so charming, intelligent, sweet-natured, guileless, could have been bludgeoned to death.

When Jessica Tate took the stand, even Holder seemed impressed. She testified in a strong, clear voice about her relationship with Scott Dunn, telling the jury how much they had loved each other and that they had planned to marry and spend their lives together. It would be easy for the jury to see that, in this young woman, Scott had the hope for a new and better life for himself. It would be hard for them to believe that he would let Leisha come between him and this beautiful woman; it would be even harder for them to believe that he voluntarily would have disappeared without ever contacting Jessica again.

The prosecution presented the scientific evidence they had used in Leisha's trial in an orderly and concise manner and the jury seemed to pay close attention. When it came time for closing arguments, Ladd felt that they had presented the case well and they had gotten their point across. Tim Smith might not have struck the blows that took Scott Dunn's life, but he helped, at least to clean up the blood and remove the body, to protect the woman he loved.

When, after only forty-five minutes of deliberation, the jury returned a guilty verdict, Jim felt Scott had been vindicated. Judge Hancock immediately began the punishment phase of the trial, which proved lengthier than that of Leisha's. Throughout the trial, the courtroom had been packed with members of the charismatic church to which Tim and his wife now belonged. The group had been vocal every day about their belief in Tim's innocence and they had solicited the prayers of Christians all over the city for a verdict that would clear Tim's name. Holder called several character witnesses from among this group in an attempt to win leniency for Tim.

Holder also informed the jurors that not only could they assess a minimum punishment, five years in prison, but they could also recommend probation, in which case, Tim would be free to take care of his family.

Because the guilty verdict had been returned in a remarkably short time, Jim, Barbara, the prosecutors and courthouse observers expected the jurors to assess punishment in a record time as well. More than two hours dragged by, however, before the jury could agree. When they did, the courtroom exploded in disbelief.

The jurors imposed upon Tim Smith a sentence of five years for participating in the death of Scott Dunn and they wanted that sentence to be probated, so Tim would never go to prison. In addition, they wanted Smith fined ten thousand dollars. Jim shuddered, his heart palpating wildly. Impossible. They had found Tim guilty of murder, but they didn't want to send him to prison?

Even Judge Hancock seemed shocked, but he had an alternative. Under Texas law, a person sentenced to only five years for murder could not have his sentence probated. If Tim Smith were to receive probation, ten years was the minimum mandatory sentence. Judge Hancock warned Smith that he must adhere to every rule of his probation, that if he ever wanted to appeal the sentence and get it shortened, he would first have to reveal to the court where Scott Dunn's body was or prove to the judge's satisfaction that he did not know where Scott was.

Afterword

After both trials were over, Jim Dunn had hoped to experience a sense of freedom from the vow that had driven him since Scott had disappeared, but he didn't. Though he felt a sense of solace at Leisha's conviction, he felt outraged that Tim Smith, convicted of murdering Scott, was free to walk the streets of Lubbock. Free to enjoy his life with his wife and son, while Jim's son was condemned to indignity, to limbo, the location of his earthly remains still unknown to anyone except his killers.

Jim knew even Leisha Hamilton might not know where Scott's body was. Tim Smith might be the only person who knew whether Scott lay in an obscure, unmarked grave somewhere on the wild West Texas prairies or had become a part of the limestone at the Lubbock Landfill or had been reduced to ashes in an incinerator to which Tim had access, as Leisha had once suggested to Karl Young. Jim felt that now that Tim was free, Tim would have no incentive ever to reveal his guilty knowledge and those who were still looking for Scott's body would have no leverage over him.

Ladd tried to quell Jim's indignation, saying that Tim might yet tell them where he had put Scott's body. After all, ten years is a long time to serve on probation, which can be revoked if the probationer violates the terms of his probation in any manner. At some point, Tim might violate probation and Judge Hancock had made it clear that if that happened, Tim would go to prison—unless he revealed where he had disposed of Scott's body. Jim didn't have much hope that this would happen, though. Apparently, Tim had given up alcohol and drug use, which would have been a violation of probation. He didn't have a reputation for consorting with felons, he had not been known to carry guns or other weapons. The only hope Jim had, and it was slim, was that Tim would not be able to pay his ten thousand dollar fine. Jim knew, though, the State of Texas allows a great deal of leniency in that area, setting ridiculously low monthly payments for fines, so paying it probably would not be a serious hurdle for Tim.

The concept that a person convicted of murder could be given probation was abhorrent to Jim and to everyone to whom he talked about it. This was a law that needed to be obliterated from the books, as his son had been obliterated from the earth. He had promised Barb that after the trial he would let his battle to gain justice for Scott go. But now he knew he could not give up. He had to try to eradicate this obscene law that had let one of his son's killers go free, so that other families of victims would not suffer as he was. However, though he tried, Jim was unable to stimulate interest among legislators to eliminate a state law that was, in Jim Dunn's and most other people's view, a disgrace to the state.

Now Jim turned to, in his eyes, an even more imperative concern: bringing closure and peace to victim's families. He had become a member of the Vidocq Society and he became active, encouraging its members to do even more to help other families such as his. The Society named Tal English Investigator of the Year for his work on Scott's case. Tal and his wife, Tonya, flew to Philadelphia for the award ceremony and Jim tried to express to him again his limitless gratitude for Tal's perseverance during those six long years.

Later, Vidocq named Rusty Ladd Prosecutor of the Year for his work on the case.

Both Jim and Richard Walter had become members of the national group Parents of Murdered Children. Richard was named to its Board of Directors. Jim traveled and gave talks to various chapters, trying to comfort grieving mothers and fathers. He encouraged them to get involved in the investigation of their children's deaths as he had. No matter how dedicated to solving a case police officers are, no one cares as much as the parents of the murdered child, Jim told them. No one has as much at stake in gaining justice as the parents have.

Time passes and Jim Dunn looks forward, ever encouraging Vidocq, POMC and everyone he can influence never to give up. He knows that he cannot. There is an empty grave site in a Lubbock cemetery that reminds him of his quest. There is a headstone bearing the likeness of Scott Dunn's Camaro, the one that roared through West Texas like thunder—thunder now silenced—that tells Jim Dunn he must keep searching. Until the remains of its driver, his son, are buried in the plot of ground beneath the Camaro, he cannot rest; he will not give up.